EMBODYING IDENTITIES

Migration is also a matter of generational acts of story-telling
about prior histories of movement and dislocation.
Sara Ahmed (2000, p 90)

One can never escape the way in which one's formation lays
a kind of imprint on or template over what one is interested
in, and what kind of take one would have on any topic, what
linkages one wants to make and so on.
Stuart Hall (1994, p 271)

...what is the use of studying philosophy if all that it does for
you is enable you to talk with some plausibility about some
abstruse questions of logic, etc, and if it does not improve your
thinking about the important questions of everyday life.
Ludwig Wittgenstein in a letter to Norman Malcolm
(16 November 1944)

Social reality is lived social relations, our most important
political construction, a world changing fiction.
Donna Haraway (1991, p 190)

For Anna,

for Lily who suggested the original project,

for Daniel and Rebecca,

for Sammi and Marilyn,

for all the Brazilian family,

and for all those, struggling in different ways,

with questions of identity.

EMBODYING IDENTITIES

Culture, differences and
social theory

Victor Jeleniewski Seidler

This edition published in Great Britain in 2010 by

The Policy Press
University of Bristol
Fourth Floor
Beacon House
Queen's Road
Bristol BS8 1QU
UK

t: +44 (0)117 331 4054
f: +44 (0)117 331 4093
e: tpp-info@bristol.ac.uk
www.policypress.co.uk

North American office:
The Policy Press
c/o International Specialized Books Services (ISBS)
920 NE 58th Avenue, Suite 300
Portland, OR 97213-3786, USA
t: +1 503 287 3093
f: +1 503 280 8832
e: info@isbs.com

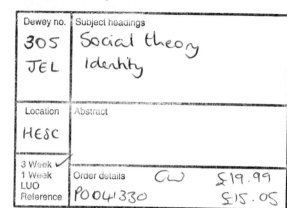

British Library Cataloguing in Publication Data
A catalogue record for this book is available from the British Library.

Library of Congress Cataloging-in-Publication Data
A catalog record for this book has been requested.

ISBN 978 1 84742 381 8 paperback
ISBN 978 1 84742 382 5 hardcover

Cover design by Qube Design Associates, Bristol
Front cover: image kindly supplied by Ferdinando Scianna/Magnum Photos
Printed and bound in Great Britain by MPG Books Group

Mixed Sources
Product group from well-managed forests and other controlled sources
www.fsc.org Cert no. SA-COC-1565
© 1996 Forest Stewardship Council

Contents

Glossary

Biological determinism A theory that understands actions, feelings and behaviours as emerging from, and being determined by, biological or instinctual factors. It has re-emerged through a focus on genes as a possible explanation for the determining of social behaviours, but can be a form of reductionism that fails to appreciate how genes interrelate with diverse environments.

Body politic A term that imagines society and politics through narratives of the body. A notion that feminism and sexual politics in the 1970s reclaimed; to think across the boundaries of public and private life showing that power and emotions move across these boundaries.

Cartesian tradition A philosophical tradition emerging from Descartes that assumed a mind–body dualism and a notion of the rational self framed through a distinction between reason and nature. It is assumed that we have an inner relationship to reason, mind and consciousness and an externalised relationship with bodies deemed to be part of an external disenchanted nature.

Cognitive dissonance An idea that we can hold contradictory ideas and feelings that remain in tension with each other although we are barely aware of the tensions. A psychological theory focusing upon the tensions within mental life in cognitive terms, so contrasting with psychoanalysis and its appreciation of emotional life.

Colonialism A relationship of power established between European powers and the non-European countries that they ruled and governed. This became a marker of white European superiority and the notion that it was only through accepting subordination to European rule that the 'uncivilised' non-Europeans could make a transition from nature to culture, so becoming independent self-governing states.

Complex identities A notion that recognises that in postmodern societies people often have complex inheritances, with families having migrated across different space, thereby shaping their identities and experiences. Acknowledging how these diverse inheritances help to shape identities in the present helps appreciate the significance of histories and cultures.

Demonisation A term produced within a dominant Christian imaginary, initially framed around the figure of 'the Jew' as radically other and to be identified with the supposed work of the devil. It shows how traditions of racism and anti-Semitism have been interrelated and the ways that 'others' so often come to be blamed, ridiculed and undermined in their humanity.

Diaspora A term that was initially framed in relation to the dispersion of Jews because of the destructions wrought by the Romans; now generalised to reflect the connections that peoples can feel to their diverse 'homelands' and ways this can be an important feature in generational senses of embodied identities.

Disembodied rationality An idea that reflects how Western philosophical traditions have often been shaped through disembodied notions of mind, reason and consciousness. This is reflected in social and cultural theories that assume that knowledge exists in an abstract realm of its own that is neutral, impartial and objective. Such assumptions are often challenged by feminism and sexual politics.

Distributive This is a term that refers to the distribution and circulation of goods and resources, including moral and spiritual goods, across societies. It often refers to notions of distributive justice that tend to think of notions of justice through ideas of fairness alone.

Durkheimian tradition This is a tradition of social and cultural theory that flows from the French sociologist Durkheim and which tends to assume that the 'social' is a category that can be grasped as 'sui generis'. The social is often framed in functionalist terms as independent of individual psychologies. But it is also a tradition that challenges the 'common-sense' individualism of liberalisms and allows for the significance of context.

Enlightenment A tradition of thought that goes back to the 17th century Scientific Revolutions and the idea that social life can be organised as a realm of reason alone. It argues for a scientific method that can be used to grasp the laws that supposedly govern both nature and culture while also drawing a distinction between the sciences and the humanities. Descartes and Kant remain central figures in framing the disenchantment of nature and the autonomy of morality.

Essentialism A term often framed through a poststructuralist tradition within social theory to contrast identities as being inner and somehow 'essential' as opposed to being 'socially constructed'. Exploring instances where people feel as if they are acting 'against' their natures shows complexities that a simple dualism does not allow.

Fixed identities The idea often associated with 'identity politics' that identities are somehow given either in nature or through particular social categories of class, 'race', ethnicity, gender, sexuality and able-bodiedness. Often issues remain about how identities are fluid and fractured, and how also they might be invented, created or constructed around particular histories and inheritances.

Fundamentalism Ways in which the literal reading of religious texts within diverse religious traditions have fostered a sharp distinction between 'good' and 'evil', 'right' and 'wrong', and thus believers assume that they alone are the bearers of 'truth' and 'goodness'.

Hegemony A term developed by the Italian Marxist Gramsci to refer to the dominant or hegemonic ideas, values, institutions and practices within a capitalist society, and the ways that these are challenged through creating alternative counter-hegemonic practices and ways of living that sustain more equal and humane values.

Individualism The assumption that society exists as a collection of discrete individuals who shape their own lives through their individual energies and abilities, so disavowing the social relationships of power and subordination within which their histories and experiences are shaped.

Kleinian A tradition of psychoanalytic theory and practice that follows from the influential work of Melanie Klein that recognises the intensity of early infant emotions and ways they are reflected in adult life. She draws attention to issues of guilt, loss and reparation and so to moral realities within psychic life.

Liberal democratic polity The political theory and practice of liberal democratic societies that depend upon notions of democratic representation and the rule of law and which are organised around the sovereignty of the people and notions of civil and legal rights.

Liberal humanism Draws on a contrast between humanisms that have depended on the flourishing of human capacities, needs and potentialities and a more narrowly defined Enlightenment liberal humanism, which depends on a distinction between reason and nature, and where, for Kant, reason alone comes to be identified with morality.

Modernity A historical and cultural transition shaped through the 17th-century Scientific Revolutions, which framed a disenchantment with nature, and the Enlightenment tradition, which sought to make society an order of reason and to identify freedom, history and progress with a dominant European modernity. Modernity comes to be contrasted with a past that is pre-modern and governed by tradition, habit and religious authority and a postmodern present where people are supposedly free to invent their own identities.

Moralism A tradition that allows people to legislate what is morally good for others and insists that they alone are the bearers of a reason that others somehow lack. It claims an authority to legislate for others that was framed in patriarchy by the authority of fathers to reflect divine authority within the family so that questioning was a sign of disobedience that deserved punishment.

Nationalism A social and political theory of enormous significance in the 19th and 20th centuries through which particular nations made claims of belonging in relationship to particular spaces. The nation-state claimed sovereignty and established terms of belonging so that people were organised to feel a primary loyalty to the nation-state. The 'international' came to be defined as the relationship between clearly defined states, but with population movements people in the 21st century are increasingly shaping transnational identities with complex senses of inheritance and belonging.

Ontological security This is a term drawn from phenomenology and psychoanalysis to frame the sense of trust and security people can feel in relation to their own embodied sense of self-worth. It is a term that was deployed by R.D. Laing, and also invoked by Anthony Giddens, to explore the relationship between self-identity and modernity.

Orientalism Points to the ways that Europe often imagined itself against its vision of an Oriental 'other', which was conceived as lacking in reason, judgement and future planning – qualities taken to be critical to the traditions of European modernity. Often these visions of the 'Oriental' are projections that reveal more about the unspoken insecurities and anxieties of a dominant white European masculinity.

Patriarchal society Refers to societies that have traditionally been organised around the authority of fathers who have taken themselves to be representatives of divine authority on earth. Feminism has been vital in naming the structures of a patriarchal society that have so often been taken for granted and its effects on undermining the self-worth of women and children.

Performative Often refers to ways identities come into being through the ways in which they are performed, so that it is through actions and behaviours that feelings and identities are formed. Also recognises the ways that language is not just descriptive of an 'external world' but itself performs certain tasks within specific contexts.

Phenomenological A tradition of social and cultural theory that emerges out of the focus given to the creation of production of meanings as forms of interpretation. Draws upon the philosophical work of Husserl, Heidegger and Merleau-Ponty who influenced phenomenological traditions within social theory as they developed through the interpretative work of Max Weber and Alfred Schutz.

Positivism A tradition within social theory that holds that the social and cultural world can be understood using the same scientific methodologies that have been developed to reveal laws governing the natural world. Positivisms seek impartial, neutral and objective forms of knowledge, which tend to take for granted certain masculinist epistemologies that disavow emotions and feelings as sources of knowledge.

Postmodern Social and cultural theories have tended to imagine the postmodern as a break with a modernity that has assumed an identification between history, freedom and progress and so certain possibilities of emancipation. Within the postmodern there are few hopes for social transformation and a sense that identities can be created in the present.

Poststructuralist As a tradition poststructuralism has developed as a break with the historical legacies of Hegel and so with a reading of Marx that was framed through Althusser and a reading of Freud through Lacan. With the antropologist Levi-Strauss they focused on the structures of language and the ways that they helped frame experience and fractured identities. The more recent social theories of Foucault have been understood as a development, at least initially, within a poststructuralism.

Rational self Within an Enlightenment modernity people learn, following Descartes and Kant, to identify themselves with their reason, mind and consciousness. In this way they learn to assume they can control their lives through reason and so find freedom, meaning and happiness through fulfilling ends established through reason alone.

Rationalist tradition Teaches that knowledge comes through impartial and objective reasoning, so discounting emotions and feelings as sources of knowledge. It tends to sustain disembodied notions of identity and assume that experience can be controlled and shaped through reason.

Reflexive identity politics An awareness that people can reflect upon their histories and experiences as they shape their identities. Challenges a liberal moral tradition that assumes that societies are made up of collections of discrete individuals who are free to make their own lives and recognises how questions of class, 'race', ethnicity, gender and sexualities help shape embodied identities. But these are not imagined not as fixed or given categories but as reflexively shaped as people make their own journeys through life and feel a need to come to terms with aspects of their histories and cultures.

Reflexivity A recognition that the 'common sense' notions that we use to shape meanings and relationships carry certain assumptions that we can become critically aware of. As we trace their histories and cultural roots so we appreciate the complex and unspoken inheritances we so often take for granted. A process of critical self-awareness that takes time to develop and cannot simply be activated as a matter of will.

Saussurean linguistics This is a theory of language that has been framed through a relationship between signifiers and the signified. Meanings are established within an autonomous sphere of language through the contrasts established between a system of signs.

Semiological As a theory of signs semiology as a tradition has been significant in the interpretation of advertisements and cultural codes, particularly through the influential writings of Roland Barthes. Rather than see 'truth' as a matter of correspondence between language and an 'external reality', truth comes to be established through systems of signs and cultural codes.

Social constructionism As a social theory the idea of 'social construction' has developed to encourage the notion that meanings are not given in nature or somehow 'essentially' but that they are socially and historically 'constructed'. This encourages a sensitivity to social and historical context and a recognition of how ideas do not remain unchanged over time but need to be traced through their breaks within particular historical 'conjunctions'.

Social justice A recognition that justice is not merely a matter of the ways individuals freely choose to treat each other but that their relationships are also shaped through the social relationships of power and subordination that move across gender, 'race', ethnicities, sexualities and able-bodiedness. A concern for social justice also moves across the boundaries of nation-states to global relationships of social justice and the terms of trade through which nations negotiate with each other.

Social movement As people gather together in groups to effect social change so they shape social movements around issues of class, 'race', ethnicity, religion and sexualities. Through black-consciousness movements that influenced feminism and sexual politics in the 1970s there was a recognition of how social movements had become central to a revival of democratic politics and to a refiguring of the nature of the 'political'.

Somatic A recognition of how bodies do not exist as parts of a disenchanted nature and so as 'objects' of a medical gaze as a rationalist modernity might assume but exist as sources of knowledge. So bodies have emotional lives as Freud and Reich came to understand and carry traces of their cultural and social histories and memories. A tradition of body psychotherapies has developed to explore the emotional lives of bodies.

Subjectivism A theory that assumes that there is no external world that exists independently of the interpretations we make and the meanings we create. A recognition that there is no such thing as objective 'truth' and that people are free to create their own truths and so establish their own sense of reality.

Totalitarian A social and political theory that argues that people cannot be trusted with their own authority and so is sceptical about the assumptions of liberal democracy. Rather it argues for a certain authoritarian leadership that needs to control every aspect of life. Often an emotional identification with the leader is encouraged, as happened in Stalin's Russia and Hitler's Nazi Germany, although we also have to be careful to recognise what differentiates different forms of totalitarian rule.

Voluntarism An understanding of individual freedom that wants to assume that people are always in control of the lives they make for themselves and are free to shape their lives in ways they want. Lives are not shaped by history, culture and tradition; people are free to separate from these diverse inheritances.

Zionism A political and cultural theory initially developed by Theodor Herzl, who felt that the revival of anti-Semitism in Western Europe as marked by the Dreyfus case[1] in France showed the limits of the project of Jewish emancipation and assimilation. Zionism argued that Jewish people needed a homeland that they could consider as their own, and from which they could not be excluded on the principle of national self-determination. With the creation of the State of Israel in 1948, and so a realisation of Zionist aims, post-Zionism questions expansionist forms of Jewish nationalism and argues for a just settlement with the Palestinians.

Endnote

[1] The 'Dreyfus case' came about when a military officer of Jewish background was falsely accused in a case that divided France in the 1870s.

Acknowledgements

Many people have offered invaluable support in the many years that it has taken to bring this project to completion. Anna my partner has been constantly there offering more insights than I could possibly appreciate as we worked together to bring up our children with the strength and understanding to create their own identities. At different times, the paths of Daniel and Lily took them through sociology and it was to illuminate Lily's concerns about culture and identity that this writing was initially stimulated. With understanding and editorial tact Karen Bowler and others at The Policy Press have helped to bring it to light.

The Sociology Department at Goldsmiths has continued to be a supportive and inspiring environment where, over the years, people, some of whom have carried the spirit to other departments, have been ready to listen with patience across the many theoretical traditions that thrive there. Over the years conversations with Brian Alleyne, Vikki Bell, Les Back, Andrew Barry, Chetan Bhatt, Kirsten Campbell, Violet Fearon, Ben Gidley, Ross Gill, Paul Gilroy, Moncia Greco, Sally Inman, Michael Keith, Celia Lury, Kate Nash, Doreen Norman, Caroline Knowles, Pam Odih, Nirmal Puwar, Caroline Ramazanoglu, Nikolas Rose, Marsha Rosengarten, Bev Skeggs, Mary Stiasny, Brett St Louis, Fran Tonkiss and Bridget Ward have found their ways into my thinking and writing. Although many may not agree with the directions I have taken these conversations, it shows the vitality of an intellectual community that people can draw quite different conclusions from the same conversation. Over the years Howard Caygill and Josh Cohen who have helped shape the different events of the Philosophy and Human Values group at Goldsmiths have been constant sources of inspiration and support.

Many of my postgraduate students and others will also recognise themselves in some of these pages and the conversations that help shape some of the ideas. In their different ways they have helped to renew my experience in the department and hopefully keep me in touch with the thinking of different generations as they find their ways into social theory and philosophy. In relation to some of the issues explored I would like to remember the 'Mexican group' of Luis Jimenez and Teresa Ordorika, in a later time joined by Monica Morena; the 'Cultural Memory group' that consists of, among others, Viki Skiftou and Alice Hohenloe; the 'Body group' that consists of Demitris Latafikos, Beckie Coleman and Dellia Duna; and much more work recently with Daniela Jara, Stephen Jones, Shamea Mia, Clair Morrow,

Ben Sanders and Jaray Singhakowinta. These were loose groupings of PhD students who would come together for occasional seminars and who make up part of the vital postgraduate community. Earlier supervisions with Danny Kelly who was working on issues around men's health in relation to prostate cancer, and Dean Whittington on working-class masculinities, drugs and violence in Deptford, helped to sharpen my sense of working with complex identities and the many different kinds of difficulties people face in creating their identities as they move through different moments in their lives.

I have also learnt a great deal in recent years, from working with Richard Sennett and Craig Calhoun in the NYLON Culture Project. This has brought together postgraduate students from London and New York to engage in dialogues around diverse narratives of engagement with transformations in a globalised new capitalism. After 9/11 and the London bombings that I wrote about in *Urban fears and global terrors: Citizenship, multicultures and belongings after 7/7* (Routledge, 2007), questions of complex identity multicultures need revisioning. The pressures identities are under and how they make themselves felt at different levels of embodiment and lived experience, rather than disappearing, have become more urgent to engage with in new and creative ways.

We need to be able to listen and to attune not only to what is said but also to what remains unspoken and silenced although felt at some level as part of a traumatic inheritance. As we learn to think across the boundaries of the secular and the religious, the psyche and the social, we need to refigure social theories. We need to make space for diverse histories, traditions and spiritualities so often devalued within traditions of European modernity that for so long legitimated slavery, colonialism and genocide as part of its dark shadows that still haunts the contemporary West despite the freedom, democracy and justice it has fostered.

Preface

Uncertain lives / complex identities

If some people argue that the very language of identities implies a kind of 'fixity' from which we ought to be escaping in postmodern times, preferring instead to think of the different kinds of identifications people make from the particular positions from which they speak, this can make it difficult to appreciate the pain and suffering that people from diverse backgrounds face in relating different aspects of their identities. It can make it difficult for social workers to listen to different levels of experience and understand how people shape identities over time. Rather than 'working through' feelings of shame, isolation and difference, people can feel encouraged to disavow whatever difficulties or ambivalences they feel to present a certain image of themselves to others. They might be concerned with presenting an adequate self in public but feel unsupported in working on the emotional issues that help shape precarious, and complex identities.

Sociologists and social workers must also become aware of the generational character of identities so that they do not unhelpfully generalise from their own experience or find others 'lacking' because they do not conform to their expectations. Within the generational experiences of young women and men who have been able to grow up taking the advances of feminism for granted there is often an assumption that gender equality has already been realised. Often this conceals the inner tensions people learn to live with as they present images of themselves within workplaces. They have often implicitly accepted a new demarcation between 'private' and 'personal' life within the new capitalism and feel obliged to present images of competence and efficiency in public.

Young women and men can often feel estranged from themselves in ways that have been made difficult to name in a post-feminist generation. Their experiences no longer seem understandable within the theoretical frameworks of 1970s feminism and sexual politics but they can also be unconvinced by the freedoms to create their own identities suggested by postmodern social theories. Sometimes it is only once they have children that heterosexual couples are faced with this and find it difficult to negotiate their new relationships, when women are literally left 'holding the baby' as men return to work. Sometimes these conflicts are assuaged, for a time at least, through the employment of other women to look after their young children. There is a sense, though, that women today live in a radically different world from their mothers' feminist generation and they might find it difficult to discover a language that illuminates the tensions of their own gendered lived experience and relationships.

If we follow the 'common sense' of the human sciences that have also shaped different traditions of social and community work, we can be left thinking that identities are 'socially and historically constructed' and so are shaped within the terms of particular societies and cultures. For example, we might reflect on the egalitarian notions of friendship we discover in Scandinavian countries, assuming that the terms of friendship are set and that it is a matter of individuals adjusting to social expectations. But this can make it difficult to understand *how* friends can be important in sustaining a sense of identity and the fears that people might have about, for instance, expressing anger that might be deemed as threatening. The aspiration towards equality might conceal a fear of intimacy that can only be revealed if we can open up a politics of friendship that recognises not only how friendships might be gendered but also how friendships might wane and die as people grow apart and discover that they want different things out of life.

We need to open up a critical and morally engaged exploration that can reveal tensions which are so often closed down within the radical 'social constructivism' of discourse theories, so moving beyond the terms of a poststructuralist theory. There are often tensions between the identities people feel obliged to assume at work and the ways they feel about themselves in different spheres of life that cannot be illuminated through thinking how people are positioned within particular discourses. The internet and the global media have spread images of relationships and possibilities for alternative identities and intimacies across the planet and have also provided a crucial virtual space for exploration, for example, for gay men who may find freedom to explore their gay feelings and desires in a virtual world, that they might feel obliged to conceal within the masculinities they perform at work, or for young transgender people who are able to reach out for support that they might feel is lacking in their families and school communities.

If this involves thinking differently about complex identities it helps us to *make connections* between the personal and the theoretical that have often been implicitly disavowed within poststructuralist theories, which have otherwise been so important in revealing the fragmentation and fluidity of identities. Drawing on the strengths of poststructuralist recognitions of the uncertainties and fluidities of fragmented identities, we can explore a different kind of relationship between the 'psyche' and the 'social' that can think across the boundaries of minds and bodies and engage critically with the familial frameworks of traditional forms of psychoanalysis.

In also drawing connections between the 'personal' and the 'political' we are recognising how people can *transform* their identities in the present through engaging in collective actions and social movements. People can define their individualities more clearly as they clarify their own beliefs and values and so explore ways of being that promise consistency in the relationship between their beliefs and actions. For example, people who feel committed to social justice might become clearer about their own identities as they take actions with others in a movement to 'make poverty history'.

Identities / dis/placements / globalisations

Drawing on a variety of histories, identities and experiences within modern and postmodern cultures, this book explores how diverse traditions of social theory have been shaped through a relationship between a dominant European white masculinity and a rationalist modernity. This has shaped how we have tended to inherit disembodied visions of identity as *rational self* that have found it difficult to acknowledge emotions, feelings and desires as sources of knowledge. Through a critical engagement with diverse traditions of social theory, including psychoanalysis and postcolonial theory, we can recover resources that help to illuminate the very different realities and aspirations with which people live in postmodern consumer cultures in the West. Not only do we need to rethink relationships of power within a globalised world, but we also need to appreciate the rapid circulation of media images across national boundaries in the shaping of transnational complex identities.

Immigrant communities in urban spaces often live in everyday contact with different national spaces through media images and can feel that they live and make their homes across different spaces. The existence of global media can make a difference, for instance, to young Bangladeshi children in east London, who find it easier to maintain different languages than their older siblings who have grown up with pressures to learn English and a different kind of desire to assimilate. The 'war against terror' since 9/11 has produced its own fears for Muslim communities who no longer feel the same kind of safety on the streets for which they once hoped. As we become used to living in dangerous times, new tensions and insecurities are created that can help to produce more defensive identities where people are less trusting of their neighbours and more suspicious of strangers.

Religious identities have also assumed a particular significance for a second generation who cannot identify with their parents' connections to a distant home with which they have little relationship. They might feel more identified with their cities and friendship groups than they do with wider notions of a reaffirmed 'British identity'. They might identify with Islam as a transnational identity that is not tied to a particular nation state even if they are not particularly religious. They might feel as if they can be 'British Muslims' in a way they do *not feel*, as their parents might, like 'British Pakistanis', instead feeling that their home is in London, Birmingham, Leeds or Leicester for example. With possibilities of travel and global media they might feel more relationship with their families that they have visited while also being aware of the different lives they are living despite the influence of globalised music and aesthetic cultures.

Within a newly globalised world, where there is a quickening of time and an acceleration of experience, young people in the West can be both cynical about the possibilities of change and constantly networked through social network sites. Some are reflective about the meaning of their own lives as they become less identified with their work and careers than an older generation who had definite futures and so less precarious lives. In their twenties, young people, particularly in times of relative prosperity before the global financial crisis that hit in 2009, show a greater willingness to give up well-paid jobs when they feel they are no longer learning new skills or getting what they need for themselves. They might choose to travel and will take risks in putting themselves back in the labour market when they get back that would have frightened their parents' generation, who would have held tight to jobs that offered a future career. With the potential for recession we can expect different behaviours to develop.

Young people often live with a sense of insecurity and uncertainty that goes together with a freedom to create their own identities. They can feel burdened with feelings of guilt as they feel responsible for whatever unhappiness or isolation they experience. Having learnt to discount issues of class, gender, 'race' and ethnicities they are responsible for their own futures. Since they feel they can *create* their own identities they feel responsible for whatever decisions they make, as if they themselves are always to blame within this new individualism: if only they had made different choices, life would have turned out differently.

Individuals have been made more responsible for their fates within postmodern cultures.

The disciplines of the global market economy produce their own insecurities as people can feel that they are constantly being 'appraised' and must somehow 'prove' their 'worth' to the organisations for whom they work. This shows a refiguring of a Protestant ethic within corporate and managerial cultures in which people can feel that their lives are segmented as they are broken into discrete activities which must be separately regulated and appraised. A younger generation that has grown up to take these *insecurities* for granted, never having been offered the idea of a long-term job and accepting that their skills will need to be constantly updated and their lives will constantly change, form their own identities in relation to these pressures, mediated through relations of class, 'race' and ethnicities. Often they learn to look only to the future and it can be difficult to acknowledge their complex inheritances, especially if they threaten to be 'excess baggage' that produce loyalties which may make it harder for them to take whatever opportunities are available in the present.

Traditional forms of social theory need to be re/imagined if they are to illuminate the predicaments and precariousness of people lives in a newly globalised world of new capitalism. With mass migrations there are such widespread population movements across national boundaries that diverse communities are forced to learn to live together within multicultural spaces. If new social theories are to be able to engage ethically and politically with these new realities they must imagine new forms of cosmopolitics and transnational identities that can appreciate discourses of global human rights and democracy. If solidarities are to emerge between the global North and South, with global justice and more equal trade relations produced, we must re-vision the relationship between 'the West' and its 'others'.

This means engaging critically with dominant master narratives of the nation and nationalism and also the identities produced and sustained within traditional forms of social theory. We need to re-vision *the human* in ways that think outside the boundaries of a European modernity shaped through disembodied visions of the rational self. We must allow for visions of human vulnerability and precarious lives that allow us to recognise the fragility of the planet in a time of global warming and allow us to create identities that can make a difference through a recognition of individual responsibilities for global justice and a re/enchantment of nature.

Victor Jeleniewski Seidler
August 2009

ONE

Introduction: identities, bodies and differences

Thinking identities

When we think about identities we are thinking around the question 'Who am I?' We are asking this question at a particular time, a particular moment in our lives and at a particular place, within a particular culture or setting. This is a question that we are asking of ourselves and often something has happened to provoke this self-questioning, which marks a certain level of awareness. In the West, this is sometimes a question we ask ourselves in our early teenage years when we suddenly experience ourselves as separate from our parents. Somehow we experience ourselves as different from them, as having our own lives and future. Often there is a moment of self-realisation when we become aware that we have a life of our own and that at a certain moment this life will end. Possibly for the first time we become aware of our own mortality. This can be a disturbing realisation because we can feel suddenly *apart* and separate from those around us. It might be difficult to share this new thinking about ourselves and we might feel uneasy and fearful, unsure about where such self-questioning might lead.

Sometimes, if we grow up with brothers and sisters in the family, we can become aware that we are different from them too. We like doing different things and different activities make us happy. We might also think that we have a different character or personality from our siblings and so we aspire to live different kinds of lives. Even this awareness can feel threatening and unsettling because at some level we might feel that we do not really want to be different from others, rather we grow up wanting to be 'like everyone else'. It is this ambivalence that partly forms and shapes what we inherit as a sense of individuality, and it partly defines modern times.

This is a form of individualism that Erich Fromm (1991), a social theorist influenced by Marx, Freud and the Frankfurt School but who also took questions of religion seriously, has explored in *The fear of freedom*. Individualism marks a historical break between feudalism and capitalism, and means that we know ourselves as individuals and believe our fate to be determined by our individual abilities and talents. This helps to shape what we know under the influence of the Enlightenment as 'modernity'.

Fromm argues that within feudal society in Europe people did not have to ask themselves questions about their identities, because they were born into a particular position within society that defined their duties and obligations and their fixed identities. Traditional European societies were organised according to a distinct hierarchy in which people were born into fixed positions and responsibilities. The boundaries between these feudal orders were fixed as a matter of birth and blood. You knew what was expected of you, given the position you had been born into; you already knew in what position and in what labour you would die. The future was very much to repeat the present. There were moments of resistance and challenge, as with the peasant revolts in different parts of Medieval Europe, but these rarely challenged the dominant vision that the natural order was somehow ordained by God and that the social order was also part of this 'great chain of being' (Lovejoy, 1936). Such visions shaped what historians of Europe still identify as the 'pre-modern', when feudalism gave way to the economic relationships and cultural imaginations of Enlightenment modernity.

Capitalism and modernity

It was with the transition from feudalism to capitalism that questions about identity came to be framed in different terms. With the development of capitalist market relations land came to be conceived of as a *commodity* that could be exchanged on the market. As Fromm (1991) explores, with this historical shift of the breakdown of feudal orders there was also a new individualism expressed within a Protestant tradition which allowed individuals to have their own relationships with God, no longer mediated by the Church as it was within a Catholic tradition. The ambivalence emerges in the forms of recognition that could be given to *individual* abilities and capacities. It was gradually argued that different positions in society should not be inherited but should be decided based on talent and ability. Individuals were left to compete with one another for the available positions of power and authority. If these structural positions remained, the individuals who could fill them were, in theory, chosen based on their individual abilities and talents.

But, as Fromm (1991) crucially recognises, this Protestant tradition had also sharpened the Christian idea that people were 'born into sin', since the Protestant Church had broken with Catholic rituals and practices of confession. Under Protestantism there was no option for penance that could bring a new beginning, rather, one would be made to suffer eternally in hell for one's sins and evil deeds. Within a dominant Christian symbolic that had fractured into different churches, there opened up different ways of thinking and experiencing identity which related crucially to issues of authority. Within the Catholic tradition there is a clear sense that authority lies with the Church that defines the difference between 'good' and 'evil'. This was thought to be something that individuals could not legislate for themselves because it had already been decided by the authority of the Church as God's representative on earth. 'Goodness' became fundamentally a matter of obedience, of obeying the orders of authorities who knew what was expected of you better than you could know yourself. Of course, individuals might stray from the religious path, but they could always confess their sins and, if they did the necessary penance, they could begin again on a righteous path. Within Catholic cultures there can be less firm control and regulation of individual behaviours and identities because there is always the possibility of confession and so of a new beginning. Paradoxically there might be more freedom to sin.

Within a Protestant tradition, however, there is a greater awareness of individual conscience, which means that individuals can supposedly discern for themselves the difference between 'right' and 'wrong', 'good' and 'evil'. As Luther and Calvin made clear in their own ways people therefore had to silence their 'evil natures', so that they could directly listen to the authority of God's voice. There was a radical split between earthly and spiritual identities in which people had to destroy their 'animal' natures that were deemed to be sinful.

In *The Protestant ethic and the spirit of capitalism* Max Weber (1930) explores Calvinist doctrines of predestination: whether people would be 'saved' or not had been predetermined, so that they could only work in the hope that their success and achievement might serve as a sign of whether they had been redeemed, rather than left to dwell in hell. People learnt to *distrust* their own desires and inclinations, which they sought to suppress and silence so that they were not led astray. People were locked into a struggle against their 'animal' natures, fearful of what these natures might reveal if they were not controlled and silenced.

Modernity and protestantism

Social theories assumed that secularisation would follow in the wake of industrialisation. Even though many people in the industrialised

West have grown up within secular cultures, in which religion seems to have been marginalised, religious traditions (even in secularised forms) continue to influence and shape identities in the present and tacitly inform ways we think identities and how we feel about our bodies, appetites, desires and sexualities. This is to recognise the ways that modernity has been shaped through the secularised terms of a dominant Christian discourse, which in different ways continues to shape identities even though we might be largely unaware of its influence and uneasy about tracing the lines of its continuing presence. It remains a continuing strength of Weber's work that he can remind us of *how* capitalist societies remained indebted to forms of identity and character produced within the terms of a Protestant ethic. He was less aware that he was also describing the conditions for a dominant white heterosexual masculinity that could alone take its reason for granted. It was men who supposedly had the strength of character, because they were 'independent' and 'self-sufficient', to *resist* the temptations of their animal natures. Women were deemed to be the 'weaker sex' because their behaviour was likely to be more influenced by their emotions, feelings and desires.

Within a Protestant moral culture we learn to think identities in dualistic terms. When we think about the question 'Who am I?' we already split the idea of 'self' from a nature which is deemed to be 'animal'. This echoes a symbolic Christian tradition in which there is a radical disdain of the 'animal' that is identified with the 'earthly', set in contrast with the 'human' that is identified with the 'spiritual'. This rejection of the 'animal' and 'earthly' has set the terms for dis/embodied notions of identity whereby the disembodied spiritual self came, within modernity, to be identified with the **rational self** as outlined by **Immanuel Kant**. Kant's dualistic vision, as I explored in *Kant, respect and injustice* (Seidler, 1986), reinforced the idea that it was through reason that identities were established and sustained; it was through ideas and learning to think for themselves as free and autonomous rational selves that people would occupy their own identities. This reinforces a vision of personal identity that focuses on memories and thoughts, as if to lose one's memory is to threaten a sense of self.

As I argue in *Jewish philosophy and Western culture* (Seidler, 2007a), this is where a Greek/Christian tradition in the West has set itself in opposition to a Jewish tradition that has been identified as 'Carnal Israel'. As it sought to consolidate its opposition to Judaism so Christianity tended to understand itself more in these dualistic terms with a rejection of bodies and sexualities. This made it difficult for a dominant Christian tradition to understand its Jewish roots and Jesus as a Jewish prophet to be understood within the context of Jewish prophetic sources. Rather this disavowal of the Jewish sources of Christianity produced a form of radical denial in which historically Christian is set against Jew as denigrated 'other' and so as 'enemy' that led, eventually, through long traditions of Christian anti-Semitism, to the Holocaust and the idea that the 'enemy within' had to be destroyed so that the nation state could be 'purified'. The ways we learn to think identities in the West have often been set in terms of understanding what we are not – of the rejected 'other' or aspects of self. The terms of Christian anti-Semitism have also set the terms in which uncivilised 'others' were to be identified as 'animal' and so as 'uncivilised' and 'less than human' within colonialism (see Goldberg, 1993; Mufti, 2007).

Nature / culture

The disdain for nature that has been so much part of Western culture has framed the relationship between nature and culture. In secularised Christian societies nature has been identified with the earthly and the animal and set against the spiritual and the human. This dichotomy has helped shape inner anxieties and feelings of guilt and shame, and framed the struggle of emotionally divided and fragmented human beings who have asserted their 'humanity' by denying their animal natures, including their bodies and sexualities that have been associated with 'sins of the flesh'. People could only aspire towards their identities as 'spiritual selves' if they were ready to disavow their bodies and sexualities. Sexuality was deemed sinful, only justifiable for procreation within relationships of marriage. Human beings were born through sin, since they were born through sexuality. Christianity reinterpreted the 'Book of Genesis', as part of its more general appropriation of Jewish texts, and it was as if the expulsion from Eden was being re-enacted with each new birth. Since celibacy was framed as an ideal within Christian societies people were haunted by a sense of inadequacy and fear that their sexual desires somehow revealed an untamed 'animal nature'.

This meant that for a dominant Christian tradition within the West the body and sexuality were *not* part of identity – part of who we are – but rather were part of a disdained 'animal nature'. Individuals had to 'rise above' or transcend their 'animal natures' if they were to be able to recognise themselves as spiritual selves. This produced a tacit and often unrecognised hostility towards the body and also to embodied forms of knowledge that were regarded as 'subjective' and 'anecdotal'. It set the terms for a rationalist tradition that disdained emotions and feelings as sources of knowledge.

The Renaissance and humanism

There were moments in the early humanist tradition, for example in the works of Desiderius Erasmus, that linked back to the Renaissance when it was appreciated that people should develop their natures rather than suppress them, in marked contrast to the Enlightenment rationalism that followed. During the Renaissance, the recovery of Greek and Gnostic texts in Europe prompted scholars such as Marsillo Ficino to propose a different vision of identity as *self-realisation*. It was through coming to terms with your emotional life, rather than disdaining the emotions as 'feminine', that human beings could grow and develop. There was still an organic vision of human identity that had not yet been replaced within modernity with René Descartes' mechanistic notions of bodies and minds (see Rée, 1974; Williams, 1978). There was a sense, alive within the Renaissance in Italy, that human beings could create a sense of balance between different aspects of the self. There were practices to help bring thinking into balance with feeling, as reason was not to be threatened by emotions. This represented a moment when self-knowledge within **Gnostic traditions** was deemed as providing knowledge of God. Self-knowledge was not feared for revealing a threatening 'animal nature', instead there was a recognition of different levels of experience and the need to integrate different aspects of self. There was a sense of individual growth and self-development through different stages of life and an awareness of the importance of love and intimacy.

Within a tradition of European humanism there were complex inheritances that promised quite different visions of identity, growth and development and which questioned straightforward assumptions about a fixed or given conception of human nature. Renaissance humanism advocated that individuals should develop their qualities in a balanced way. If people developed their mental faculties, but failed to develop their emotional lives, this would create disharmony within the self. Rather than thinking about the self separately, as a distinct category, it was connected with the development of natural qualities. Even if the humanist vision of human development was different from the rationalist assumption of control over an 'animal nature' it remained critically gendered. Women were still deemed to be closer to nature and therefore more likely to be governed by their emotions and desires, so it was a dominant masculinity which was still more likely to sustain a sense of balance. There was at least a recognition of the growth and development of different aspects of identity and of human beings developing both within the realm of culture and within the realm of nature.

Rationalism and the Scientific Revolutions

Rather than learn about our identities as human beings through our relationships *with* nature, in the rationalist tradition nature came to be regarded as a *threat* which needed to be controlled, even suppressed. We inherited a language in Europe that reflected a dominant Christian narrative that talks about the need within modernity to *control* both 'internal' nature and 'external' nature. Somehow progress was to be measured through the instrumentalisation of control as regulation. Progress was to be measured and there were to be instruments that could deliver objective measures. The Scientific Revolutions of the 17th century worked to reduce nature to 'matter' and to identify progress with the control and domination of nature. Carolyn Merchant (1980) tracks gendered transformations of nature, so often regarded as 'feminine' in the West, in the ways we imagine relationships between nature and culture. Merchant recognises how the denigration of nature within the West has gone hand in hand with the denigration of women. While women have traditionally been regarded as sexual objects who are 'closer to nature', living nature has been reduced to dead matter with 'the death of nature' (see also Griffin, 1981, 1982; Midgely, 1989).

The 17th-century Scientific Revolutions led to a reordering of gender relations of power (Easlea, 1981; Roper, 1994; see also Warner, 1976). In stark example, in early modern Europe women with medical and herbal knowledges were deemed to be threats to the new masculinist sciences, and accused of being witches. Linked as they were to nature and therefore to the body and sexuality, they were considered to be doing the work of the devil. Also, being deemed to be closer to nature, these women were somehow identified with Jews in the dominant Christian imaginary and were forced to wear three-pointed hats similar to those that Jews were forced to wear to mark their difference. They had to be exposed and were often punished through the witch-burnings that took place across Europe in the 16th and 17th centuries. Along with the enslavement of people of African descent, this was the dark side of modernity, rarely explored in conventional histories of the Scientific Revolutions.

Modernity, reason and nature

Within an Enlightenment vision of modernity that grew out of the world-view created during the Scientific Revolutions of the 17th century there was a sharpened distinction between nature and culture. We learned to think about nature as given, as if it could somehow only generate *fixed* identities while it was within the realm of culture alone that identities could be *created*. Culture was the sphere of language and discourse as it is framed within poststructuralist theory. This is represented in a particular cartography of the person whereby, when we are asked to point to ourselves, we learn to point to our minds as the space of identity. As rational selves we learn to disown the body and sexuality as part of an 'animal nature'. It is as if there is an invisible line at the neck; the body being part of a disenchanted nature and so the object of medical sciences, while the head and mind is alone part of culture.

Within structuralist and poststructuralist traditions in social theory we inherit a categorical distinction between nature and culture and find that, rather than being challenged, the **Cartesian tradition** is sustained through the primacy given to culture as framed through language and discourse. We learn that if animals remain part of a sphere of nature, then human beings alone live and shape their identities within the realm of culture. Where the 'animal' is to be explored, through fixed and given desires and needs, the 'human' is to be regarded as having mutable and fluid needs and desires that characterise freedom. This encodes the disdain for the 'animal' that has defined the category of the 'human' within the West. We learn to define the human through a relationship of hierarchy and superiority in relation to the animal, so it is through an independent and autonomous faculty of reason that the human is defined. We learn to accept a radical distinction between reason and nature which becomes a defining feature of Kant's moral theory that did so much to shape the classical social theories of Emile Durkheim (see Chapter Eight) and Max Weber (see Chapter Four).

For Kant, the distinction between reason and nature remains crucial to the ways in which he conceives the very notion of 'human nature' (Seidler, 1986). He makes clear that it is reason which allows us to be 'human', while the nature element is to be disdained as 'animal'. It is only as rational selves that we have identities as human beings. This establishes a crucial dualism that is taken for granted in different ways by Durkheim and Weber: that it is reason alone that is an independent and sovereign faculty radically separated from nature.

Echoing a Cartesian tradition, the body and sexuality are deemed to be part of a disenchanted nature, as they are reduced to matter. For example, the body becomes the *object* of the medical gaze and the doctor alone comes to have knowledge of our bodies, while we are left with 'mere' *subjective* experience. This encodes a pervasive distinction between knowledge and experience whereby knowledge is taken to be 'objective' and 'rational', while experience is 'subjective' and 'personal'. In its own way such a rationalist tradition serves to undermine our self-confidence, because it means that we cannot learn to trust the experiences we have as a basis for knowledge. We learn to be silent as we stand before the doctor who alone can have reliable (and objective) knowledge, which sustains a hierarchy of medical knowledge.

We cannot even trust all of our own thoughts, as we learn that our negative or 'evil thoughts' do not really come from us, but from an animal nature that seeks to influence and determine people's behaviours and actions. For Kant this means that we must learn to silence 'inclinations' – emotions, feelings and desires – so that we can listen to the inner voice of reason (see Seidler, 1986). As Kant frames the distinction, emotions and desires are placed in the body and so are *external* – not really part of who we are – while it is reason alone with which we have an *internal* relationship and which is the source of freedom and morality. This means that we must learn to suppress our 'inclinations', since they are seeking to influence behaviour externally and because they can only lead us astray. They play no role in the freedom and autonomy that rests in reason alone, and therefore no part in defining our identities.

Modernity and identity

If these distinctions shape a Cartesian tradition and its notions of personal identity, it is challenged in different but related ways by both Sigmund Freud and Ludwig Wittgenstein (see Chapters Two and Three).

Freud recovered a Renaissance humanism, at least in part, in his critique of a modernity shaped around the repression of sexuality (Freud, 1930). He gave voice to the sufferings that were created through the repression of 'animal nature' and thereby questioned the moral theories of identity that had been encoded within theological traditions. Freud recognised the ways in which modernity had encoded the contempt of the body and sexuality. Modernity was framed within the terms of a secularised Christianity, even when it presented itself in opposition to religious authorities. An Enlightenment modernity carried a vision of freedom that had encouraged individuals to think

9

for themselves, so escaping from what Kant framed as the 'childhood dependency' of feudal authorities. While this allowed people as 'free and equal' autonomous selves to imagine they could create their own identities, according to reason alone, Freud helped give voice to the silent sufferings, anxieties and neuroses that followed in the wake of sexual repression.

Freud challenged the prevailing rationalist forms of social theory and refused the sharp distinction between nature and culture. He explored how identities are shaped both within the terms of nature *and* culture, by biology as well as by social relations. In opening up these questions that have remained crucial to the difficult relationships between psychoanalysis and social theory, he has challenged the Cartesian tradition that has framed identities as a matter of mind, reason and consciousness. Rather than suppressing our 'inclinations', our emotions, feelings and desires, Freud and post-analytical psychotherapies would encourage us to learn how to come to terms with them and to acknowledge them as part of our identity.

The Cartesian tradition is also questioned by Isaiah Berlin when, in conversation with Steven Lukes, he questions the idea that "The self, the human subject is simply whatever acculturation makes of it." He also believed that human nature sets limits to the intelligible ends that human beings can pursue so that "the number of ends that human beings can pursue is not infinite ... in practice human beings would not be human if that were so" (quoted in Lukes, 2001, p 55).

Wittgenstein recognised something similar in his later philosophy, that in order to understand what 'I am afraid' means on a particular occasion one might have to take into account the time of voice and the context in which it is uttered. This is something with which social workers might be familiar. In his biography of Wittgenstein, Ray Monk recognises that:

> There is no reason to think that a general theory of fear would be much help here (still less a general theory of language). Far more to the point would be an alert and observant sensitivity to people's faces, voices and situations. This kind of sensitivity can be gained only be experience – by attentive looking and listening to the people around us. (Monk, 1991, pp 547-8)

When Wittgenstein was walking with his friend Drury in the west of Ireland, they came across a five-year-old girl sitting outside a cottage. Wittgenstein implored, "Drury, just look at the expression on the child's face", adding, "You don't take enough notice of people's faces; it is a fault you ought to try to correct" (quoted in Monk, 1991, p 548). Monk recognises that this piece of advice "is implicitly embodied" in Wittgenstein's philosophy of psychology:

> An inner process stands in need of outward criteria. But those outward criteria stand in need of careful attention. ... What is 'internal' is not hidden from us. To observe someone's outward behaviour – if we understand them – is to observe their state of mind. The understanding required can be more or less refined. (1991, p 548)

Can one learn the difference between a genuine and affected expression of feeling? Wittgenstein says: "Even here there are those whose judgement is 'better' and those whose judgement is 'worse'." As sometimes happens in his philosophical writings, he goes on to answer his own question:

> Can one learn this knowledge? Yes; some can. Not, however, by taking a course in it, but through 'experience'. – Can someone else be a person's teacher in this? Certainly. From time to time he gives him the right tip. – This is what 'learning' and 'teaching' are like here – What one acquires here is not a technique; one learns correct judgements. There are also rules, but they do not form a system, and only experienced people can apply them right. Unlike calculating rules. (quoted in Monk, 1991, p 549)

In this way Wittgenstein moves beyond those who would interpret Freud's psychoanalysis as an exploration of an 'inner psychic life' that exists in autonomous space of its own and begins to suggest affiliations with post-analytic forms of body psychotherapies that move across the boundaries of 'inner' and 'outer' and so help frame a **reflexive identity politics** that is also a life politics.

Morals and ethics

In his biography of Isaiah Berlin, Michael Ignatieff comments:

> we are moral beings: we would not qualify as human if moral considerations, however false or inadequate, were absent from our deliberations. And from this ground – of

> a shared body and a shared language of moral discourse –
> we know the inhuman when we encounter it. (Ignatieff,
> 1998, pp 249-50)

Returning to our 'rational self', for Kant, it is only when we act out of a sense of *duty* that our actions have any moral worth. Kant struggles with the idea that within a capitalist society everything has a price, so he wonders what this means about human worth and dignity. This Kantian vision is echoed in different ways within a modern and postmodern sensibility where the focus is often on the freedom that people have to create their own identities. Rather than imagining identities to be fixed, as if they subsist through time and across place, identities become fluid and constantly changing. In modernity people can choose to adopt different identities in different settings, or at different times (see Bauman, 1991; Giddens, 1991; Freidman and Lash, 1992).

Within postmodern societies there is a growing realisation that people are no longer fixed by their inherited identities, in ways that, say, political party allegiance used to fall along class lines. People no longer appear to be so determined by the structural positions that they occupy within class, 'race' and gender relations of power and subordination. This has meant that questions of identity and allegiance have become more pressing, not so easily predicted, so we need new ways of thinking about the complex relationships between identities and cultures. This can also question assumptions so often taken for granted within modernity, which, within Kantian terms, would treat culture and history as forms of 'unfreedom' and determination.

Today, we often learn to think that rather than being *fixed* by nature, identities are 'socially and historically *constructed*' within the realm of culture and of our own choosing. But often it is difficult to explain the contrast or to fully appreciate the *disdain* for nature that this sustains. We should not conclude too crudely that a humanist tradition assumed a singular and shared vision of human nature, while a structuralist tradition allows that 'human nature' is not 'given' but is socially and historically constructed. We must be aware that there are more complex relations between nature and culture, biology and society, as the neurosciences and techno-sciences are discovering. Therefore, treating nature as 'constructed' and 'artificial', and so as a feature of culture and discourse, does not illuminate those complexities. Rather, we need new languages that can appreciate *how* identities are embodied and how they are shaped through senses as well as through relationships with objects, and how they are also shaped by journeys that families make across space and transnational memories of losses embodied as traumatic histories.

Further reading

Erich Fromm

Erich Fromm's *The fear of freedom* (1991) draws on a critical reading of Max Weber's *The protestant ethic and the spirit of capitalism* (1930) to explicate the individualism that has characterised competitive capitalism, which has left people often feeling isolated and alone, unable to trust and constantly having to prove themselves in their competitive relationships with others. In reality this presents the history of a particular dominant European Protestant masculinity.

Enlightenment modernity

Classical Social Theory was traditionally taught around the distinction between feudalism and capitalism and the different accounts offered of this transition by Marx, Weber and Durkheim. More recently this transition has been framed through an understanding of 'Enlightenment modernity'. For a helpful reading of the feudal relationships and how they blended nature, culture and political hierarchies, see Lovejoy (1936). See also Charles Taylor's *Sources of the self* (1989).

Max Weber

For some discussions that acknowledge relationships between Weber's writings on the protestant ethic and the exploration of dominant masculinities within capitalist societies see, for instance, David Morgan's *Discovering men* (1992), Bologh's *Love or greatness* (1990) and Seidler's *Unreasonable men* (1994) and *Transforming masculinities* (2005).

Immanuel Kant

I explore the structure of Kant's moral theory and the implications for our sense of morality that follows from the denial of emotions, feelings and desires in *Kant, respect and injustice* (1986). I argue that emotions, feelings and desires are sources of human dignity and self-worth and so fundamental to notions of identity.

Gnostic traditions

For some appreciation of Gnosticism across diverse religious traditions see, for instance, Elaine Pagels (1982) *The Gnostic Gospels* and Gershom Scholem (1990) *Origins of Kabbalah*. For a sense of Sufi traditions within Islam that share certain Gnostic elements see Nasr (1991) *Islamic spirituality II* and Trimington (1973) *The Sufi origins of Islam*.

Sigmund Freud

Freud's exploration of the relationship of civilisation in the West to the repression of sexuality is explored in *Civilisation and its discontents* (1930). For an illuminating biography of Freud's intellectual development which helps to place this theme within the broader context of his work see, Peter Gay's *Freud: A life of our time* (1988).

Isaiah Berlin

For some helpful reflections on the nature of freedom and identity within modernity see, for instance, Isaiah Berlin's *Four essays on liberty* (1969) and *The age of enlightenment* (1979). For a sense of views that have challenged an Enlightenment modernity and so helped shape the Counter-Enlightenment and Romanticism see Isaiah Berlin's *Vico and Herder* (1976) and the essays collected as *Against the current* (1981). See also Charles Taylor's *Sources of the self* (1989) and Zygmunt Bauman's *Modernity and ambivalence* (1991), *Liquid modernity* (2000) and *Liquid times* (2007).

Modernity

For some helpful discussions about the relationships of modernity to cultural notions of identity see Friedman and Lash (1992) *Modernity and identity*; Bauman (1991) *Modernity and ambivalence*, (2004) *Identity*; Giddens (1991) *Modernity and self-identity*; Taylor (2004) *Modern social imaginaries*; Beck and Beck-Gernsheim (2002) *Individualization*.

Judaism in Christian imaginary

For some interesting reflections on ways Judaism was identified with carnal Israel in the dominant Christian imaginary so helping us think about the ways other religious traditions including Islam are framed, see Boyarin (1992) *Carnal Israel: Reading sex in Talmudic culture*; Seidler (2007) *Jewish philosophy and Western culture: A modern introduction*.

TWO

Challenges: complexities / diversity / self-worth

This chapter explores how issues of identity, power, bodies and self-worth developed through the challenges that feminism and gay liberation, which in turn learnt from the Black Power and Civil Rights movements, made to an Enlightenment modernity.

Challenges: complexity / diversity / self-worth

Within modernity we learn that people have to establish a sense of individual identity through *separating* from collective identities that might seek to influence and determine their behaviour externally. In Kantian terms identity becomes a matter of will, so that you can *resist* the collective identities that might otherwise claim you. The context of liberal individualism means that, for example, children often learn that they have to 'think for themselves' in ways which mean they must resist the influence of traditional cultures and identities.

With the development of new social movements helping to shape postmodernities in the 1960s and 1970s there was a break, in practice as well as in theory, with certain modernist assumptions which would think identity, dignity and self-worth in the disembodied terms of the rational self. With the feminism and gay liberation movements there was a recognition that gender and sexual identities involve coming to terms with personal and emotional histories which have been framed by larger social and historical contexts of patriarchal and homophobic cultures and in which particular identities had been shamed or denigrated. This also questioned forms of male violence that had sustained the implicit power of dominant heterosexual masculinities, so normalising a particular order of gender and sexual power (see Brittan, 1989).

These movements questioned the disavowal of bodies and sexualities that had been regarded as part of a despised nature that could not help shape and define embodied identities (see Chapter One). They challenged a liberal moral culture to recognise that as a young woman learnt to think of herself not just as a person, but also as a woman whose gender had been subordinated and its meanings silenced, she was defining herself *more clearly* as an individual, not simply identifying with a collective identity. As a young man refused to be shamed about his sexuality at school but started to take risks to share his sexual orientation with his friends, he was *affirming* his identity, rather than denying it. This was to take an ethical position thereby helping to shape new conceptions of the relationships between ethics, identities, sexuality and power, at the same time as it challenged prevailing patriarchal and heterosexual relations of power.

These movements for sexual liberation had learnt from the black consciousness and Black Power movements of the late 1960s in the US which realised that individuals had to transform their sense of self-worth as they challenged a white supremacy. According to Darcus Howe, we must appreciate the particular histories of migration and different experiences that have shaped generations. Forty years ago in Britain:

> every move was haunted by the overwhelming race prejudice which dominated the landscape. Huge energies were trapped in an isolated way of life in which police malpractice was a major feature. Things began to loosen with the new generation, which was as comfortable with toad in the hole as it was with fish and chips. School, and school dinners, drew us out of isolation and into direct social relation with whites. This proximity prompted huge demands for racial equality, especially when American Black Power movements began to stalk the international stage. (Howe, 2000, p 29)

Identity and difference

In Britain, the riots in Brixton and Toxteth in 1981 were a watershed in race relations and the politics of difference, although, at the time, they were not properly understood:

> The riots of 1981, which appeared on the surface only as mass destruction, concealed another much more important factor – a major escape from the isolation of the generation which preceded it. In the last 20 years, we have appeared alongside whites in places hitherto reserved for whites alone. There are black and Asian faces on the television screens,

police officers of rank, leaders of trade unions, bishops and vicars, scribes and novelists, teachers and managers. You name it and we occupy it. And the demand for more is on the agenda as never before.

The myth of white superiority and its engaging partner – black incompetences – has taken a huge beating in this movement. Colour of skin is becoming less a determinant of capability. It merges at a moment in history where class superiority is being undermined by a new meritocracy. (Howe, 2000, p 29)

If this is a hopeful presentation, it does not suggest that the structures of racism have been completely overturned. This does not have to be reiterated in the face of the brutal murder of Stephen Lawrence on the streets of south-east London and the inquiry that followed, which presented the reality of institutional racism in the police force. Although the Macpherson report (Macpherson, 1999) did not label individual police officers as racist, it highlighted that the police culture and institutions needed to adapt to the realities of a multicultural society. In an interview with *The Spectator* Sir William Macpherson acknowledged that he had hesitated before using the 'institutional racism' charge. Macpherson stated that the phrase was not his and expressly denied that every Metropolitan police officer was racist; he insisted, however, that it was the only way he could sum up a systematic failure of policing in which unconsciously racist assumptions had played a part at several stages:

It was a collective failure, little groups of people. Not just one person, not just the rotten apple in the barrel, but each infecting the other. I could have bottled out. I could have decided not to mention racism at all, and stuck to all the policing questions. But as this procession of coppers came in, our mouths sort of fell open, and we thought, we are bloody well going to have to say it publicly. (*The Guardian*, 5 January 2001, p 6)

A liberal moral culture that wanted to wish away the realities of 'race', ethnic, gender and sexual oppression, assuming that people could abstract themselves from these collective identities to relate to one another as equal individuals has been forced to question some of its fundamental assumptions. Gradually a discourse of human rights that can challenge traditions forms of discrimination that have been in place for years has gained authority. If people are not harming others then they should not be discriminated against. An example of this is the Wolfenden Report (Committee on Homosexual Offences and Prostitution, 1957), which helped to decriminalise homosexual relationships between consenting men in private and opened up a cultural space in which gay liberation movements could argue that people should not be discriminated against for their sexual orientation. This was to question the normalisation of a single pattern of heterosexual marriage and was eventually to lead to the recognition of civil partnerships as a form of gay marriage.

Complex identities

Within a postmodern culture we need to appreciate that identities are complex and that people often carry diverse identities, histories and traditions as a result of mass immigration and a globalised economy. Often people inherit hybrid and 'hyphenated' identities as they come to terms with the different cultures, religions and ethnicities that are present within their own families. Within the increasingly multicultural Britain that developed in the 1980s and 1990s there were new spaces for identity that had not existed in earlier times when a politics of assimilation ruled. Different generations carry their own anxieties about identity and belonging and often there are conflicts between different ethnic groups who might for a time seek alliances with one another, as African-Caribbean and Asian migrants did in the 1970s and 1980s under a shared political category of 'black' only later to seek out distinct identities of their own. As second-generation Asian migrants born and educated in Britain feel less connected to their parents' country of origin, which their parents still regard as 'home', so some, particularly after 9/11, have identified themselves more strongly as British Muslims distinguishing themselves still further.

   Often these dual or mixed positions that people occupy come to represent a separate category that demands recognition, such as British Asian or African-American. Despite globalisation and mass migration changing the nature and authority of the nation state (Seidler, 2007b), it can still feel uneasy in a post-9/11 world to accept that people increasingly live transnational identities in multicultural societies and so feel complex loyalties that reach across different spaces. In the face of the 'war against terror' there has been a return to notions of national identity and the master narratives of the nation as there has been a crisis in confidence in multiculturalisms and the idea of Britain as a multicultural society. Politicians have looked towards the US for different models and practices of belonging, such as introducing 'citizenship ceremonies' as a way of marking a significant moment of changing identity.

When we talk in terms of multiple or **complex identities** we are acknowledging a *range of differences* that people can feel they need to come to terms with or somehow integrate in their lives. Young people might be coming to terms with the mixed racial, religious, ethnic or sexual inheritances in their families as they might be with their gender and sexed identities. They may still have to deal with the scenario Ien Ang describes:

"Where do you come from?"

"From Holland."

"No, where are you really from?" (Ang, 2001, p 29)

A focus on a person's ethnicity as a way of categorising national identity is problematic for 'hyphenated' individuals, for whom the issue of 'where one is from' might be much less relevant, at least for the present than 'where one is at'. But it is not always easy to identify 'where we are at' with ourselves at any time, since at different times and at different ages we might be subject to quite different pressures. Different identities might become significant and so come into play at particular times. For example, it might be difficult for young people who are coming to terms with their gender identities in the early years of secondary school to really take on issues around sexuality, which for older adolescents might be more significant.

It is difficult to generalise and we need a theoretical understanding of embodied identities that can illuminate the *different temporalities* through which people come to terms with aspects of their experience. The impact of divorce is often minimised by young people, especially boys, only to return in later years as a much more significant influence in their lives than they might have been willing to acknowledge at the time, when they were mainly concerned to show that they could 'deal with it'. It might be easier for young women to reach out to friends for support, while young men can still feel they somehow 'should be' *in control* and able to handle whatever life throws at them.

For, as a young man coming to terms with his gay identity appreciates, 'coming out' can take time and is part of a process of engaging with significant others in your life. There are spaces in which you might feel safe to share aspects of yourself and others in which you feel you have to be more guarded and self-protective. These are judgements people will have to make for themselves and they will be framed differently in different cultural settings. For instance, in Spain it might be more difficult to think you could come out to your family, who may already know about your sexuality but do not want to be confronted in this way. We must be careful not to universalise on the basis of particular anglophone experiences and to appreciate the different cultural and historical settings through which identities are shaped and the different kinds of compromises that people might feel appropriate. This can reflect different Protestant and Catholic traditions predominant in the north and south of Europe, as well as the different moral cultures (as discussed in Chapter One). A Protestant culture tends to focus more on individual moral consistency and so would support the process of 'coming out'. In a Catholic culture, such as that in Spain, while it might be possible to come out to friends who are able to offer support, one might feel quite wary of upsetting or even dishonouring parents. Under these circumstances, people can be so used to being 'flexible' and living different identities in different spaces that it hardly bothers them (Jimenez, 2002).

People have to come to terms with multiple or complex identities that are often in tense and ambivalent relationship with each other. It might be easier to come to terms with certain aspects, rather than others. In my own experience, I was struck by how a generation of men were influenced by feminism to come to terms with their inherited masculinities. These were universal experiences to do with the power and authority of heterosexual masculinities and we were challenged by feminists to deal with our own identity issues rather than emotionally depending on them in intimate relationships. This was a way of providing more balance within a relationship as men learnt to draw emotional support from other men, with whom they were finally learning to talk.

In the early 1970s partly as a response to feminism men got together in consciousness-raising groups to explore our often ambivalent relationships with a dominant white heterosexual masculinity that had remained strangely invisible and unnamed within the dominant culture. We would explore our own feelings for other men and fears of gayness that could make it difficult to express the love and affection we felt for our friends. In some ways we were 'queering' heterosexual masculinities and, through naming our own fears and sharing them with other men, we were shaping new masculinities which allowed men to explore our emotional lives and cultural inheritances. This was a process that took time and we used to meet every couple of weeks for a number of years until some of us felt confident enough to produce the journal *Achilles Heel* to publicly explore what we had investigated about the tensions between men and masculinities. Theoretically, this allowed me to grasp how a dominant masculinity was taken for granted, also in philosophy and social theory, as it alone could take its reason and rationality for granted and it provided the standard against which 'others' were to be defined and judged as 'lacking'.

Masculinity, like whiteness, was a structure of power that did not need to speak its name; masculinity provided a norm in which men often found it difficult to define what it meant for them to be men, only being able to say that being a man meant that you were *not* a woman. It is an identity that traditionally defined itself against the *threat* of the feminine. As discussed in the previous chapter, since emotions and feelings were regarded as 'feminine' they were not allowed to a dominant masculinity. It may have been because Jewish men in Western Europe were often defined as 'feminine', as were Asian men in Britain in the 1970s, that this marginality made it possible for Jewish men to understand claims which early feminism was making. There was also a question about the racialisation of 'Jewishness' and about whether or not 'Jewish' could be 'white'. Early Jewish immigrants into the US made efforts to claim whiteness for themselves, against the resistance of the dominant powers that framed a racial politics that has been traditionally divided between 'black' subordination and 'white' supremacy (see Biale et al, 1998; Jacobson, 1998; Goldson, 2006).

In the 1960s, within a culture of assimilation, you would show your respect for someone's Jewishness by generally ignoring and not making an issue of it – it was through indifference that you demonstrated respect, although tacitly this was often to leave identities shamed. So, while I was able to challenge my understandings of masculinities in the 1970s, it seemed to take longer, for me personally in the 1980s, to be open about questions of Jewishness, especially when they linked back to my family's traumatic histories of loss in the Holocaust. Exploring similar issues, Eva Hoffman describes how her parents' experiences of the war unwittingly infiltrated and affected her own psyche:

> I have not known what peace of mind feels like…. Is it that
> I come from the war, while my parents were born before it?
> Is it that I have only struggled with spectres – their spectres
> among others – while they have battered themselves against
> the hard realities? (Hoffman, 1991, p 129)

Often it is questions that can take time to formulate that help shape identities. If there *are* answers these might come a lot later, if at all.

Issues present themselves in their own time and identities that might have been difficult to affirm in the 1970s could become much easier to acknowledge within the multicultural spaces that people growing up in the 1990s took very much for granted. Young people today do not, at least on the surface, appear to have the same issues around embracing diverse racial, ethnic and sexual identities. A younger generation are more likely to be 'out' about their differences and, rather, feel obliged to act as a kind of 'representative', answering the questions of their friends. They take different identities very much for granted and seem better able to support one another emotionally.

Self-worth

As we acknowledge that different generations shape complex identities within the context of different orders of social relations, so we appreciate the breaks in the communication and contact that take place between parents and children. Often children and young people feel that they live in such a different world from the one that their parents have known that the instruction and counsel they receive carries little weight with them. This is a recurrent theme but it takes on a different intensity in different times, especially in today's globalised world, when new technologies and the internet give young people access to virtual worlds that their parents could hardly have dreamed of.

As postmodern culture is increasingly shaped by global media and new technologies, identities are shaped by very different forces. While at some level young people might feel more open and able to visually present themselves on social networking sites such as Facebook, there are also choices they make about to whom they will give access to particular levels of personal information. Young people become skilled in self-presentation and they recognise that these skills are transferable within the new capitalism (Sennet, 1998). There are increasing numbers of new means by which people can communicate with one another, but also diverse approaches to establishing ways of belonging. As the owner of a mobile phone of a distinct brand or through wearing designer clothes with particular logos people make distinct claims to belong. In this way they also exclude others who might not be able to afford similar models or brands. The branding of a technological world has also meant that there is access to information and support on the internet which can help people in exploring their uncertain identities. Fearful of sharing with friends young people can often reach out more easily on the impersonal spaces of the internet to explore emerging feelings and desires.

But there is also a darker and more risky side to these new technologies. In a recent report by the charity Young Voices, which questioned 7,000 pupils in rural and inner-city schools, one in ten reported severe bullying, including physical violence. Many felt that they could not tell anyone what was happening to them as their treatment by other children had sent them into a spiral of depression: "I hated myself. I felt there must be something I'd done wrong or terrible for this to happen. I felt ashamed", said one 14-year-old girl. With many children now owning mobile phones, harassment can be conducted by phone and email: "They send sick messages to your mobile", one girl said. It was torment by text messages and silent calls that was believed to have driven 15-year-old Gail Jones to take an overdose at her Merseyside home in 2000 (reported in *The Observer*, 7 January 2001, p 10).

According to Adrienne Katz of Young Voices racism appears to be a factor, with 25% of children from minority ethnic groups reporting having been severely bullied, as opposed to 13% of white pupils. One of the most heart-rending cases that highlights the interrelation of issues of class, gender and race in bullying, was that of the 13-year-old Manchester schoolboy Vijay Singh whose parents found the following entries in his diary:

Monday: My money was taken.

Tuesday: Names called.

Wednesday: Uniform torn.

Thursday: My body pouring with blood.

Friday: It's ended.

Saturday: Freedom.

Saturday was the day Vijay was found dead, hanging from the banister of his home (*The Observer*, 7 January 2001, p 10).

As Katz understands it: "There are factors which protect children: being bolder and having high self-esteem and positive, warm parenting is overwhelmingly linked to those who are not being bullied" (*The Observer*, 7 January 2001, p 10). The Young Voices study found that home life plays a vital part in determining whether a child will be a bully or a victim:"For both the victims and the bullies, parenting was markedly less positive, colder and more controlling. Bullies were far more likely to see aggression at home" (Katz quoted in *The Observer*, 7 January 2001, p 10). This link confirms the significance of early childhood experience in shaping identities and the importance of children being able to develop their own self-esteem and self-confidence. It shows the complex factors that are helping to shape young people's identities, which also highlight the kinds of sensitivities that social workers and youth workers need to develop to work effectively with them. The complex interaction between issues of gender, 'race' and self-worth all help shape the complex and multiple identities that young people live with in their everyday lives. Often these are pressures that a dominant white culture finds difficult to understand, because they often do not have to live with them themselves. The functionalist theories that have for so long underpinned social and community work training find these hard to illuminate.

In 1997, Kelly Yeomans, aged 13, took an overdose of painkillers to end an 18-month bullying campaign. At the time, her mother Julie said, "We keep going over the same question: 'Why didn't she tell somebody?'" (quoted in *The Observer*, 7 January 2001, p 10). Often young people can feel shamed by being the objects of bullying, as if it reflects that there is something wrong with them. They might not want to tell anyone, because this feels as if it will only make them feel worse about themselves. This reflects the unease within wider culture about communicating emotions and feelings that are so often, especially for young men, deemed to be signs of weakness and threats to their male identities. This is where we have to be able to question prevailing cultural assumptions rather than assume in functionalist terms that they shape identities.

The ways in which these different pressures come together in young people's lives help shape their identities but also put young people under increasing stresses. Suicide among adolescents has risen in the past decade, and now attempts among under-14s appear to be increasing too (Brophy, 2006). Often young people will not speak about these pressures, because they do not want to appear weak in front of their fellows. This is why we need to develop countercultures of modernity that can acknowledge the *moral* work involved in sustaining gender, 'race', ethnic and sexual identities. Within a modernity shaped by a Kantian moral tradition, we can only acknowledge moral work involved in resisting the 'external' influences of culture, history and tradition so that we can exist as individual rational selves in our own right. But if these traditions emphasise the need for self-control and the significance of will and determination they simply reinforce silences. This suppression of emotions and feelings needs to be questioned, especially for young men.

As we learn about processes of embodying identities, an Enlightenment rationalism presents us with an ambivalent inheritance because it encourages people to suppress the anxieties they have about how they are to define themselves within a multicultural society in which they want to feel a sense of belonging. Rather than share their anxieties and seek support, say for the emotional conflicts at home or the racial or sexual harassment they experience in school or on the streets, they will often learn to keep these fears to themselves. Young men feel a particular pressure to sort things out for themselves, thinking that to need support is a further threat to their male identities. Young men can also feel uneasy about what is expected of them in relationships, since feminism has shifted the rules of acceptable or 'normalised' behaviour between men and women. It is important for them to be able to imagine new masculinities that can allow them to reach out for the support they need, knowing they can offer similar support themselves to their friends.

We need a recognition of *identity politics* that does not fix people in pre-given identities but allows for young people to be supported in the mixing or *queering* of their diverse identities. Rather than simply thinking that identities are either 'given' or 'socially and historically constructed' we will begin to appreciate the dynamics of emotions and power that help sustain feelings of self-worth and clarity as our complex identities take shape. We will learn to appreciate that *identity work* is always in process and that there are life decisions we have to make for ourselves, as well as clarity gained through talking with others who know how to listen. Working through our identities has a rhythm and timing of its own that we also need to respect as we learn that we do not have to make it on our own and that others can really be there to support us in times of need.

This calls for social theory as life thinking and life politics in which young people feel listened to and supported as they seek to come to terms with different aspects of their complex identities. As we learn to recognise the identity work in which people are engaged within a postmodern culture where they no longer inherit identities from their parents, we appreciate the complex interactions between identities, culture and politics. Sometimes these come together in hybrid identities that people can feel good about, but often there are unresolved pressures as people feel pulled in different directions. Identity work as moral work will take diverse forms and it will often involve an extended cultural grasp of the 'emotional work' that Freud largely conceived of as taking place within familial relations. In part this will involve challenging prevailing cultural expectations, as well as the creation of new social relationships which can sustain diverse identities.

Further reading

Feminism and gay liberation

For some discussion of the ways feminisms and gay liberations questioned the terms of a prevailing gender and sexual order see, for instance, Arthur Brittan (1989) *Masculinity and power;* Sheila Rowbotham's *Woman's consciousness, man's world* (1973) and *Dreams and dilemmas* (1983); Jeffrey Weeks' *Coming out* (1977) and *Sexuality and its discontents* (1985); Judith Butler's *Gender trouble* (1999) and *Undoing gender* (2004).

Men and masculinities

Early explorations in the UK of a critical relationship to men and masculinities that helped set the terms for a wider international discussion emerged in the collective deliberations in the journal *Achilles Heel* (so named after much discussion). This work has been collected in two volumes: *The Achilles Heel reader* (Seidler, 1991c) and *Men, sex and relationships: Writings from* Achilles Heel (Seidler, 1992). See also *Rediscovering masculinity* (Seidler, 1989) and *Recreating sexual politics* (Seidler, 1991b).

THREE

Histories: beliefs / diasporas / belongings

This chapter explores issues of belief, citizenship, diaspora and complex belongings. It traces the impacts of diverse historical inheritances, memories and journeys, and the ways we think about the fixity, fluidity and fragmentation of postmodern identities.

Modernities, identities and beliefs

Does my identity change if I change my beliefs or do I remain the same person who just happens to have different beliefs? In what sense is our identity at least partly defined by our beliefs? These remain troubling questions that we have learnt to think about in different ways within an Enlightenment vision of modernity. We have learnt that as long as someone acts with *good intentions* or with goodwill, then their actions are likely to be *moral*, at least in their eyes. We have also learnt within a liberal moral culture to acknowledge that different people have different goals and purposes in life and that the freedom offered within the terms of a capitalist democracy allows people to find what will bring them happiness and fulfilment. We no longer believe that these things can be defined for individuals in advance but rather that they have to explore their needs and desires for themselves. These views roughly characterise thinking about identities as rational selves within modernity.

Within the pre-modern European world there was a dominant Christian representation that took for granted that it knew the difference between 'good' and 'evil', between 'right' and 'wrong'. As a Catholic country, this ideology was dominant in Spain which, under the reign of Ferdinand II and Isabella I from the mid-15th to early 16th centuries, was to become unified through military activity against Muslim communities in the south. The forming of what was to become modern Spain from two previously separate regions with the marriage of these 'Catholic monarchs', meant that there was a new enforced identification between being Spanish and being Catholic. As part of this

Reconquista, under the rule of Ferdinand and Isabella, Spanish Christians were to fight against the Muslim presence and so bring to a close the period of *Convivencia* – of different communities living together in an uneasy respect for their religious and cultural differences (Baron, 1957; Peters, 1980; Zakhor, 1982). The Jewish community that had also been long-established in Spain had found ways of living together with Christian and Islamic communities and of learning from one other. For example, Jewish scholars took the responsibility for translating Greek texts that had only survived in Arabic and so returned these texts to Europe. But this multicultural polity in Andalusia was never without friction and conflict and was to be broken by a revitalised Catholic **hegemony**.

With the creation of the **Spanish Inquisition** in 1478 people's faith was tested using various technologies that were developed to prove the 'truth' of people's beliefs. There was an intolerance of different beliefs, as those who believed differently were understood as a threat and their heresy had to be punished. It was only a heretic who would dare to question Catholic beliefs, as the beliefs provided the criteria through which 'truth' and 'falsity' were judged. If a person intentionally held to different beliefs that went against a Catholic orthodoxy this *proved* that they were evil as heretics. A 'good' person could only have orthodox Catholic beliefs, so if they ceased to hold these beliefs it proved that they had become 'evil'. Those in power did not want to listen to what people of different religions had to say because this could only threaten; rather, such people had to be punished for wilfully holding beliefs that were heretical. It was not enough to prove that what they believed was false, because if they held different beliefs this demonstrated that they had wilfully questioned what people knew as the one and only true religious belief.

To believe differently in Catholic Spain was to condemn yourself as evil, since it was always open for you to see the *self-evident* truth. Rather, what needed to be explained was *how* people could refuse to accept the truths of Catholicism: it could only be because they were evil or like the Jews, who were taken to be a 'blind' and 'stiff-necked' people.

So, with an intensification of Catholic authority, anyone presenting different beliefs was therefore deemed to be a heretic or else mad, and the Inquisition set about gathering evidence to determine how non-believers would be judged.

For a time there was a tension between theological discourse and a medical discourse that was attempting to establish itself independently. This new way of thinking recognised that although heresy was a matter of evil, madness was not. People who were mad were considered to be 'lacking judgement' and therefore could not be held as responsible for their actions. There was a widespread fear, however, that people were presenting themselves dishonestly, for instance, that people were feigning or pretending to be mad in order to avoid punishment.

While the *Reconquista* of 16th-century Spain may seem to have little relevance today, the relationships between religious beliefs and identities has returned as a central concern in a post-9/11 world in which we are aware of the return to **fundamentalism** across diverse Western and Eastern religious traditions. There is a **totalitarian** strain within traditions that insists that they provide the only true religious path and reflecting on these historical experiences can help to shape responses to the renewed prominence of religious identities in the contemporary world.

Punishment and expulsion

There were no different paths to God in Catholic Spain; there was one true religious path. Other paths were false and could only lead people astray from God. It was difficult to explain how a person could hold different beliefs, unless they had *wilfully become evil*, since no good person would refuse to accept beliefs that were so self-evidently true. If a heretic persisted in their beliefs, even when the heresy had been pointed out to them, this proved they were evil and so *deserved to be punished* since evil must always be punished. Punishment therefore becomes a means of purification through which we might seek to punish the body so that the spirit can be purified. It was the drive towards 'purification' that was to produce the master narrative of Spain as a Catholic nation that no longer had space for those who believed differently. In Catholic Spain, Jews were given the chance to convert or else to leave the country.

Jews presented a threat to the **body politic** and such differences could not be tolerated, rather, they had to be destroyed. What we need to understand is why differences that might formerly have been accepted were now deemed to be too threatening to tolerate. It is this intolerance that eventually led to expulsion of Jews and Muslims from Spain, and this totalitarianism that ties the expulsions of Catholic Spain to the expulsion of Jews from Hitler's Germany. This is the dark and dangerous side of **nationalism** that has reasserted itself in more recent decades in the 'ethnic cleansing' that we witnessed in Bosnia and Kosovo with the destruction of the former Yugoslavia and in the genocides in Rwanda and Darfur.

Although we have looked here at the Spanish Inquisition as a historical example, we could also look to an earlier period of English history when Jews were expelled, and from which later technologies of expulsion seem to have a source. According to Simon Schama's *History of Britain* (Schama, 2003), Edward I's expulsion of the Jews and the execution of hundreds of the elders of the community in Clifford's Tower in York made England "the first country to perform a little act of ethnic cleansing" . Schama stresses the support of the Church and the populace for anti-Semitic violence and describes an incident when a ship's Jewish passengers – Jews being expelled from England – were deliberately drowned "to the entertainment of the crew and all who heard about it" (quoted by Jason Burke in *The Observer*, 1 October 2000, p 6). Schama also claims that 300 Jewish leaders were hanged in the Tower of London under Edward's reign. Although Jeremy Ashby, assistant curator at the Tower of London, highlights that there is no mention of this in any display, other senior curators take a stronger line. One called such atrocities "frankly marginal, given the range of what Edward achieved. You have to doubt their relevance and interest to the public" (quoted in Burke, 2000, p 6). Possibly then it should be of little surprise that there is no mention in the website of the British Royal Family on the less seemly activities of Edward I.

Histories / cultures / identities

Taking into consideration an Enlightenment vision of modernity as illustrated by the histories above it becomes easier to understand why someone whose grandparents immigrated from Russia or Poland at the turn of the century might want to disavow any connection with Jewishness. They perhaps do not want to be reminded that their grandparents were immigrants who had suffered from discrimination and anti-Semitism as they worked long hours in the sweatshops of Whitechapel and Stepney in east London. Second and third generations often want to forget the harsh realities of immigrant working-class life, as they make their transitions from the run-down city to the suburbs, to pass on nostalgic memories of a past that has been severed from the lived experiences of their children. They can legitimately argue within the secular terms of modernity that, as Judaism is a religious belief and that they personally hold all religions to be forms of superstition with no place in a rationalist society (see Chapter One), they have only an *ancestral* connection with Judaism. As far as they are concerned they have been born and educated in England so that they are English 'like everyone else'. Even if they experienced mild anti-Semitism in school, this would be very different from the kind of everyday racism that black and Asian people often have to deal with. Forgetting becomes a path to *belonging*, while differences are disavowed, and those who were defined as Oriental 'other' or as 'enemy aliens' are given opportunities within liberal modernity to *become* 'like everyone else'.

They feel they have escaped from being viewed as an internal 'other' – a perception conceived within a framework of Orientalism – and who are therefore not to be trusted. They had escaped the Orientalist gaze, as Edward Said framed it:[1]

> The imaginative examination of things Oriental was based more or less exclusively upon a sovereign Western consciousness out of whose unchallenged centrality an Oriental world emerged, first according to a detailed logic governed not simply by empirical reality but by a battery of desires, repressions, investments and projections. (Said, 2006, p 8)

If Jewish people consider themselves to have finally escaped from this 'Orientalist' gaze in the post-Holocaust West, that is, to be a minority ethnic group more neutrally along with other minority ethnic groups (see Chapter Two), they still suffer from recently revived anti-Semitisms, even if they no longer suffer from civic forms of discrimination and oppression. If it is argued that someone can disavow Jewishness and so 'pass' within gentile society in a way that an African-Caribbean or Asian person cannot conceal their colour, we still have to consider the anxieties and fears of so 'passing' and thereby denying something about oneself.

When we think about the return to anti-Semitisms within contemporary European societies and ways in which they have been dangerously supported on extreme Islamist websites, it is important to reflect on the attacks on Zionism that go beyond disagreements with the unjust policies of the Israeli government and its occupation of Palestinian lands, to questions about the legitimacy of the Israeli state itself and the rights of the Jewish people to self-determination. While it is unhelpful to identify anti-Zionism with anti-Semitism and important to recall that there have always been Jews who were anti-Zionists, there are dangers in the kind of anti-Zionism that calls specifically on anti-Semitic and even Nazi imagery. There are a disturbing number of sites on the Internet that preach Jew-hatred and which serve to fan the flames of racism as anti-Semitism. Rather we need ways of opening up a dialogue between Islam and Judaism and recalling times when these traditions both suffered religious and racial discriminations and were both marginalised by dominant Christian cultures. We need to recall times when different communities were able to live in creative dialogue with one another, as they were in Andalusia, which could provide a world of multicultural dialogue that can hopefully speak to the present post-9/11 world.

Diaspora and difference

In his essay, 'Cultural identity and diaspora' (Hall, 1994), Stuart Hall talks from an experience of Caribbean **diaspora**, and suggests that:

> Diaspora does not refer us to those scattered tribes whose identity can only be secured in relation to some sacred homeland to which they must at all cost return, even if it means pushing other people into the sea. This is the old, the imperialising, the hegemonising form of 'ethnicity'. (p 235)

This is an unfortunate metaphor but it is important to recall the terrible destruction and loss of life that followed in Europe as Jews sought to identify and belong, and also the experience of other peoples today, like Kurdish or Tibetan people, who seek to return to their ancient lands.

If we are to acknowledge different experiences of diaspora, we also need to be wary of distinctions between 'old' and 'new' that can be unwittingly reproduced within **poststructuralist** styles of thinking. Hall might be right to say, "We have seen the fate of the Palestinian people at the hands of this backward-looking conception of diaspora", and there were terrible injustices and 'ethnic cleansings' perpetrated during the Israeli War of Independence in 1948. These are not excused by the threats of the Arab armies once some kind of victory had been achieved. But the contrast Hall makes is too clearly stated and categorical in poststructuralist dualities when he goes on to say more generally:

> The diaspora experience is defined not by essence or purity but by the recognition of a necessary heterogeneity and diversity; by a conception of 'identity' which lives through, not despite, difference: by hybridity. Diaspora identities are those which are constantly producing and reproducing themselves anew, through transformation and difference. (p 235)

This is confirmed by Eva Hoffman who, on her return to her native Poland, describes how her friends could detect a difference in her which she had subconsciously come to embody while living in America:

> If she sees American-ness in me, it's partly because my face has become more composed, more controlled than the faces of the women around me, I move in a more 'American' way too – with looser, more resolute strides. I've allowed my body a certain straightforward assertiveness. (Hoffman, 1991, p 236)

It can also be helpful to recall how categorical distinctions between 'religion', 'race' and 'ethnicity' were gradually established. It was in the 1930s in the US that "liberal intellectuals were able to dispel the notion of a distinct Jewish 'race' and introduce new concepts concerning group difference within American culture" (Goldstein, 2006, p 193). Goldstein notes that Franz Boas had been unsuccessful in rallying the scientific community to discredit Nazi racial theories in the mid-1930s, but he also recalls that "As the term 'race' came to be applied more exclusively to peoples of color, concepts like 'ethnicity,' pioneered by Jewish scholars in the 1920s to refer to European descent groups, were finally introduced more broadly to the American public" (p 193). W. Lloyd Warner and Leo Strole sharply distinguished non-white 'racial' groups from white 'ethnic' groups. While ethnic groups might carry "a divergent set of cultural traits which are evaluated by the host society as inferior" they explained, "racial groups are divergent biologically rather than culturally" (quoted in Goldstein, 2006, p 195). Goldstein notes how "the spread of these new theories about the differences between 'race' and 'ethnicity' all paved the way for Jews to gain acceptance as American whites during the war years" (p 195).

Belonging and fragmentation

Does this mean that some ethnic minorities can shift their identities as they shift their beliefs? If Judaism is a matter of religious belief alone with no consequences for notions of 'ethnicity', this aspect of their identity will surely disappear if people choose to assimilate into a dominant culture. This is what happened in countries such as Denmark and Sweden where, at certain points in history, Jewish communities literally disappeared as they integrated. Reflecting back to the Spanish Inquisition, even though people were given the chance to convert, these *conversos* were often still under suspicion. There was a fear that even though they professed to be 'new Christians' in their practice, in their homes and in their hearts they might remain Jewish. This was deemed to be a particular threat to the state and the Inquisition set about collecting evidence on *conversos* who carried on Jewish rituals in private. They would be tested by the Inquisition by being given pork to eat or being made to make the sign of the cross.

Where there are such strict categories imposed on 'identity', there is often a fear of the spaces in between. As there were once sharp divisions between men and women, between masculine and feminine, and an intolerance of ambivalence, so there was no middle ground between being Christian and being Jewish. It was not a matter of practices alone, but of whether you could be 'truly' Christian with a Christian soul if you had recently converted. For some people, religion was considered a matter of 'blood', so that conversion was considered significant but not defining. Sometimes there was a need to present family genealogies that went back ten generations to prove the authenticity of your Christian heritage. In some cities conversion was enough to ensure Christian status and more liberal views held. But in other cities *conversos* remained under constant suspicion.

If you were born a Jew or a Muslim in Catholic Spain then you remained a Jew or a Muslim, because people were identified through their religions and it made no difference what beliefs you chose to adopt as an individual. You might be able to change your beliefs, but it has remained a question whether or not you can change your identity – transform your spirit and soul. This explains the meaning of fixed or given identities (see Chapter One) that can be provided by religious groups. Your religion identifies *who you are* in a dominant pre-modern Christian imaginary.

It was only with *modernity* that a radical shift took place and identities as rational selves were deemed to be primary as was a status as 'free and equal' citizens within a **liberal democratic polity**. Religion became incidental and a private and subjective concern. As Kant stated it, you could treat religion as a matter of history and culture that did not need to affect your status as a rational self. What mattered was your identity as a rational self, able to discern through reason your beliefs and values. It was through reason that you could discern the dictates of the moral law.

Despite this shift, the history of **religious conversion** continues into the 21st century and there have been vital alliances between the gun and the cross that have worked to convert people away from their traditional cultures and beliefs, for example, in Africa and Asia. Although these practices were at odds with the self-conceptions of a European modernity, at another level they revealed the ways in which modernities continued to be shaped through the secularisation of dominant Christian traditions that tied colonialism to a Christian mission of 'saving souls'.

Again, reflecting on these histories can be illuminating for the contrast they offer for terms of belonging and exclusion within contemporary nation states. What kinds of language and cultural tests do people have to pass in order to be granted citizenship? What kinds of beliefs do we expect people to have? Judith Butler has already drawn attention to the test that was used for citizenship in Holland that gave people an image of two men kissing (Butler, 2008, p 3). If these images were regarded as unacceptable should this be grounds for refusing citizenship on the assumption that it somehow proves that a person does not share the same liberal tolerance that is regarded as defining of Dutch culture?

In a multicultural nation like the US it might be true that ethnicity is rarely emphasised in everyday interactions, because as Leili, a young woman of mixed Iranian parentage growing up in Britain, recognised "everyone was from everywhere, everyone was everything" (McCarthy, 2008). However, people still find it challenging when they are asked to answer the question of where they come from. In Leicester, Leili was cast as the non-white-yet-not-black-nor-Asian girl at school, and when asked to explain her identity, she said:

> "It really depends. When people ask me that question I say I'm half Iranian or my dad's from Iran because I think they're asking because I don't look English, or whatever that's supposed to look like, so I think, that's the reason, or I've decided, that's the reason so this is the answer I'm going to give because that's the explanation as to why I look this way."

Leili also found that as she was growing up she would often gravitate to people who came from mixed backgrounds, which gave her a sense of belonging:

> "I have one friend whose half Japanese, the other half Chinese. I lived with this Canadian girl whose mother was a Russian Jew and her father was Welsh … it was about hybrid identities and mixed nationalities, not specifically Iranian, but just what….There's actually this cultural Other, this experience of being an Other that we all share, so it doesn't matter if my friend's half Chinese, that has nothing

to do with Iranian culture, it just matters that we have the experience of not being quite one, not being quite the other." (McCarthy, 2008)

Creating identities

Within a postmodern culture, greater emphasis is placed on our ability to create our own identities. We learn that identities are not waiting there to be discovered, as if there were a singular identity that somehow persists through changes in beliefs and values. Rather, we supposedly define and constitute identities through the beliefs we choose for ourselves. Identity has become a matter of choice and is radically fluid. According to the **poststructuralist view**, we can go so far as to assume different identities at different moments during the day depending on the situation and what happens to be our mood. This vision of complex and fluid identities is reinforced by new technologies, where on the internet, for instance, we can create a whole new persona and choose to assume a different gender, age, class and sexual orientation (see Chapter Two). It is these possibilities that give weight to the idea of identity as **performative**, as argued by Judith Butler. We can engage with others on the internet through these differing presentations and choose to live these identities with others in everyday life.

The idea of identities as performative can be particularly illuminating when thinking about the celebrity consumer culture in which young people are often encouraged by the media to model themselves on celebrities with whom they identify, so adopting their styles and looks as their own. Some will even use surgical interventions in order to remake their own bodies in accord with what their idols look like. They become convinced that they will be happy if they can somehow live out this ideal for themselves and so *perform* these identities as their own. This is a contemporary form of self-deception. People may fool themselves that this is the way they might find joy or love, even though they might find it difficult to discern whether or not these emotions are real.

As **Ludwig Wittgenstein** wrote of himself, "But I am easily hurt and afraid of being hurt, and to protect oneself in *this* way is the death of all love. For real love one needs *courage*" (Wittgenstein, 22 October 1946, quoted in Monk, 1990, p 504; emphasis in original). A few days later he wrote "I do not have the courage or the strength and clarity to look the facts of my life straight in the face" (p 504). Having fallen in love with his friend Ben, he demanded, not just friendship, not just fondness, but love:

A person cannot come out of his skin. I cannot give up a demand that is anchored deep inside me, in my whole life. For *love* is bound up with nature; and if I became unnatural, the love would have to end.... *Love*, that is the pearl of great price ... in fact it *shows* – if one has it – what great value *is*. One learns what it *means* to single out a precious metal from all others. (p 505; emphasis in original)

As Wittgenstein says about love, "The frightening thing is the uncertainty" (p 505).

Re/creating histories

Not only can we create identities for ourselves as a means of security, but we can also create particular histories and memories. We can be encouraged to adopt a particular national history as our own, so in history lessons at school, for example, I never learnt what Edward I did to the Jews. Rather, even as young Jews (this does not seem the right expression, but possibly 'young people with Jewish religious backgrounds' fits the aspirations of belonging that were defined through the promises of assimilation) educated in British schools, we learnt to identify with the aspirations of the powerful.

Returning to Simon Schama's *History of Britain*, Schama also describes the violence and the brutality of Edward I in his campaigns to subject and pacify the Welsh and the Scots. He calls Edward's construction of castles in Wales "the most ambitious exercise in colonial domination ever undertaken in medieval Europe" (p 6). But Edward I has been revered as the king who did most to unify Britain in the Middle Ages. I learned those histories as my own, not as a history of internal colonisation, and did not know about the expulsion of the Jews enough to make me feel even ambivalent.[2]

To meet conservative objections that the great achievements of this nation are being run down by this reviewing of our accepted histories, Martin Davidson, executive producer of the *History of Britain* TV programmes, said: "We are not bringing out a heritage site gift shop. History is somewhere you go not to escape the past but to understand the present" (*The Observer*, 1 October 2000, p 6). Indeed, history, if it is not to be airbrushed out when it is not convenient, *will* challenge national myths. It will also ask questions of national identity. Since my schooldays in 1950s' London, African-Caribbean and Asian pupils have had to come to terms, through the 1970s, 1980s and 1990s, with the histories of Empire and slavery that they were also to absorb as part of embodying identities, although hopefully today all pupils are taught with more critical awareness than we were encouraged to have in the 1950s. Black and Asian communities argue that they have been omitted from mainstream histories, for example, with the contribution of black and Asian servicemen in the Second World War being generally ignored: "There is a false perception that Jews and others are newcomers to British shores.... Actually they have been here for centuries" (Reilly, quoted in *The Observer*, 1 October 2000, p 6).

As we learn more diverse histories so we have to question who writes the histories. The master narratives of the nation have served those who had the power to write traditional national histories. This is not simply a plea for inclusion of other histories into dominant narratives, but the questioning works as a deconstruction of these narratives and the identities of power and greatness that they have helped sustain, as Simone Weil appreciated (see Blum and Seidler, 1991). Weil (1972) questioned the ways in which Europe shaped its national narratives through Roman ideals of power and greatness. Why should school pupils continue to identify with Caesar rather than with those he conquered? How are we to break with Roman traditions of power and greatness that have echoed across the British Empire and also framed Hitler's dreams for his Third Reich?

As we learn to recognise different values, so we need to write *new* histories that give due weight to competing narratives and so will sustain diverse and complex identities. We will discover that there is a much richer and more complex story to tell about class, gender, sexuality, 'race' and ethnic relations of power and subordination. As we learn to recognise different histories, so we begin to see the past in different terms and learn to *listen* to those who have been hidden from history as we imagine both past and possible futures in alternative ways.

As we question the notion of a singular national history sustaining a single version of British identity, so we become aware of diverse identities connected through rich and complex histories. At the same time we can recognise that these histories should be respected and acknowledged in the present, rather than disavowed within the terms of a rationalist modernity. We must think about the *ethics* of identities in relation to memories and histories. This can mean questioning prevailing modernist visions of identities as rational selves and so the possibilities and limits of change, as well as the relentless postmodern emphasis on fluidity and fragmentation. At the same time we need to acknowledge that people can sometimes get stuck in historical hurts and memories from which they feel unable to escape, as we learn from the painful experiences following the break-up of the former Yugoslavia.

—

Endnotes

[1] Edward Said explains his method saying, "My principle methodological device for studying authority here are what can be called *strategic location,* which is a way of describing the author's position in a text with regards to the Oriental material he writes about, and *strategic formation*, which is a way of analysing the relationship between texts and the ways in which groups of texts, types of texts, even textual genres acquire mass, density and referential power among themselves and therefore in the culture at large" (2006, p 20).

[2] For some alternative historical accounts reviewing Jewish histories in Britain see, for instance, Sacks (2000, 2002).

Further reading

Convivencia
Some helpful historical and cultural discussion that relates to the period of *Convivencia* in Spain is provided by Baron (1957), Peters (1980) and Zakhor (1982). See also Trachtenberg (1943) and Cohen (1982).

The Spanish Inquisition
For some illuminating discussion about the nature of the Spanish Inquisition and the different rituals and practices that it developed to legitimate its authority see, for instance, Lea (1906-07), Kamen (1985) and Peters (1989), who explores how myths around the Inquisition developed so that by the end of the 18th century the Inquisition 'had become the representative of all repressive religions that opposed freedom of conscience, political liberty and philosophical enlightenment ... as the enemy of modernity' (Peters, 1989, p 231). Moore (1987) argues that between the 10th and 13th centuries Christian Europe became a persecuting society that shaped forms of state and ecclesiastical persecution down to the 20th century.

My thinking around the Spanish Inquisition was developed through supervising the Phd thesis of Teresa Ordorika (2003) entitled 'Madness and heresy in the Spanish Inquisition'.

Totalitarianism

For an influential discussion of the nature of totalitarianism that explores some of these connections across the divide of otherwise religious and secular nation states, see Arendt (1951). Arendt was thinking in the aftermath of Nazi rule and the Holocaust but she was also concerned to reflect on the experiences of Stalinism in the Soviet Union. For helpful reflections that explore the use of medical metaphors of 'purity' within Nazi Germany see Robert N. Proctor's *Racial hygiene* (1988).

Religious conversion

For some interesting discussions on the nature of conversion and different ways it was historically and culturally framed see, for instance, Mills and Grafton (2003) *Conversion: Old worlds and new*, Hefner (1993) *Conversion to Christianity: Historical and anthropological perspectives on a great transformation* and Morrison, K.F. (1992) *Understanding conversion.*

Judith Butler

For a sense of the development of Butler's work see *Gender trouble* (1990) and *Undoing gender* (2004).

Ludwig Wittgenstein

An interesting historical background to the development of Wittgenstein's philosophies is provided by Ray Monk in *Ludwig Wittgenstein: The duty of genius* (1990).

Simone Weil

In her work, Simone Weil was looking for alternative visions of 'civilisation' in Europe, in France in particular, that might reveal contrasting historical values of those who might have been silenced through defeat but who can be helpfully remembered in the present. Writing at a time of national crisis, *The need for roots* (1972) is a plea for a different kind of France to be created out of the ashes of defeat. See also the further discussion in Blum and Seidler (1991).

FOUR

Experiences: realities / psychologies / discourse

This chapter explores relationships between voice, language, experience, power and fragmentation. It also traces connections between the psyche and the social.

Identities / psychologies / fragmentations

A phenomenological tradition in sociology, developed in the 1970s, taught that reality was a subjective construction and that individuals were free to create their own identities through assigning particular meanings to their experience. This individualistic and subjective voluntarism was challenged by an emphasis on *power* as presented by new readings of Karl Marx as suggested by Georg Lukács, Karl Korsch and Antonio Gramsci and with their sources in Husserl and Schutz. There was recognition that if people *can* create their own identities, it is not in circumstances of their own choosing.

There were also other more internal challenges to phenomenology, since the very relations of teaching and learning were questioned in a phenomenology that, while helping to focus on lived experience, could not explain why one version of reality should be given more legitimacy and power than any other. It also proved impossible to sustain a meaningful distinction between 'sanity' and 'madness', as became an issue for R.D. Laing's work (Laing, 1961a) and the anti-psychiatry movement. These could be presented as different realities that had their own legitimacy and could not be evaluated according to any singular scale.

As Wittgenstein was to write after visiting long-stay patients at St Patrick's psychiatric hospital in Dublin, "See the sane man in the maniac! (and the mad man in yourself)" (Monk, 1990, p 388). In his diary he also wrote, "Freud's idea: In madness the lock is not destroyed, only altered; the old key can no longer unlock it, but it could be opened by a differently constructed key" (p 387). He also wrote to Drury, who was spending his period of training residence in the hospital, "Look at people's sufferings, physical and mental, you have them close at hand, and this ought to be a good remedy for your troubles.... Look at your patients more closely as human beings in trouble" (p 389).

While there were important insights in the phenomenological critique of **positivism**, there were dangers in the resulting **subjectivism**. There was little grasp of the realities that were attached to the disintegration of mind, either through madness or dementia. These were not simply conditions that could be celebrated in their difference, as Ronald Laing was later to come to acknowledge. It is not just that people live in different realities of equal value, but that we need to recognise that the different worlds people create for themselves have meanings when understood in the context of the pressures and tensions of the lives they are living. This questions a rationalist tradition in psychiatry which would dismiss forms of language and behaviour as irrational and thereby lacking any possible meaning (see Laing, 1961a, 1961b, 1982; and Seidler, 1994).

Laing crucially questioned this assumption and learnt to listen, as Wittgenstein was also attempting to do, to the people with psychotic experiences. He discovered that it is possible to interpret these experiences if you were willing to listen and give time and attention as well as recognise anguish and mental suffering. As Wittgenstein understood, Freud's idea that dreams are wish fulfilments is important because it "points to the sort of interpretation that is wanted". As Monk explains Wittgenstein's view:

> This again is connected with Freud's determination to provide a *single* pattern for all dreams: all dreams must be, for him, expressions of longing, rather than, for example, expressions of fear. Freud, like philosophical theorists, had been seduced by the method of science and the 'craving for generality'. There is not one type of dream, and neither is there one way to interpret the symbols in a dream. (quoted in Monk, 1990, p 449)

Wittgenstein constantly stressed that it was "the understanding which consists in seeing connections" (p 451). Wittgenstein thought of using Bishop Butler's phrase "Everything is what it is, and not another thing" as a motto for his book *Philosophical investigations* (1958b).

Laing also recognised the reality of mental pain and suffering and the ways this should help shape thinking about identities. He learnt to identify the suffering that went along with the fragmentation of identities (see Chapter Three). His book *The divided self* (1961a) draws on notions of **ontological security** that can be undermined and threatened through the ways in which people communicate with one another. He knows the importance of people *feeling recognised* and their experience being validated, partly through a process of exploring how the dynamics of family relations so often worked to undermine and attack a sense of self-worth through the invalidation of experience. This is not to assume that experience is somehow given, but it does question a prevailing poststructuralist dualism, which would have us think that experiences are provided through language or discourse alone.

In the group analytic approach of psychotherapy, as it came to be practised by Robin Skynner, there was also an appreciation of a dialogical relationship in which as the therapist exposes themselves to the dynamics of those they are treating, they must remain closely attentive to their own emotional and bodily responses which they might pass back as information about themselves in a careful and considered way (Skynner, 1976). According to John Schlapobersky, a friend and colleague who wrote Skynner's obituary:

> Skynner had a rare capacity to compose himself in the presence of others' emotions and to master the terms of their predicament in terms that were often very practical. He belonged in the tradition of the Cornish miners who designed and built the London underground, but this capacity for dealing with things below ground was applied to human dilemmas. (*The Guardian*, 28 September 2000, p 24)

This analytic approach in which we are constantly encouraged to step back and examine the ground on which we have been standing has been explored within a phenomenological tradition as an issue of **reflexivity**. But even within the rationalist terms of postmodernity there has been a resistance to acknowledge the emotional and bodily resonances that are often brought into play within an interview situation, such as that described by Schlapobersky above or, for example, in research. If there has been a readiness to acknowledge the fragmentation of identities, this has too often been celebrated as reflecting complex subjectivities so often closing down further reflections. At the same time, a research project drawing on postmodern methodologies has to reflect more, rather than less, on notions of objectivity. Since they can never assume that their position is one of neutral and impartial truth, a researcher must always be ready to interrogate the positions from which they are speaking. As Hall frames it, "We all write and speak from a particular place and time, from a history and culture which is specific. What we say is always 'in context', positioned" (1994, p 222).

However, within the Cartesian emphasis on consciousness, we have tended to assume an integrity of consciousness within a phenomenological tradition. This was an assumption that Antonio Gramsci and Michel Foucault helped to question in different ways. As Stuart Hall acknowledges:

> Perhaps instead of thinking of identity as an already accomplished fact which the new cultural practices then represent, we should think instead of identity as a 'production' which is never complete, always in process and always constituted within, not outside representation. (1994, p 222)

I think this is helpful, but we also need to move across the boundaries of 'inside' and 'outside' so that through making connections, we appreciate also what is forming and shaping representations. Recognising this we can affirm with Hall that:

> Cultural identity is a matter of becoming as well of being. It belongs to the future as much as to the past, It is not something that already exists, transcending place, time, history and culture. Cultural identities come from somewhere, have histories. But like everything which is historical, they undergo constant transformation. (1994, p 225)

There is a tendency within postmodern writing to resist notions of identity as somehow essentially fixed, and so to prefer talking in terms of processes of identification or to give up on notions of identity completely. This can make it difficult to understand relationships between identity, power, bodies and culture. Helping to question this tendency, Wittgenstein recognised that seeing an aspect, understanding music, poetry, painting and humour are reactions that belong to, and can only survive within a culture; a form of life. According to Monk:

[Wittgenstein's] pessimism about the effectiveness of his work is related to his conviction that the way we look at things is determined, not by our philosophical beliefs, but by our culture, by the way we are brought up. And in the face of this, as he once said to Karl Britton: "What can one man do alone? Tradition is not something a man can learn; not a thread he can pick up when he feels like it; any more than a man can choose his own ancestors. Someone lacking a tradition who would like to have one is like a man unhappy in love." (p 533)

This can also work to make identities too provisional and at the same time can render invisible the emotional pain and suffering, as well as the traumatic histories and memories, that can come with the fragmentation of identities and can be 'passed on' *transgenerationally*. Returning to Skynner, Schlapobersky explains in terms that Laing would have appreciated:

His inquiry was focused by his struggle to deal with the confusion and distress of his own upbringing and he remained profoundly interested in the life of the family. "It has enormous creative potential including that of life itself," he observed, "and it is not surprising that, when it becomes disordered it possesses an equal potential for terrible destruction."

These destructive forces, he believed, led to and derived from a fragmentation of consciousness complicated by the need to deny the underlying divisions. Denied problems were then transmitted across generations. (*The Guardian*, 28 September, 2000)

We also need a sense of the integrity of the person, not as something given but as in a process of growth and development through the validation of experience and the recognition of self-worth.

Language and experience

Although there has been an awareness within the postmodern of *how* language is crucial in articulating experience, we also need Johann Gottfried Herder's insight that different languages also carry profoundly different visions of the world (Berlin, 1976). This can make it difficult to translate across cultural traditions. A striking example, given by Jonathan Sachs in his article 'Seeing evil, facing evil', is that:

Judaism is a religion of commands, yet biblical Hebrew contains no word that means simply 'to obey'. The closest is the verb 'shema'. Yet 'shema' means more than to obey. It also means, 'to listen,' 'to hear' and 'to understand'. This tells us something highly significant – that in Judaism the Divine commands already contain an appeal to human understanding. (*Jewish Chronicle*, 29 September 2000, p x)

Sachs draws on the example in the Book of Genesis of Abraham and his argument with heaven when God reveals his plan to destroy the cities of the plain. Sachs points out that Abraham does not speak on his own accord but that God invites the dialogue and even specifies its key terms – 'right' and 'just' – in advance. God knows that Abraham is wrong to suppose that there might be any innocent households in Sodom but he invites Abraham to argue against the verdict. This is a dialogue for the sake of heaven that we do not associate with a faith so often defined in terms of piety, acceptance and submission to the will of God. But rather than being marginal to Jewish thought, it is one of its most characteristic expressions, as Sachs recognises. In a spirit that cannot be translated into a Greek tradition so crucial for Christianity, God yearns for dialogue. As Sachs quotes the sages, "God longs for the prayers of the righteous" (2002, p x). Sachs explains what he takes to be Judaism's unique voice in the conversation of humanity, acknowledging, "Only slowly over the years have I begun to see how radical it is" (2002, p x):

For the Greeks, Plato especially, truth is harmony. For Judaism, truth is cognitive dissonance, the conflict between the world that is and the world that ought to be. That is where the argument between earth and heaven begins.... What the prophets speak about, however, is not the world to come, but the here-and-now. They do not aspire to the perspective of God. They speak – God empowers them to speak – from the perspective of mankind.

Jewish faith, therefore, is not acceptance of the evil in this world. It is a sustained protest against it in the name of God and (His) image, mankind. There is only one resolution to the conflict between the existence of evil and the existence of God. It is not to be found in logic. It lies, and can only lie, in action. Every act of justice, every fight for freedom, every gesture of compassion, reduces the dissonance between the world that is and the world that ought to be. (2002, p xi)

This might partly explain why Wittgenstein contrasted Drury's 'Greek' religious ideas with his own thoughts, which were, he said "one hundred per cent Hebraic" (quoted in Monk, 1990, p 540). Monk suggests that:

> Central to Wittgenstein's 'Hebraic' conception of religion (like that of his favourite English poet, Blake) is the strict separation of philosophy from religion: "If Christianity is the truth then all the philosophy that is written about it is false." (1990, p 540)

Even if I feel uneasy with the notion of **cognitive dissonance** you can recognise a tradition of justice and equality out of which Marx was speaking, even as he disdained his Jewishness. When Sachs allows himself to say that, "Judaism is the revolutionary moment at which humanity, hearing the voice of the world that might be, refuses to accept the world that is" (2002, p xi) he still resists thinking about issues of gender and sexual justice as he argues for traditional notions of family values that so often bring religious traditions together in their oppositions to modernity and discourses of human rights.

But the tradition he defends also seems to provide, as Islam and Christianity do in their own ways, resources to envision justice and equality in more democratic and inclusive terms. Rather than dismiss religious traditions as somehow 'backward' and unable to speak relevantly in the secular present, we can also recognise their moral values and engage critically with their patriarchal and homophobic traditions. In a post-9/11 world we need to shape forms of transcultural dialogue that can respect the dignity of difference/s while reaching across the boundaries of the secular and religious and insisting on a discourse of human rights in shaping democratic moral and political traditions.

Identity and experience

In *Man of reason*, Genevieve Lloyd argues that within 'the West' reason has usually been conceptualised as a transcendence of the feminine. This is firmly embedded within a Greek tradition but it is tacitly questioned within a Hebraic tradition, as Wittgenstein acknowledges. It is not a matter of establishing ideals against which reality is to be judged and found wanting, as if notions of equality and justice exist as ideal forms within a transcendent sphere of their own. Within modernity, as we have reviewed earlier, this resonates with a rationalism that supposes that we can, through reason alone, become clear about the meaning of the concepts before we apply these concepts to particular cases. Within Jewish sources, as with Wittgenstein's later writings, it is through exploring contexts of use that we can begin to recognise a complexity of family resemblances in the meanings within concepts. As Wittgenstein wrote, "If language is to be a means of communication there must be agreement not only in definitions but also (queer as this may sound) in judgements. This seems to abolish logic but does not do so" (1958b, p 242).

There is no technology that can cut through this necessary philosophical investigation. We need to question the idea of truth as existing within a reality of its own, against which empirical reality is to be found lacking. It is the connection of reason as transcendent and the feminine being defined as 'lacking' that has been so crucial to a Western tradition that has been encoded in a secularised Protestantism. It shapes the ways in which people think about their identities and the kinds of relationship they form with their bodies, desires and emotional lives. This is an issue which Avtar Brah appears to be addressing when she describes "a notion of experience not as an unmediated guide to 'truth' but as a *practice* of making sense, both symbolically and narratively; as *struggle* over material conditions and over meaning" (Brah, 1992, p 141). These are not separate struggles, but are part of the same investigation.

We also need to recognise a tension with the poststructuralist influence in Joan Scott and Theresa de Lauretis that Beverley Skeggs takes as her starting point, as being "Not individuals who have experience but subjects who are constituted through experience" (2004, pp 27-8). Naming this distinction does not make it clear, even if it draws a contrast between 'individuals' and 'subjects', for you could argue that individuals both have experience at the same time as they are constituted through experience. We can question possessive notions of experience, while also acknowledging that people have to 'dwell on' or 'learn from' their experience if it is to 'make a difference' to the ways they think, feel and behave. In part this was what Wittgenstein was doing in his arguments against 'private language': questioning a certain picture of inner mental states as 'a foundation of knowledge'.

In the Platonic dialogues Socrates seeks to answer philosophical questions such as 'What is knowledge?' by looking for something that all examples of knowledge have in common. This is reflected in the ways that we might be tempted to think of identities as something that people from a particular gender, 'race', ethnicity or sexuality somehow have in common. This is a move that poststructuralism makes in its critique of essentialism to end up in a position which assumes that it proves that identities are discursive constructions. Wittgenstein, however, seeks to replace this notion of *essence* with the more flexible idea of *family resemblances*:

> We are inclined to think that there must be something in common to all games, say, and that this common property is the justification for applying the general term 'game' to the various games; whereas games form a family, the members of which have family likenesses. Some of them have the same nose, others the same eyebrows and other again the same way of walking; and these likenesses overlap. (1958a, p 17)

The search for essences is, Wittgenstein states, an example of "the craving for generality" that springs from our preoccupation with the method of science:

> Philosophers constantly see the method of science before their eyes. And are irresistibly tempted to ask and answer questions in the way science does. This tendency is the real source of metaphysics, and leads the philosopher into complete darkness. (Monk, 1990, p 17)

This might be related to what Skeggs is aiming for when she states, too categorically, that:

> It is through the experience of subjective construction that we come to know and be known. This enables the shift to be made from experience as a foundation of knowledge to experience as productive of a knowing subject in which their identities are continually in production rather than being occupied as fixed. It also suggests that not all experience produces knowledge; this depends on the context and the experience. It also means that women can take standpoints (on particular issues such as feminism, for instance) rather than being seen to own them through the accident of birth. (2004, pp 27-8)

The focus on the 'production' of identities would both be understood as well as challenged by Wittgenstein who would draw attention to the *different kinds* of production as well as a diversity of sources out of which identities are being produced. Similar issues are also present when Hall quotes Frantz Fanon:

> A national culture is not a folk-lore not an abstract populism that believes it can discover a people's true nature. A national culture is the whole body of efforts made by people in the sphere of thought to describe, justify and praise the action through which that people has created itself and keeps itself in existence. (1994, p 188)

An example should help to clarify what is being discussed here. It is partly an argument against essentialist notions of identity which would hold, for example, that if someone is born a woman then she will have a *particular experience* as a woman which will serve as a foundation to a particular form of knowledge. There is nothing necessary in these connections, although we could argue that it might be easier for women to understand certain things, given, for example, their different relationship with their bodies. We would have to be careful to refuse a too sharp a structuralist distinction between nature and culture, as if identities are exclusively constructed within the realm of culture and language alone.

Mary Kenny makes a strong opposing argument when she rejects 1970s 'social conditioning feminism' as outdated, and states that Simone de Beauvoir (1968) was wrong to say that "one is not born a woman – one becomes one". Rather Kenny has come to accept the neo-Darwinian arguments of Anne and Bill Moir: it is because men's brains are not wired up that way that they will never take a 'fair share' of homecraft or childcare; men are ill-adapted for carrying out caring and sharing domestic duties at the same level as women. She no longer accepts that human behaviour is the result of social conditioning so that:

> Bring little boys up like little girls and we will have a new generation of men who play with dolls, dress in frocks and prefer consensus to conflict. Bring little girls up in a gender-neutral way and they will stop their spending money on silly things like cosmetics, breast enhancement and Versace handbags. (*The Guardian*, 23 March 2000, p 22)

Rather than explore the complexities in the relation between the biological and the social and look for new languages in which to explore gender and sexual difference Kenny simply reverses the duality and gives little weight to the social. As far as she is concerned:

> de Beauvoir was wrong: one *is*, except in rare cases of chromosome disorder, born a woman. Female-ness is not a 'social construct'. It is biologically determined from an early stage in foetal development.... Men will never do the same amount of housework as women (with some exceptions) because their brains are not programmed for domestic detail. Although males virtually always perform better on spatial tests – there is a direct correlation between spatial ability and the male hormone, testosterone – they also have 'tunnel vision' when it comes to the arrangement of domestic space. Men quite literally don't 'see' domestic disorder in the same way. (*The Guardian*, 23 March 2000, p 22)

If Kenny no longer expects men to share the care of the home and the family equally, we have to realise how easy this makes it for men to say that their brains are 'just not programmed for domestic detail'. Even if we accept her scepticism, we are challenged to rethink the terms of gender equality so that we do not think about equality as sameness, but acknowledge the significance of gender difference (see Chapter Five). As we reject **biological determinism**, it can at least encourage us to ask different questions and so create different languages with which to think the relationship of the 'biological' and the 'social'.

This is something Theodor W. Adorno recognised in his appreciation of Freud. He was suspicious about the visions of social engineering that so often politically accompany notions that identities are socially and historically constructed. He learnt from Freud the limits of social conditioning. Freud's recognition of the biological helped Adorno to appreciate the harm and suffering that is done when we think that people can always *adapt to* prevailing social and cultural conditions. As we think of identities "not as individuals who have experience but subjects who are constituted through experience" (1974) we can face analogous insensitivities.

This is the force of Freud's emphasis on the misery that was created in modern Western societies through the repression of sexuality. Foucault misses this in his critique of Freud's understanding of repression as involving a hydraulic vision of sexual and emotional life. It limits his thinking about identities and the ways in which they are also formed through different levels of experience; he also misses the mental anguish and emotional suffering that is too often forgotten in an emphasis on regulation and governmentality. This could partly explain the shift of emphasis in Foucault's later writings, that he felt he could not really account for, when he turns to explore relationships between ethics and the self.

But as we think about processes through which people at different moments embody identities, so we begin to think about the different *levels* of experience and ways these interact with one another in spoken and unspoken ways, as *tension* between language and experience. These are so often missed within poststructuralisms, as are the impacts of both unresolved emotional histories and the effects of historical traumas that can accompany migrations.

Further reading

Theodor W. Adorno
A helpful discussion of Adorno's relationship with Freud is provided by Russell Jacoby (1975) in *Social amnesia*. See also the important selection of Adorno's writings in *Can one live after Auschwitz?* (Tiedemann, 2003).

Karl Marx
For a helpful historical introduction to Marx's theory that helps place his theoretical development in the context of changing historical conditions which helps shape his theoretical concepts, see, for instance, Raya Dunayevskaya (1971) *Marxism and freedom*; McLellan (1980) *The thought of Karl Marx*; and Seidler (1994) *Recovering the self*.

FIVE

Differences: feminisms / enemies / equalities

This chapter discusses the women's movement, the 'personal is political', men and masculinities, poststructuralist feminism(s), identity politics, difference/s and gender equality.

Identities and enemies

With the emergence of the **women's liberation movement** in the early 1970s there was a recognition that a tradition of **liberal humanism** needed to be challenged in new thinking about gender and identities. This challenge was because even where a liberal moral culture assumed equality between women and men, this served to conceal the relationships of power and subordination that structured women's experiences and identities. Through the practice of consciousness-raising women could begin to frame their *individual* experience as emerging out of a partly *shared* experience of women's oppression. If there was an 'enemy' against which women could come together in a vision of sisterhood, it was men who continued to maintain power within the institutions of a **patriarchal society**.

It was tempting to think that there were qualities that women shared, which defined their identities as women. The focus was not on some inner essential quality but on a shared experience of subordination and oppression, which seemed, in part at least, potentially to cross boundaries of 'race', class and sexuality. There *was* recognition of difference within the early feminist movement but these were to be named through the shared practices of consciousness-raising and an initial refusal to set identity against difference. There was an *openness* within the practices of consciousness-raising to acknowledge, say, **differences of class, 'race', ethnicity and sexuality**, while there was also an aspiration to look towards what women shared, for instance, men's traditional control over women's bodies and sexualities. Rather than women internalising and accepting responsibility for their experiences of unhappiness and low sense of self-worth as reflecting their personal inadequacy, they recognised how they had emerged out of a shared experience of subordination and oppression. The strength of the early movement lay in its recognition that *the personal is political* and that, through a personal sharing of suffering and pain as well as joy and laughter, women could rename their histories, experiences, fears, shames and anxieties. In naming the details of their individual experience they recognised *how* their experience was political and had been structured through larger gender relations of power and subordination.

It was through maintaining a tension between the 'personal' and the 'theoretical' that a particular relationship between politics, criticism and theory was sustained. At some level there was a suspicion of theoretical language that could not be grounded in everyday experience. In part this was an understandable response to a **disembodied rationality** that a dominant masculinity had taken for granted within an Enlightenment vision of modernity. Men could so easily feel that they alone could take their reason and rationality for granted and so could legislate what was good for others. Often they had been able to reduce their female partners to silence within heterosexual relationships. Women were made to feel that, unless they could defend what they had to say rationally, they had to keep their silence. They were also made to feel that it was somehow disloyal to discuss their personal feelings and relationships with other women outside the space of the relationship. Men often felt threatened and sought revenge. The language and experience of women was devalued and denigrated as 'emotional' and 'subjective' when set against the 'impersonal' and 'objective' language of men (see also Chapter Two).

There is a resonance here between feminist insights and Wittgenstein's suspicion in his later work that language can so easily become *empty* as it dis/connects from any *grounding* in lived experience. Wittgenstein learnt to trace the meanings of words to their context in use, as he encouraged people to think back to childhood contexts in which they had initially learnt to use certain words. As he says in *The blue book*, "Language games are the forms of language with which a child begins to make use of words" (Wittgenstein, 1958a, p 17). In this way, when we ask 'What is identity?', we no longer assume that we can answer the question by naming some *thing*. This was to break with a tradition which stated that words had a *singular* meaning that could be clearly defined. Wittgenstein questioned a kind of linguistic rationalism that sustained a vision of the autonomy of language. Implicitly he questioned a **semiological** tradition that treated language as a system of signs, in which meaning was established through the relationship between these different signs. Rather we have to "look at the role this word plays in our usage of language, but it is obscured when instead of looking at the *whole language game*, we only look at the contexts, the phrases of language in which the word is used" (Wittgenstein, 1958a, p 108).[1]

Meanings could therefore no longer be legislated through reason alone, rather they had to be explored in their diversity through tracing the *different* uses they had within everyday life. Rather than search for metaphors that seemed to resonate within a poststructuralist feminism, which assumes experience is articulated through language, there is a space for exploration in which we illuminate tensions *between* language and experience and so a 'family resemblance' between diverse contexts in which words are used (see also Chapter Two). This involves a different practice of reading from a rationalism that often reasserted itself within a poststructuralist rendering of feminism. We learn often to disengage and impersonalise and so to read texts as if these ideas need to be evaluated at a distance – a fear that if we *let them in* they might bring emotions that are 'personal' to the surface and cause us hurt or damage.

A rationalist tradition teaches us to read within particular rhetorics of criticism: we weigh ideas on the scales of reason and we reject them if we can identify a 'weakness' in them. There can be a fear of being touched by ideas or of really letting them in and living them for a while, to see *what difference* they are making to the ways we think, feel and live. Women who came to feminism through a poststructuralist reading learned to give a specific interpretation to the notion 'the personal is political' which often worked to conceal the 'personal' and the 'emotional' as somehow threatening to academic rigour. They have grown up with a different generational experience and often this has been reflected in tensions between different generations of feminists. Acknowledging that theoretical work is a form of political practice can help to develop significant and politically relevant theory, but it can also work to weaken connections between theoretical developments and the experiences and political struggles of women to transform their everyday lives. A younger generation growing up in the 1980s and 1990s often feel that the insights of the feminisms of the 1970s, effectively a generation they might identify with their mothers, do not really speak to the gender equality that they have learned to take for granted both in their schooling and in their work lives. If they identify as feminists – the f-word – they are often looking for something different.

A sense of the personal, cultural and political experiences that have shaped lives and identities can help us acknowledge the intellectual and political generations in which we have grown up and can hopefully open up a dialogue across generational differences. It can help to position both intellectually and politically and to illuminate what we have so often learnt to take for granted. An early generation of feminists might have insisted the personal could no longer be separated from the theoretical and later generations might have learnt to take these insights for granted. Through their own experience they understand that we can intellectualise and rationalise experience as a form of self-defence. This reflects a form of *dissociation* that Wittgenstein wanted to heal through returning abstract notions to their contexts of use and helping us to question pictures that encourage us to falsely generalise. For different but related purposes, Freud also sought to return us to childhood experience through a regression to help people engage more deeply with their own experience, so acknowledging what wider culture has encouraged people to *disavow* when it has urged the denial of painful emotional experiences so that the focus can be on living in the present.

In his *Philosophical investigations*, Wittgenstein (1958b) questions a picture of mental life that informs thinking about 'private languages' as if we are comparing words with the 'mental images' we hold in our minds. He holds that what is 'internal' is not hidden from us. To understand someone's outward behaviour – if we understand them – is to observe their state of mind. At a basic level: "If I see someone writhing in pain with evident cause I do not think: all the same, his feelings are hidden from me" (para 223). In different ways Wittgenstein questions a notion of 'interiority' sustained within a Protestant tradition, that is, that my 'true' self somehow lies hidden within an interior space. The idea that others cannot really know who I am or what I think and feel, and that I alone can know myself; people can only know those aspects of self that I am prepared to show them. This is a cultural anxiety which feminism only partly came to terms with. Within consciousness-raising it created an alternative space in which women (and later men) could explore shamed and hidden aspects of self. Rather than be left feeling how these reflected individual inadequacies, you could begin to recognise *how* these feelings of inadequacy are formed through a shared structural experience.

Sometimes, of course, you might fail to connect with other people, but there was recognition in feminism that others who had lived through similar experiences, say of abortion or of abuse, are more likely to understand what you are communicating about that experience. It is not enough to understand the language of what is being said, but one must be able to meet others on the same level. This was a moment of critical imagination in which women could recognise one another in their sufferings, but also in their joys. There was a recognition of the structures of patriarchal power and how they *worked to* undermine and diminish women in their own eyes. Exploring new possibilities, women could refuse to evaluate their experience according to prevailing patriarchal values and insist on creating their own meanings and values. This involved recognition that individual women could want very different things out of life, but this was something they had to explore for themselves as it involved an awareness of the difference/s across identities of class, 'race', ethnicities and sexualities.

Identity politics

Within poststructuralist feminism there has been a refinement of the idea that men are the enemy against which women have to define themselves. A younger generation of women have experienced greater gender equality in schooling and have grown up to feel that they could compete with men on equal terms. Today, women can appreciate that feminism has succeeded in creating conditions of gender equality, and that women have been empowered and given access to previously blocked professions and careers within the public realm. They might feel grateful for the achievements of the women's movement, but consider these identity politics to be part of a past that has little relevance to the lives they live in the present. Within a postmodern culture there is a new individualism, in which young people believe that their achievements will be down to their skills and abilities. They do not want to see themselves as in any way limited by their inherited identities – either in terms of gender, 'race' or ethnicity – rather they will be free to create identities for themselves within a new multicultural world. They are often critical of ideas around 'identity politics', which they assume means fixing people into given categories of identity.

Often poststructuralist feminisms learn to identify modernity with a vision of the rational self and liberal individualism. They tend to think of 'postmodernity' as shaping a different kind of identity politics with a challenge that feminism has initiated around questions of gender that unsettle a unified notion of 'woman', thereby encouraging thinking that is 'beyond gender' (see Butler, 1990, 1993; and Narayan, 1997). Similarly, the black movement has questioned the stability of categories of 'race', which is assumed to imply a certain fixity that denies the fluidities and possibilities of hybrid identities, so shaping thinking that is 'beyond race' (see Gilroy, 1993, 2000; and Chakrabarti, 2000). The gay movement, under similar influences and global changes, has questioned the settled nature of gay and lesbian identities, seeking greater flexibility and ambivalence in queer identities in relation to issues of sexuality (Duncan, 1996; Brett et al, 1997; Cruz-Malave and Manalansan, 2002). The disability movement has also questioned assumptions around able-bodiedness, so contesting the ways that institutions and public spaces have long been constructed around certain normalised assumptions of physical ability. These changes could be framed as a movement from identity towards *difference/s* so shaping a different kind of 'identity politics'.

Sometimes such theoretical developments rely too easily on certain constructions of the past. The early women's movement, for example, is often presented as committed to a vision of equality as that of sameness, and to women's identity as one of essentialism in which there had to be a shared equality across differences of class, 'race', ethnicities and sexualities and in which women as a gender are set against men. When women's equality was imagined as a matter of making women *equal* to men, through opening up opportunities and spaces so long denied to them within a patriarchal society, there was a 'normalisation' of male experience. Rather than challenging the terms and powers of a dominant masculinity, these structures themselves could become naturalised. This was an early focus in Scandinavia where women were encouraged to compete on equal terms with men and were provided with state-run childcare to enable them to do so. The state would take over responsibility for childcare as women entered the world of work on equal terms. However, women were still largely expected to take responsibility for childcare and domestic work, but gradually there were demands for a more equal distribution between women and men of domestic and intimate labour within the home (see Chapter Four).

Women and work

The early women's movement in Britain insisted that work had to be transformed so that it no longer simply reflected the needs of men within a patriarchal culture. It was understood that work was not a gender-neutral space but a space that men had been able to construct in their own image. These demands for the transformation of work relations and cultures were soon forgotten as younger women felt that they could and should compete on whatever terms were set for them. They did not want any 'special allowances' to be made for them as women. This has opened up a tension within the workplace where women can sometimes despise female colleagues with families who they might feel get benefits or do not seem to be so *identified with* the workplace. They can feel that they give women a 'bad name' and that when they have to take time off, say when children are ill, it is the single women who often have to cover for them. Young women, like men, can become so identified with their roles at work that, although they talk of wanting relationships, they have little space for them in their lives. With the rise of speed-dating, for example, we see the creation of new spaces to minimise the time required for heavily pressured single people to make opportunities for meaningful relationships.

The strategy of New Labour when it came to power in Britain in 1997 was to focus on giving access to work and encouraging women to enter the workforce as a space of equality and empowerment. They sought to encourage women to return to work through gradually improving state childcare provision as per the Scandinavian model discussed above. Culturally, however, there is still a significant difference with Scandinavia where women are expected to be equal economically

In Norway, for example, it has been recognised that a feminism constructed around a notion of gender *equality* has often sustained a masculine norm which has left women feeling that, however hard they try, they inevitably fall short. Often these conflicts have become privatised as women feel uneasy about sharing their personal anxieties and conflicts (see also Chapter Four). They may talk to their friends but without support of shared consciousness-raising, such struggles are seen very much as part of a past that is over; women therefore often feel that they have to solve these issues on their own. In the public world of work it is crucial for women to present themselves as being effective and in control; emotions are still deemed a sign of weakness, as masculine norms have become universalised within this new regime of gender equality.

Gender differences

A focus on *difference* has allowed for women to discover a new space in which they could more easily acknowledge differences with men. It could bring a rediscovery of a feminist ethics that envisioned alternative values and meanings. These cultural insights have been sustained within lesbian cultures, but often lost elsewhere. As Judith Butler states:

> I would argue that any effort to give universal or specific content to the category of women, presuming that that guarantee of solidarity is required in advance, will necessarily produce factionalisation, and that 'identity' as a point of departure can never hold as the solidifying ground of a

feminist political movement. Identity categories are never merely descriptive, but always normative, and as such, exclusionary. This is not to say that the term 'women' ought not to be used, or that we ought to announce the death of the category. (Butler, 1990, p 15)

This is an interesting quotation from Butler because many people have accepted that the tendency that flows from her work is to question the very category of 'women' as if it *has to* imply qualities that all women can be said to share. Butler is at least helping us think about the danger of a 'factionalism' that was so much part of 1970s sexual politics. If we assume with Melucci that an identity always needs an 'outside/r' which is an 'enemy' against which the identity comes to be defined then we can fall into the trap of fixing identities. There was a **moralism** in feminism that also needs to be named, which suggested that there was a singular path that had to be followed.

For radical feminists this often meant a *separatist* politics in which women who had sexual relationships with men were somehow deemed to be 'traitors to the cause' because they continued to have relationships with 'the enemy'. Since feminists' struggle had to do with taking away the power which men claimed as their own, there could be no meeting ground or solidarity with anti-sexist men. In some ways these men were deemed to be more dangerous because they were pretending to be other than what they were: men sharing in the benefits of patriarchal power.

We can name this as a form of *identity politics*, without concluding that we have to dispense with the notion of identity. Rather we can think about questioning ideas of 'given' and 'fixed' identities, as we appreciate how people so often live with multiple, complex and flexible identities. Some identities people learn to share, while others can remain concealed because it feels too threatening to share them. People learn to protect their vulnerable identities, which they might practise only in specific, personal spaces.

As I have already mentioned in Chapter Two, I personally know how I learnt to conceal aspects of my Jewishness that I *could* practise at home. This became an automatic process as I moved between different spaces, which would also show itself in the language on which I would happily draw. With other Jewish people I might more easily talk about Jewish festivals like Pesach or Chanukah, without needing to watch for the response I might get. It appears to me that something similar has happened with British Hindus and Muslims who may feel easier talking in general theoretical terms about their hybrid identities than sharing details of the religious traditions in which they have been brought up. At some level these aspects of their identities remain shamed.

When Butler says that "Identity categories are never merely descriptive, but always normative, and as such, exclusionary" she is making this a matter of definition. This is the very kind of definitional rationalism Wittgenstein helps us question. The distinction between 'descriptive' and 'normative' is not as clear as Butler describes it, nor does it follow that identity categories are "always normative, and as such, exclusionary". There is a danger of identities becoming exclusionary, as we saw in the 1970s, so that, for instance, you could not be a 'real' feminist if you were involved sexually with men. There was a moralism that came with feminism that very much dictated how you were supposed to look, dress and present yourself to others. Unless you were prepared to make these concessions, you could not expect to belong. Of course this is put too bluntly, but it illustrates features of the kind of 'factionalism' that Butler identifies.

To follow Butler and assume that any talk of the identity of women must be normalising should make us think about the deconstruction of the category of 'women' in feminist politics. This is a kind of forgetfulness of the difficulties many women can *still* confront in coming to recognise (or come to consciousness of) their 'individual' experience as gendered. This remains a moment of potential revelation because it positions you differently in relation to power and social life and opens up a different way of thinking about identities, relationships and experience. In placing feminism in the past – as a feature of a modernity which assumed a shared category of 'woman' and which has given way to the fragmentation of a postmodern culture – young women can assume that they do not have to *work* to establish their own feminist consciousness.

Kate Nash wants to argue that identity should not be a central issue for feminism, that it is a term that we should leave behind so that we can concern ourselves with *conflicts*, which, as far as she is concerned, do not emerge in relation to *identities* but in relation to *resources* that are unequally distributed (Nash, 1999). She gives as an example the international feminism campaigns around the idea that 'women's rights are human rights', which have dealt with issues of domestic violence without making appeals to questions of identity. She acknowledges that, at the same time, these campaigns draw on a sense of the vulnerability of women and men's traditional power over women's bodies and sexualities.

She draws attention to the influence of a postcolonial theory that recognises that you cannot easily translate across different cultural contexts. Western feminist movements have been criticised when Western norms of gender equality are universalised and established as markers of the superiority of the West in relation to 'the Rest', where women are supposedly still trapped within traditional patriarchal relationships. Although Nash resists Gayatri Spivak's challenge to these programmes that human rights is a feature of an Anglo-American white supremacy (see Spivak, 1990, 1999), she is nevertheless forced to acknowledge that some of these critical issues echo earlier concerns about bodies, violence and sexuality. Nash also conceded that because rape and sexual abuse have been considered *personal concerns* they are not accepted by Amnesty International, for example, as grounds for rape victims being regarded a 'prisoner of conscience' or for being granted asylum or refugee status.

When Spivak points out that legislation against child labour within a globalised economy can serve to undermine the very basis of these economic relationships, say in Bangladesh, we have to be careful how childhood is conceived in this argument. We must think about the different forms of family relationships and the ways in which women can sometimes be empowered through being able to earn for themselves, even in these oppressive conditions. As young women feel their increased economic power so they might also expect more for themselves within relationships. Again this demonstrates that we should not so neatly divide, as Nash would, questions of identity from issues of conflict and resource allocation. Rather we need to acknowledge *how* concerns with social justice inevitably move across the boundaries of the personal and the political.

This leads us to Simone Weil's concern that we recognise injustice *as violation,* as somehow prior in establishing the terms for distributive concepts of justice which so often take individual freedom and autonomy for granted (Weil, 2005). As we recognise injustice as relational, so we can recover within feminism a non-distributive vision of injustice as violation. Rape can be a form of violation in which injustice is done: not just the infliction of 'psychological' damage, as Weil insisted, because this is *a moral reality* in which a woman is being violated. This understanding of bodily integrity and violation was a critical feminist insight that potentially transforms our sense of injustice. This is related to identity, but not identity as fixed or given. Rather we learn about human vulnerability and ways in which this is connected to *how* people learn to relate to one another. For example, a young man today might feel able to use his mobile phone to send an abusive text message to his female partner saying things that he might never dare to say directly. This message can be hurtful and can break the trust that was in the relationship, as the recipient never expected to be addressed in this way by someone she cared for. This is an abuse of his patriarchal power of which he might not be aware.

This example also shows how new technologies can also be used to bully others and damage their sense of self-worth and identity, which can be so easily undermined (see also Chapter Twelve). The ease with which people will *show* aspects of their identities depends on trust, making it important to be able to recognise different *levels* of experience and different ways in which people can hurt one another, even though they might feel they have to hide or conceal that hurt so as not to lose face.

Inclusion/exclusion

Within the spaces of a re-imagined identity politics we might also be concerned with issues of inclusion and exclusion: who should count as friend and who remains as enemy? Who can be trusted and relied on? Even if we want to leave behind the kind of identity politics which was associated with the moralism and legislative identities of the 1970s, we might still be struck by the ways women remain 'invested' in particular identities as women. Even if we are tempted, with Butler, to give up the category of 'woman' as carrying necessarily essentialist implications, we must still explain how and why women come to be invested in these particular identities. Sometimes this language of 'investments' frames the issues too voluntaristically, as if people are free to withdraw these 'investments' at any time as they are to shape their identities as they desire.

Wendy Brown talks about these investments as 'wounded attachments' to traumatic experiences of inequality and subordination (Brown, 1995). This can help to explain the continuing investments in particular identities which women find it difficult to 'leave behind' and possibly therefore unable to 'move on' in their lives. This can help explain a sense of being 'trapped' in a particular history or identity, for example, as a victim of abuse or sexual violence. A woman might be continually replaying the violence in her relationship with her partner, as this is an identity in which she has 'invested', but this leaves her unable to let the relationship go, even when it is over, so that she can move on in her own life. Rather she can feel trapped into replaying her old relationship, even if the hurt is long past (Brown, 2006). This is something that Freud knew, recognising that when people are able to engage in 'emotional work' they might be able to leave the past behind and not feel so victimised and fixed by it.

This is one way in which people can be 'fixed' in identities, but it is only through exploring ways of 'working through' their experience, rather than disconnecting as a matter of will and determination, that they might find greater freedom. Freud believed that what we deny and repress will often *return to haunt* our dreams and this can produce its own forms of culturally displaced resentment as people find it difficult to dis/invest in particular histories and identities. Brown is much less clear about *how* we are to move beyond these histories of suffering. She talks about a movement from identity – from 'I am' towards an agency of imagined desire, or 'I want'. If this does not get us far it does allow the possibility of imagining different futures. It offers a chance of 'moving beyond' these 'wounded attachments' as, to some extent, feelings can follow behaviours and we can become clearer and more defined in our identities as we free ourselves from 'wounded attachments' that block possibilities for meaningful relationships. But, as Freud knew, this often involves an *acknowledgement* of the influence of such 'wounded attachments' in our lives. This does not need to involve a return to childhood experience, as if there is a single causal key waiting to be discovered, as alternative psychotherapies have explored, we can also work to *transform patterns* in relationships as we can be open to different behaviours and feelings in the present.

Beyond gender?

We need to think about what difference it makes if we accept the death of the category of 'women' or whether we go along with Butler's suggestion that calls for a different kind of emancipation: an escape from gendered identities. Often there is a flight from the personal and the emotional that connects to an aspiration to leave considerations of identity behind, to move *beyond* gender as others have asked that we move beyond 'race'. In some ways this gives a different form to an Enlightenment modernity framed within the terms of a secular Christian tradition that would 'leave behind' the earthly conditions of our lives. This reflects an inheritance of a particular vision of *freedom as autonomy*. Wittgenstein and Freud both questioned this inheritance, drawing on Hebraic/Jewish sources that would, in contrast, countenance a 'coming to terms' with the conditions of our earthly and sexual lives

For Freud, it is only through 'coming to terms' with our emotional histories that we can find more freedom; we should be suspicious of tendencies that encourage flights from identity as denials and evasions of the emotional and cultural histories we often carry into the present. At the same time we can appreciate Hall's poststructuralist insight that pushed the limits of this inheritance when he views identification as a discursive process of construction:

> it does not mean that we do not have any connection with what went before. But it does mean that this connection is not something that can now be naturally summoned up as if it exists in all of us, somewhere down there in our bodies, in our genes, as a force of nature. It has to be recreated, has to be sustained in the culture, reconfigured in the new historical circumstances which confront us. It has to be sustained in the mind, or the connection cannot be made. (p 285)

Through the work of **Michel Foucault** feminists learned to think of power not as something that men possessed in their relationships with women so that women would be framed as subordinated to male power. Rather we learned to think about how 'masculinities' and 'femininities' are constructed through relationships of power that run through all social relations. Power is no longer concentrated in the state, but exists and runs through every sphere of social life. This important insight also carried its own consequences, for if it allowed for an inclusion of issues around men and masculinities and for a discourse around masculinities to become acceptable within social theory, at the same time it reflected a silence in relation to gendered relations of power. Paradoxically, if this made 'masculinity' a reference in post-Foucauldian work, it also meant that everyday struggles of men in relationships with women were somehow rendered invisible.

There was also, under Foucault's influence, a kind of 'depersonalisation' of social theory – an appeal to telling metaphors as a way of providing alternative descriptions of social life. Foucault also talked in important ways about the disciplining and regulation of bodies, particularly in *Discipline and punish* (1975), which marked a break with his assumption that discourses somehow organise the identities of those who find themselves subject to them. His political work with prisoners allowed him a fuller awareness of the counter-discourses that prisoners had developed for themselves; they refused to see themselves exclusively through the discourses of criminology but produced for themselves a sense of their own resistant identities. Paradoxically, this reflects an insight of 'second-wave' feminism that valued women's resistant voices by validating the different voices that were often silenced and ridiculed within the dominant culture, which in masculine terms discounted emotions and feelings as legitimate sources of knowledge.

Endnote

[1] For some illuminating reflections on the changes in Wittgenstein's thinking about language and meaning see Norman Malcolm's (1986) *Ludwig Wittgenstein: Nothing is hidden.*

Further reading

Women's liberation movement

For some accounts of the development of the women's movement in the early 1970s in the industrialised West see, for instance, Sheila Rowbotham's *Woman's consciousness, man's world* (1973) and *Dreams and dilemmas* (1983); Michelle Wandor, *The body politic* (1972); Robin Morgan's anthology *Sisterhood is powerful* (1970); Mary Daly, *Beyond God the Father* (1973); and Sara Evans, *Personal politics* (1980).

Differences of class, 'race', ethnicity and sexuality

Some interesting explorations of the difference/s across identities of class, 'race', ethnicities and sexualities that is alive to their relationship with lived experience is provided by bell hooks in both *Yearning* (1991) and *Sisters of the yam* (1999). (See also Ahmed, 2000; 2004; Knowles, 2004; Puwar, 2004.)

Feminism

For a helpful introduction to the poststructuralist turn within feminism and the ways it helped shape the thinking of a generation of feminist theorists see, for example, Lennon and Whitford (1994); Flax (1990); Collins (1991); Butler and Scott (1992).

For an investigation of different generations of feminist theory and practice, and the tensions that often exist between them see, for instance, Natasha Walter's (1999) *The new feminism*; Lisa Adkins' (2002) *Revisions* and Angela McRobbie's (2007) article 'Top girls?'.

Identity politics

For some interesting reflections on identity politics and the shaping of identities within post-traditional societies see, for instance, Beck et al (1995) *Reflexive modernisation*; Beck and Beck-Gernsheim (1995) *The normal chaos of love*; Beck (2000) *The brave new world of work*; Anthony Giddens' *Modernity and self-identity* (1991) and *The transformation of intimacy* (1993); Paul Gilory, *After empire* (2005); and Zygmunt Bauman's *Liquid modernity* (2000) and *The individualized society* (2001).

Gay and lesbian identities

For some helpful discussion of the queering of gay and lesbian identities and the ways this was helping to shape new forms of queer theory see, for instance, Ingram et al (1997) *Queers in space*; Nancy Duncan's (1996) *Bodyspace*; and Arnaldo Cruz-Malave and Martin F. Manalansan (eds) *Queer globalisations* (2002). For a critique of the uses of diaspora or hybridity see Tom Boellstorff, *The gay archipelago* (2005) and Ruth Vanita (ed) *Queering India* (2002).

Michel Foucault

For some interesting reflections on Foucault's intellectual development see, for instance, David Macy's *The lives of Michel Foucault* (1995). For a sense of how *Discipline and punish* marks a break in his work as a result of his political work with prisoners, see interviews with Foucault in Colin Gordon's *Power/ Knowledge* (1980). Foucault's relationships with feminism are explored in Lois McNay, *Foucault and feminism* (1992) and *Gender and agency* (1994), and Caroline Ramazanoglu, *Up against Foucault* (1992).

For some discussion of the developments and breaks in Foucault's writings see his essay 'Technologies of the self' (1988). For an interesting exploration of the developments of Foucault's work see Dreyfus and Rabinow (1982); for some feminist responses to Foucault's work see McNay (1994) and Ramazanoglu (1992).

Men and masculinities

For some discussion of men's early responses to feminism and the experience of a generation of men who sough to reflect on tensions within their inherited masculinities see, for instance, Victor J. Seidler, *Rediscovering masculinity* (1989), *Recreating sexual politics* (1991), *Man enough* (2000) and *Transforming masculinities* (2006); Jeff Hearn, *The gender of oppression* (1987) and *Man in the public eye* (1992); R.W. Connell, *Gender and power* (1987) and *Masculinities* (1995); and A. Brittan, *Masculinity and power* (1989).

SIX

Genders: desires / self-rejection / recognition

This chapter discusses people's desire and capacity to change their identities, gender, sexuality, self-rejection and recognition.

Gender/s

How do people think that they can become different? In what sense are these processes gendered in the West? Does the West continue to be influenced by a secularised Christian culture in which women and men, in different ways, learn to reject aspects of their natures as evil? How does this influence young people growing up in diverse secular and religious traditions? Do people grow up with a sense of inadequacy, feeling that if only they could *change* aspects of themselves then they could find happiness? In what sense is psychoanalysis conceived of as a *technology of transformation* that helps people to become different from what they are? These are questions that still haunt social theories and philosophies in the West and they continue to shape conceptions of identities and how people think they might be able to change.

To what extent is the dream that people can *become* radically different and somehow alter who they are still central to self-conceptions within the West? Shaped within the terms of secularised Christian traditions people may feel that they can only affirm their identities as rational selves through rejecting their 'animal natures' – their bodies and sexualities that are still at some unconscious level tied to the 'sins of the flesh'. Max Weber explores these themes in the *Protestant ethic and the spirit of capitalism* (1970). Weber understood that people are always left with a sense they have to prove themselves, because they are haunted by a sense of *inadequacy* that derives from an unspoken belief that their natures are evil so that they can only redeem themselves through a process of self-rejection.

Traditionally, it has been through work that a dominant masculinity has learnt to prove itself and thereby assuage feelings of inadequacy. But, in contemporary capitalist and meritocratic societies, men can be left with a feeling that however much they do, they could still have achieved more. This has left men identifying with their lives primarily within the sphere of work since these were the spaces in which they could prove themselves in competitive relations with others. This has also meant that men have learned to take their intimate relations for granted. Often they happily leave it to their partners to organise their home and social lives, knowing that their identities are largely shaped by work. Further, while men often feel at odds with themselves, focusing on their work identities, they often do not recognise their own needs for nourishment. Rather, since masculinities are often identified with self-sufficiency, men have learned to disavow their own emotional needs because they are experienced as a sign of weakness. It can therefore come as a revelation for men to recognise that it is possible for them to be nourished in their relationships, as they can often be trapped into feeling they have to be strong for others. Men might find it difficult to show vulnerability even in their intimate relationships. If this is not a sign of self-rejection it is at least a denial of their emotional needs.

It has also been difficult for men to give time and attention to themselves, learning that this is a form of (inappropriate) self-indulgence. Since masculinities are identified with 'being active' there is also a fear of passivity as this tends to be identified as 'feminine', and so can be experienced as a *threat* to male identities. Men can feel that they must be constantly active to assuage the feelings of anxiety and inadequacy that might otherwise arise. At the same time, men can feel *entitled* to get their way in heterosexual relationships and in this way their needs are met. They often end up getting to do what they want to do, although this can still have little to do with fulfilling their emotional needs that they find so difficult to identify. When they insist on taking time to offload the events of the day, they assume their partners will be there to listen and often fail to acknowledge the emotional labour involved, also failing to give similar attention to their partner's work stories.

Within postmodern cultures in the West the influence of the women's movement has meant that women have had greater access to the workplace and have therefore been able to compete on more equal terms with men (see Chapter Three). Even if work cultures have changed so that they are more appreciative of communication skills (traditionally 'feminine' skills), women can feel an *unspoken* pressure to present themselves in gender-neutral terms. Women are obliged to compete on terms still largely set by dominant masculine cultures, with little acknowledgement of their lives and responsibilities outside of the sphere of work. This can make it difficult for women to find a balance between work and domestic life and encourages them to sustain a vision of gender equality in their intimate relationships, particularly through postponing the time of having children. Women can feel a sense of inadequacy as they compare themselves to the 'superwomen' (mostly thin women) portrayed in the mass media who supposedly have few difficulties 'juggling' different areas of their lives. The pressures on women increase to compete with men at work while also assuming caring responsibilities at home and competing with other women in their physical appearance.

Self-rejection

Does a woman feel inadequate because she compares herself with other women and feels she does not perform as well? Is she more likely to hate how she looks, feeling that she is 'too fat', when she compares herself with the thin models she sees on the covers of magazines? In what ways is self-rejection gendered? Do women and men learn to hate themselves in different ways?

The terms of competition and self-rejection have shifted within a postmodern culture in which there are no longer clearly demarcated gender roles for women and for men. A younger generation of women feel that they are growing up in a very different world from their mothers and can therefore feel estranged from their mother's advice. They take it for granted that they will have work lives and hope for more equal relations with their partners. They no longer feel that relationships are likely to last and think it likely that they will have a series of more-or-less monogamous relationships through their lives. This can make it difficult for women today to invest as much emotionally in their partners, knowing that they have to be prepared for relationships to end and prepared to support themselves and possibly children on their own (see Smart, 1992).

Young women might be clear in their expectations for greater gender equality and at the same time more tolerant of gender differences than their feminist mothers. They might well expect their partners to take a more equal share of responsibilities for cooking and cleaning, especially if they are making equal financial contributions. But they will often have a stronger demarcation between their personal lives and their work lives, keen to prove themselves within the world of work. Adopting the terms of a rationalist culture they can assume a relationship towards their emotional lives that has traditionally been more expected of men. Women can feel equally displaced in relation to their emotional lives, unsure of their emotions and feelings. They are more inclined to interpret their emotions as a sign of weakness having learned to expect themselves to be more independent and self-sufficient. If they are still more adept at interpreting the emotions of their partners, feeling compelled at some level to ensure their partner's happiness, they can have difficulties in identifying their own emotional needs as women. It can be easier to continue blaming their partners for not being more emotionally expressive, while concealing their own emotional difficulties. This may also explain the interest that women have in studies of men and masculinities, because these have been focused on emotional lives.

I can recall a young man once telling me how he hated himself because he was so thin. He did not like himself and wanted to become a different person, as he expressed it; he did not want to accept the way he was because he hated how thin he was. He became interested in bodybuilding because he felt that if he built his muscles and changed his appearance then he would become a different person. Identifying with the personal struggles in Sam Fussell's *Muscle*, he, like Fussell, got into conflict with his father who could not understand his obsession with bodybuilding. He felt that this was a *technology of transformation* through which he could replace his old 'thin' self with a new 'strong' self; he would become a different person who would be respected by others because of the body he had built for himself. He endured considerable pain, but this effort helped to affirm himself in his own eyes. He felt that he was no longer the same person, and that he had proved himself so that others would no longer be able to reject him.

Some women have also chosen this path, but more often turn their hatred in against themselves. This has encouraged more women to self-harm as a way of *feeling* some of their inner pain and making it visible to themselves. As a self-harmer cuts into their skin they can feel a sense of relief, as if they are letting some of the 'poison' out. They can find it difficult to accept themselves the way they are, especially within a moral culture that so often leaves people feeling bad about themselves. Not only can women feel that they will only be loved if they somehow transform into something different from what they are, but they can also feel undeserving of the love of others. This is a feeling that can be intensified within a religious tradition that teaches that people are 'born into sin' and can only achieve redemption if they can deny their 'animal natures'.

Within a Catholic tradition there is at least the possibility of confession that can allow people to feel that they can at least 'begin again' after they have confessed their sins. Foucault (1976) argued that psychoanalysis can play a similar role within a secularised culture, by encouraging people to confess their dark emotions and intentions about which they might otherwise remain silent. Within a Protestant moral culture there is no such release and people can feel uneasy about pleasure. Catholic traditions are more at ease with pleasure (even if not with sexual pleasure); people seem more able to enjoy themselves and there are particular festivals at different times of the year when people can escape from the moral demands of everyday life. This tends to produce a different technology of self-rejection.

In Foucault's later work (see 1985, 1986) there is a greater awareness that we cannot separate social relations from a concern with inner emotional lives. These connections could not be explored within a framework of knowledge/power, which encouraged Foucault to assume that there has to be a "dissociation of the self" as it is recognised as an 'empty synthesis' as we "make visible all of those discontinuities that cross us" (1978, p 162) Foucault later comes to appreciate that this duality is part of the problem if we need to think about the relation between subjectivities and ethics, and the ways in which identities and experiences are shaped within particular moral traditions. This encourages him to explore the continuing echoes of Christian disdain for bodies and sexualities within secularised visions of modernity and the ways in which they sustain cultures of self-rejection (Foucault, 1985, 1986; see also Rabinow, 1998).

These self-rejections are built into classical forms of social theory (as I explore in Seidler, 1993) where, for instance, Durkheim assumes that people left to their own devices are selfish and egoistic (Durkheim, 1893, 1925). It is only through identifying with social rules that people can learn to curb their selfish natures and so *become* other than the selfish beings they would otherwise be. Society offers people a higher vision of themselves; a vision of reason and freedom that they cannot know on their own accounts. This vision of self-rejection remains implicit within Foucault's early work, in which he expresses antagonism towards a vision of self. Rather than being envisioned as 'harmonious', this inner self is cast as tainted, flawed and 'evil'. This is also related to an antagonism towards more expressive visions of self for which Friedrich Nietzsche has some sympathy. Although Nietzsche (1887) supposedly remains the inspiration for Foucault's vision of genealogy, Foucault produces in his earlier work an unhelpful duality between 'inner emotional life', which is presented somehow as 'harmonious', versus the play of external forces, which are discontinuous and so shape identities. Foucault wants to replace inner emotional life that sits uneasily with and somehow becomes identified for him with an essentialist vision of self with the discontinuities of external forces as discourses.

Poststructuralist traditions also produce unhelpful distinctions between *interiority* that is devalued and somehow identified with 'essentialism' in ways rarely explained and at some level reflect a fear of 'the personal' as 'emotional', and an *exteriority* that therefore comes to be valued. This legitimates the very forms of *disassociation* that are features of a postmodern culture in which people have very little connection with their inner emotional lives, coming to see themselves through the images of a consumer and celebrity culture. People often assume an externalised relation to themselves and can experience themselves as somehow 'locked out' of their inner psychic lives. This is also a consequence of the acceleration of urban life and new social network technologies, which leaves people feeling they constantly have to catch up with themselves because they never have 'enough time' to do what is required. The acceleration of life has also left people to develop their own strategies for releasing accumulated nervous energy, for example, in the gym where people shape a competitive relationship with themselves. The idea of walking quietly in nature has little appeal for busy urbanites who have little connection to themselves in this way.

Language

A fear of interiority as something that we need to *escape from* has been part of the appeal of Jacques Lacan's conception of the unconscious as a language governed by rules. A poststructuralist tradition questions a notion that people express themselves through language and which is often taken to assume there is a 'unified' or 'harmonious' self that somehow *chooses* to express itself through language. Within a *rationalist* tradition this follows an assumption that people already know in advance what they want to say, so that language is presented as an instrument at their disposal to use as they wish. Against this there is a tacit opposition between 'interiority' and 'genealogy', which somehow cuts across individual lives and is linked to a sense that it is through language that people have experience/s and thereby constitute their identities.

In support of this duality it is asserted that there can be no experiences that exist prior to language and so no identities that are not articulated or constituted through language. It is misleading, though, to appeal to time in this way, which works to foreclose a tension between language and experience that remains crucial for both Wittgenstein and early feminism. When we think about language exclusively in Ferdinand de Saussure's terms as a system of signs, whereby meaning is established through a *difference between* signs, we have moved away from issues of expression (see also Chapter Six). This is a duality that Wittgenstein refuses, recognising that it is often through expressing themselves in language that people can come to *realise* what they think. Something similar happens when you talk through a problem and find you already have the solution yourself. Wittgenstein questions a vision of mind that suggests that thoughts exist in a mental space of their own, waiting to be 'expressed' in language. He wants to rework the distinction between 'inner' thoughts and 'outer' behaviour. But this is a distinction in which Foucault's early work remains trapped, as he identifies interiority with 'harmony' and 'unity'.

Thinking in terms of *subjectivities* as a way of escaping this dualism Foucault does not really know how to develop his early work but feels a need to break with it. Having broken with psychoanalysis, which has traditionally treated homosexualities as pathologies that mark a failure to develop normal heterosexuality, potentially framing homosexualities as 'illnesses' that can be cured, Foucault cannot find a way back to thinking about the interrelations between inner emotional life and social and cultural relations. He recognises the continuing resonance of past traditions in shaping the ways we think and feel about our bodies, sexualities and emotional lives but finds it difficult to recognise possibilities of transformation in the present. Foucault does not want to be trapped in identities as defined by others, so he does not want to be confined in a gay identity any more than in any other identity. He does not want to be *fixed* through an identity that might dictate how others feel about him as much as how he might choose to live his life himself.

In 'Sexuality and solitude', a piece Foucault wrote with Richard Sennett, they share a suspicion of a sexual politics that encourages people to prioritise particular aspects of identity (Foucault with Sennett, 1981). Foucault's approach to sexuality is that while he might readily acknowledge that he has sex with men, he does not want this to dictate his politics or preferences in other aspects of his life. In their different ways Foucault and Sennett seem more at ease with a liberalism that would treat sexuality as one aspect of identity among many others.

This makes it difficult to think about the weight of sexual *denial*, with homophobic cultures and the self-rejections that this can produce. Nor are these issues helped when we think about identifications that people can make as a way of escaping from languages of identity that might fix people into predetermined categories. Foucault wants to insist that he does not have more in common with people because they are gay than he possibly has with other people because of their taste in music or their political views (see discussion of feminism in Chapter Five). A language of identifications is able to express the provisional nature by which people can assume particular identifications at particular times for particular purposes and not feel themselves fixed or confined by identities that would seem to *define* their experience. This can make it difficult to illuminate the stand a person is making against particular pressures in specific cultures in, for example, 'coming out' as gay. This can involve a process of self-acceptance and so a refusal to identify with the ways in which a homophobic culture denigrates gay sexualities.

As a young gay man, Wittgenstein moved towards a process of self-acceptance in relation to his sexuality but this often involved a struggle with himself (see Monk, 1990). He no longer wanted to hide what he recognised about himself and he wanted to feel proud of what others had shamed. This transition involves a process that cannot be achieved as a matter of individual will alone; often it is a decision that takes time and is marked by shifts in the ways in which people talk to themselves and relate to others. Even if Wittgenstein felt this to be an important step, it did not exclude other identifications nor did it mean that he could automatically come to feel about himself differently. He recognised that it would be important for him to tell his parents and also his friends and that he might feel anxious about how they might react. These were steps that others could not take for him.

Recognition

If others are ready to accept a gay identity, then it can make it easier for us to do so ourselves. But this process of self-acceptance has different levels and it *takes time* to move between them. A young African-Caribbean gay man might find it easier to share his gayness with some of his white friends than to 'come out' within the African-Caribbean community. He might recognise a complex dynamic between his 'blackness' and his 'gayness', knowing that in some contexts it feels much more relevant for him to identify as a black man engaged with struggles about racism. He might feel at ease with some other black gay men, but feel tense and anxious when with heterosexual black men, although there might well also be moments when he feels called on to identify himself as gay when he is with other black men because of how they are speaking. There are different forms of recognition that can come into play in different contexts.

What kind of recognition do we need and who do we need it from? A person might feel that it is important for their gay identity to be recognised by their parents even though their friends tell them that it should be enough that their parents are relaxed about it. In some cultures this might be a need that is partly felt because of its relative impossibility. In Spanish culture, for example, people may feel that they can be openly gay with their friends, but do not expect to have recognition from their parents. They might know that their parents suspect their gayness, but also know that they do not want the secret to be discussed openly. Sometimes parents are relaxed about a child's gay identity, as long as they do not have to deal with it, especially with their own family and friends. They prefer a situation of knowing privately and not knowing publicly, so it is never referred to openly. In different cultural settings *different* compromises might seem appropriate, although people might feel quite differently about whether or not they can live with them.

In an Anglo–American world people feel the need to be able to express themselves in different parts of their lives. Some people will question the notion that as long as you can accept your own identity then it should not matter what others think, even if they are your family, while others might feel that they can no longer 'live a lie' and be dishonest with themselves. We have to be careful *how we think* about these needs for expression, knowing that sometimes they can be compulsive, while at other times they just show where someone is with themselves. People find different balances between a need for self-acceptance and a need for recognition from others.

Self-acceptance is a process that can often involve different forms of self-recognition. As we learn from psychoanalysis, this can involve coming to terms with emotional histories that might otherwise be denied (see Chapter Two); it can also involve people taking responsibility for hurting others. There are different technologies of transformation and, within a dominant culture that has historically focused on strategies of self-rejection, it can be difficult to make space for change through self-acceptance, as explored in diverse psychotherapies. We could argue that psychoanalysis has created a *space* for bisexuality and so opened up possibilities of recognition for gay identities while at the same time working to normalise heterosexual identities.

Making connections

If people within a liberal moral culture learn to abstract from their gendered identities to think of themselves as 'free and equal' persons able to make their own lives according to their own abilities, it can be harder to recognise your experience as gendered and therefore to negotiate more equal gender relationships. Often women and men can find it difficult to make connections between the ways they feel and experience life and the social relationships of power in which they find themselves. Within a dominant heterosexual culture men learn to reject feelings of need, vulnerability and tenderness that can be experienced as 'feminine' and therefore as threats to male identities. Often men learn that it is only through rejecting these aspects of their experience that they can affirm their male identities. Instead they learn to identify masculinity with a vision of *control* over emotional life, so that through exerting control they can affirm their male identities. This can make men less sensitive to their emotional needs and so less able to negotiate more equal gender relations.

Since people who identify with postmodern cultures do not want to be confined or limited by difference/s they learn to abstract from relations of class, 'race', ethnicity, gender and able-bodiedness. Within a celebrity culture they can find themselves constantly *comparing* themselves with the images of a media culture, as if trapped into taking an externalised relationship with self. These images have assumed a greater significance for both women and men, as we discover just how widespread is concern with weight and body image. So many young people can feel that life is not worth living unless they can be 'thin', that they regulate their eating habits and control their bodies to realise these images of themselves.

If we are to think in new ways about complex identities and traumatic inheritances of migration and transgenerations we need to re-vision the relationship between emotional life, bodies and social relationships. We must think beyond a distinction between, on the one hand, psychoanalysis as a concern with subjectivity and inner emotional life and, on the other hand, social theory as concerned with social relationships of power and subordination. This involves thinking outside the terms of poststructuralist traditions that sustain a categorical distinction between nature and culture. As Freud understood, our identities are shaped across both nature and culture because identities cannot be constructed exclusively within the terms of culture alone. But Freud too often presented social relationships as a projection of inner emotional forces and post-Freudian Kleinian traditions have been too ready to assume the autonomy of psychic life as if it can be understood in its own terms. Although Foucault helps us to challenge traditions that focus on interiority, it was only in his later work that he looked for ways of understanding complex relations between subjectivities, ethics, culture and power.

Further reading

Max Weber

For some reflections on Weber's *The protestant ethic and the spirit of capitalism*, see Anthony Giddens' *Capitalism and modern social theory* (1971); Seidler, *Unreasonable men* (1994); Beetham, *Max Weber and the theory of modern politics* (1985); Sam Whimster's *Max Weber: A Biography* (2006); and Bologh, *Love or greatness* (1990).

Work cultures

For some interesting reflections on women's changing relationships to work and how this has been shaped over different generations see, for instance, Rowbotham, *Dreams and dilemmas* (1983); Ramazanoglu, *Feminism and the contradictions of oppression* (1989); Ruddick and Daniels (1977) *Working it out*; Arlie Hochschild's *The second shift* (1989); and Hood (ed) (1993) *Men, work and family*.

Self-harm

For some helpful reflections on practices of self-harming across different genders see, for instance Kilby's (2001) chapter 'Carved in skin'; Hewitt (1997) *Mutilating the body*; and Smith et al (1999) *Women and self-harm*.

Psychoanalysis

For some helpful reflections that can illuminate thinking about developments within diverse psychoanalytic and psychotherapeutic traditions as well as about relationships with issues of gender see, for instance, Nancy Chodorow (1978) *The reproduction of mothering* and (1992) *Feminism and psychoanalysis*; Eichenbaum and Orbach, *Understanding women* (1983); Seidler (2001) *Man enough: Embodying masculinities*.

For some helpful reflections on the ways psychoanalysis has treated homosexualties and queer identities see, for instance, O'Connor and Ryan (1993) *Wild desires and mistaken identities* and Drescher (2001) *Psychoanalytic therapy and the gay man*.

Jacques Lacan

For a helpful introduction to Lacan's psychoanalytic work that also gives a sense of how it has developed over time see, for instance, Benevenuto and Kennedy's (1996) *The works of Jacques Lacan.* For a critical take on Lacan's work, specifically in relation to women's sexuality see Luce Irigaray, *Speculum of the other woman* (1983) and *The sex which is not one* (1985); and Kirsten Campbell (2004) *Jacques Lacan's feminist epistemology.*

Foucault's approach to sexuality

Foucault explores the continuing influences of Christian traditions within the shaping of contemporary subjectivitities and the ways in which they help shape people's relationships to their bodies, sexualities and emotional lives in the later volumes of his *The history of sexuality* (Foucault, 1985, 1986). He also looks towards alternative sources of identification in aspects of Greek philosophy and literature. See also the collection of Foucault's later writings edited by Paul Rabinow (1988) *Ethics: Subjectivity and truth. Essential works of Michel Foucault, 1954-1984;* and Seidler (2007a) *Jewish philosophy and Western culture.*

Body image

For some interesting reflections on the signficance of body images within a postmodern consumer culture that has such an intense identification with celebrities see, for instance, Kim Chernin's *Womansize* (1983); bell hooks, *Black looks* (1992); Susan Bond's *Unbearable weight* (1993); Lisa Blackman's *The body* (2008); and Susie Orbach's *Bodies* (2009).

SEVEN

Explorations: 'race' / violence / shame

This chapter traces connections between European modernities and narratives of 'race', racism and the ways social theory can engage with imaginative literatures and stories of history, migration, violence, memory and loss.

Histories / narratives

Reflections about the nature of identities and how they are informed by complex histories, emotions, silences and relationships are often enriched by a consideration of literature and by ways in which particular lives are narrated. Social theory can learn from an ongoing engagement with the concrete and lived explorations of literature and narratives that portray the context of individual lives, as well as the workings of larger forces and structures. It can be illuminating to *listen* to the struggles of writers who have engaged with their own traumatic histories and lived experiences in the present and so take a step back to *reflect* on how our own lives and embodied identities might also be narrated through exploring transnational histories of our own. Writers may draw on a diversity of literary forms to explore relationships, while traditional forms of social theory might seek to generalise too quickly (see Steiner, 1967, 1975).

Literature may also remind us both of differences but also what is shared; warn us about the abuse of language and the need for vigilance in its use. On a walk in Phoenix Park, Dublin, with Wittgenstein, Drury, a close friend, mentioned Georg Hegel. "Hegel seems to me to be always wanting to say that things which look different are really the same," Wittgenstein told him. "Whereas my interest is in showing that things which look the same are really different." He was thinking of using as a motto for his book (Wittgenstein, 1958b) the Earl of Kent's phrase from King Lear (Act I, scene iv): "I'll teach you differences" (quoted in Monk, 1990, p 537).

Toni Morrison has always been concerned with the two things singular about human beings and the effort to be human: "language and love". Mindful of "'civilised' languages that debase humans", she warned in her Nobel Prize lecture of official language "smitheried to sanction ignorance and preserve privilege" (quoted in *The Guardian Review of Books*, 15 November 2003, p 20). She told Maya Jaggi that part of her avowed project as a writer has been to remake language, not least to free it from the "sinister, lazy racial codes" that still pervade it. She has helped to make it impossible to look at American history without thinking of African-American life. She not only "challenges restrictive notions of what is and is not universal in literature, but insists that US history and culture are incomprehensible without the African presence" (*The Guardian Review of Books*, 15 November 2003, p 20). Her life story is instructive because it helps to show *how* different narratives must be created to illuminate the traumatic histories that have often remained unspoken in families as children are so often protected from the sufferings through which their families have lived. Too often we learn within a liberal moral culture 'to leave the past behind' as if it does not still echo in unacknowledged ways that can *affect* the lives we live in the present. As we learn to listen to how Toni Morrison and, later in this chapter, Maxine Hong Kingston narrate their lives and make visible their inheritances, so we can gain a sense of how lives can be narrated, differences over time and space explored and identities embodied.

Toni Morrison

Toni Morrison was born Chloe Anthony Wofford in 1931 in Lorain, Ohio: a "little working class town with a big steel mill" on Lake Erie, which drew southerners, east Europeans and Mexicans. As she recalls, "It had one high school and we all lived together." Although she was the only black child in her class, she was undaunted. Her mother, Ramah, was a jazz singer and her family had been sharecroppers in Kentucky who had fled the Jim Crow South. Her mother helped thwart attempts to segregate the town:

> When they opened a theatre, if the usher led her one way, she'd go the other. They were early in the swimming pool. It wasn't like the sit-ins of the 60s; these were individuals who took it upon themselves to dare somebody to move them. (quoted in *The Guardian Review of Books*, 15 November 2003, p 22)

Her family, she explains, "were all arrogant; poor as we were, there was a feeling that we were right and they were wrong". But her parents were at odds. "My father was adamant: white people didn't come in our house. My mother thought they had to prove guilt not innocence." Only four years ago on a visit to Georgia, 25 years after her father had died, Morrison learned that her father had been displaced as a train engineer by a white rival. This is something that he did not talk about although it was an experience that helped to shape him. This helps to illustrate how *silences* can work so powerfully in families and how that which remains unspoken can have as much impact as narratives that are expressed in language. Morrison also explains that the year that her father's family left town, three black businessmen had been lynched. She questions widespread assumptions when she reminds us that "Most lynching wasn't about black guys whistling after white women but about men who owned businesses or land somebody wanted" (see also Zangrando, 1980).

Although her father, a shipyard welder, "thought white people were Nazis – true demons" and told her "THEY don't decide who you are," her own experience and friends proved her mother right: "It made more sense to me that you couldn't blanket a whole group." But as a child of the depression and working in kitchens from the age of 12, she embodied these different inheritances and says: "I felt like somebody from another planet who happened to be scrubbing floors." When she moved to Washington DC and so away from home to take up a place at Howard, the famed African-American university, she was *shocked*, not only by the segregation between blacks and whites, but also by a colour hierarchy imposed by well off African-Americans. "I was so ignorant about the world," she says. "I didn't know people who had a fear of white people, or about 'paper-bag tests': if you were darker than a paper bag you could not get into places" (*The Guardian Review of Books*, 15 November 2003, p 22).

After an MA at Cornell, Morrison returned to Howard. She knew that women's issues were being set aside by the Black Power movement, but says, "One liberation movement leads to another – always has. Abolition led to the suffragettes; civil rights to women's lib, which led to a black women's movement. Groups say 'what about me?'" As 'Black is beautiful' became a widespread slogan, her first novel *The bluest eye* (1970) probed the psychic devastations because of racism in the US that made it so necessary, through the story of a little girl in 1940s' Ohio who longs for blue eyes, and whose self-loathing is compounded by incest. This helps us to think about how inferiorities come to be embodied as people learn to see themselves through the eyes of the dominant white culture. Her second novel *Sula* (1974) went on to explore friendships between women and her heroine's right to exist for herself alone, reflecting her view of black women as "both the ship and the harbour", both adventurers and nurturers. CLR James found *Sula* astonishing in its implication that the "real, fundamental human difference is not between black and white but between men and women".

Morrison was exploring a style, as Jaggi seeks to explain, "that was as irrevocably black as black music, using orality and a neighbourhood chorus that echoed ancient Greek drama". As Morrison describes it, "I wanted to make black vernacular audible, not as illiterate but powerful." She also says, "But I was as guilty as others who made black speech ungrammatical or dropped the 'g'. I tried to get away from that." She said she wrote about black people "because that's where the aesthetics, authority, authenticity are". That, she says, is still true, "but it's been misunderstood as exclusive. I meant I'm writing for black people's sensibility, not for black buyers.... White people are seen as unraced – the norm. It's a dysfunctional argument." Shifting the focus onto conflicts within the African-American community, to "unspeakable things spoken at last", drew criticism:

> The push in any minority is to reassure and celebrate, to contradict the negatives – which is good medicine, I suppose. But that's when you're writing for the Other. Nobody has to prove to me how wonderful we are; I know it. (quoted in *The Guardian Review of Books*, 15 November 2003, p 22)

This, however, also involves a form of forgetting, by which you learn to speak in different ways within the community and within the larger society. This can create its own division that can undermine and weaken the voice. The idea of 'double-consciousness', as expressing a sense of living across different worlds, was initially framed by W.E.B. Du Bois (1903) and has been developed more recently by Paul Gilroy (1993) into a way of understanding how people within multicultural society learn to live *across* the *boundaries* of different worlds as they learn to negotiate their complex identities which can be experienced differently in different spaces.

Tony Morrison told Margaret Busby in a British TV interview in 1988: "Whatever I know as a black person, and my perceptions as a woman, aren't marginal – they're an enhancement." However, she is scornful about being praised for 'transcending' race and gender and argues that:

> In trying to break open the critical language you have to take risks. I was up against a wall of assumptions, and I was trying not to say, "I'm a writer and race isn't important to me", or to exoticise myself like Langston Hughes, or be pompously literate. And I didn't want to sneak into the non-black box; I wanted to take centre space and say: "I'm a black writer and I write about black people." I didn't win friends, but the writers who followed have a better chance of not being 'labelled' because of my generation. I thought I'd ride on the quality of the work; if that failed, the argument would fail with it. (quoted in *The Guardian Review of Books*, 15 November 2003, p 22)

In *Beloved* (1987) Morrison shares a narrative that grew from the real story of Margaret Garner, a runaway slave who killed her child rather than have her recaptured. She was tried not for murder but for theft of her master's property. In Morrison's novel the dead child returns in a ghostly form.

In her writing Morrison wants to show how the "erasure of history, and responses to it, are very much what we are still wrestling with", although she also cautions against "putting what you remember in aspic" (*The Guardian Review of Books*, 15 November 2003, p 23). She recognises that so much of history is "selecting what to remember; deifying or reifying aspects and forgetting others". She knows that those who have had the power to write history have therefore had considerable power over what is to be remembered and what is forgotten (see also Chapter Two). But at the same time she knows that these *hidden histories* do not disappear but have a way of returning. As Morrison says, "Until one comes to terms with it, the past will be a haunting – something you can't shake" (*The Guardian Review of Books*, 15 November 2003, p 23). This is something we can learn from Morrison, because so often in postmodern culture we learn to disavow the impacts of family histories and migrations as we are encouraged within liberalism to put history behind us, as if we live in the present alone.

Rememory

Toni Morrison uses the notion of 'rememory' in *Beloved* to describe the process of remembering what has been forgotten. As Homi Bhabha recognises this term has often been described as "recovering the history of the oppressed" (p 23) in a way that often simplifies the complex interplay of history and psychology in her novels. As he points out, rather than a novel "justifying the killing of Beloved as an act of emancipation or revenge by an unbalanced race heroine, it is a profound inquiry into the ethical consequences of her act, no matter how deeply pushed she was to it. She can't exonerate herself through history" (p 23).

In *Playing in the dark* (1992) Morrison argued that American literature has been shaped by an unspoken "dark, abiding, signing Africanist presence". She draws attention to the often unconscious habit, embodied in the very *forms* of language, of using black characters in literature as "metaphorical shortcuts" for what is dreaded and desired. In her view the "political correctness" debate is "about the power to define: the definers want the power to name, and the defined are now taking that power away from them" (*Guardian Review of Books*, 15 November 2003, p 23). The power to *name experience* and identities so questioning many of the ways institutions have sought to name us is again something that Morrison can teach us through example. She recalls histories of suffering that culture chooses to forget.

Morrison, who has seen some of the fissures in American society reopen along class and race lines since the advent of civil rights, mourns the collapse of many historically black institutions. "I happen not to think it's either/or: you could have black schools and integration at the same time. It should be about increased freedom, not identifying the one road." As for the continuing debate on ending affirmative action:

> We're in some insane dialogue about what's unfair, coming from the people who invented unfairness. Race was never biologically important, but some people would like to erase it a little prematurely. I don't trust the motive. (*Guardian Review of Books*, 15 November 2003, p 23)

As she tells Maya Jaggi, often she has no answers herself, "just maps and questions – an awareness of the journey and the loss".

While Morrison says that she did not grow up feeling American since, as she says, "I had limited citizenship and rights", that has changed:

"I wouldn't feel such a deep anxiety about US adventures now if I didn't feel so much an American." She found the rush to war with Iraq "reckless, sinister and unnecessary: when you don't have diplomacy, all you have left is the bullet. But waging war is unmodern; the language is puny" (p 23). Throughout her writings she is clear that "All my books were questions for me. I wanted to know what would happen if...? What do friendship and love mean under these circumstances? How far would you go? I don't want to write about normalcy, but when there's a cataclysm and conflict in belief, a complexity of emotion and behaviour" (p 20). She remains solid in her long held belief that "You have to talk, and exercise those feelings of almost witless affection for another human being. If we lose that feeling for the other, or the ability to talk to one another, there's really not much left. Personally, politically, culturally, it's death" (p 23). In this way Morrison shows not only the importance of a readiness to listen to 'others' that a dominant culture might exclude or reject, but also the importance of being *listened to* ourselves if we are to recognise our own histories and experiences as we embody identities.

Inheritances

In 1993, Morrison's main house on the Hudson River in Rockland county, upstate New York, was burnt down on Christmas day. Morrison lost hand-written manuscripts, early editions of Faulkner and Frederick Douglas, and family momentos. Similarly, Maxine Hong Kingston, another US author, had to have her house rebuilt after the Oakland hills firestorms of 1991, a month after Kingston's father died and shortly after the first Gulf War. In *The fifth book of peace* (2003) she recalls her sense, when the fire started, that her father's spirit had been unappeased by the funeral rituals performed for him. Later, running through a "black-and-white Guernica of trees", she experienced a revelation about the destruction of Iraq: "For refusing to be conscious of the suffering we caused ... we are given this sight of our city as ashes." She quotes an Oakland fire captain and Vietnam War veteran shocked by seeing his own neighbourhood in ruins. What an opportunity, he said, to show people "when we, as a country, decide to go to war against somebody, this is what we are going to get" (*The Guardian Review of Books*, 13 December 2003, p 20).

The fire consumed an almost finished novel-in-progress entitled *The fourth book of peace*, after the three Chinese lost books of peace, held by legend to be the mislaid key to ending war. Kingston had dreamed of those books since childhood, growing up in California with a Chinese heritage, and called on war veterans to help her write "a book of peace for our time". "I was traumatised and very hurt by the fire," she tells Maya Jaggi in her interview:

> In the shock of the loss, I changed. It made me understand why, when the planes went into the World Trade Center our country also changed. There was great fear and panic, and a blind lashing out – a loss of rational ability. (*The Guardian Review of Books*, 13 December 2003, p 20)

She found herself unable to read or write: "I tried, but I wrote directly how I felt; there was no shape, just expressions of pain and loss. It was the way I wrote as a child: to huddle in a corner secretly, away from people, and make sounds, whimper, while writing" (*The Guardian Review of Books*, 13 December 2003, p 20).

Voicelessness

Maxine Hong was born in 1940 in Stockton, California, the first of three daughters and three sons born to Chinese migrants. Her father, Tom Hong, had been a poet and village teacher, and her mother, Ying Lan, was a midwife trained in Western and Chinese medicine in Canton. After a number of attempts her father was able to elude the "immigration demons" and made it to New York where he worked in a laundry. After a 15-year separation, he won a visa for his wife in a gambling game and she caught the last boat out of Canton in 1939. Following the Maoist revolution of 1949, Kingston's uncles were killed and her aunts fled abroad. "My father left his valuable things in China", she says. "I've wondered whether he meant to return" (*The Guardian Review of Books*, 13 December 2003, p 22).

Her parents ran a gambling house in Stockton and later a laundry, where Maxine helped out. Her first language was Say Yup, a Cantonese dialect, shared by many in Stockton's Chinatown. "It was a very cohesive community, with a church, school and self-help association," she says, "but it wasn't a ghetto or physically in one place." Speaking no English until the age of five, although her parents "could understand more than they let on," she recalls her early years as silent and inhibited. "I knew I was different; my not talking had to do with wanting to communicate perfectly and not being able to at all." She still feels *afflicted* by a sudden shyness and loss of speech: "Suddenly nothing comes out or I don't have the right words" (*The Guardian Review of Books*, 13 December 2003, p 22).

This is an experience that children who have grown up in migrant communities where a different language is spoken at home can often relate to. They can experience the difficulty of having to learn a new language in the public space of school away from the familiarity and intimacy of home. This can make them acutely self-conscious in relation to the new language and they might feel much more comfortable with the written word, than they feel speaking before their peers. Sometimes they feel uneasy with the sound of their own voice; for example, Kingston once mocked herself as having a "pressed duck" voice.

They can feel uneasy at expressing themselves and might resist volunteering to answer questions in class even when they know the answer. They can often feel *reduced to silence* and others can interpret this as a sign of lack of understanding, although this is quite often a mistake, as the second generation migrant child is often acutely self-conscious and aware of what is going on around them, if only as a means of self-defence. Those who are made to learn the 'foreign' language of their parents from an early age often do so unwillingly, not fully understanding the implications of what they are doing:

> Mother always felt exceedingly guilty about our language deficiency and tried to make us study Chinese … [but] I suppose that when I was young there was no motivation to study Chinese. (Ho 1975, cited in Ang, 2000, p 33)

As Furman (2005) notes, not speaking the language of their parents is a common phenomenon among immigrant youth, challenged as they are by the demands of their new culture (see also Ang, 2001).

Maxine Hong Kingston attended Chinese school everyday after 'American school', where she was in a tiny minority and bullied by young Americans of Japanese ancestry, who had been released from internment after the Second World War: "They looked like me but spoke English well, and ganged up because they were together in the camps" (*The Guardian Review of Books*, 13 December 2003, p 22).

While her father knew Confucius by heart, Kingston's mother inherited the ancient art of 'talk-story' from her own father, a professional storyteller in the village square. She told bedtime stories of liberated women, because she was "liberated and successful" herself, but also of going to a market to buy female slaves. Kingston comments that "there was a sense that something was wrong with the status of girls in both Chinese and American culture in the 40s"; she was brought up on such sayings as "girls are maggots in the rice" (*The Guardian Review of Books*, 13 December 2003, p 22). Recently I was told by a young Korean student of a popular Korean saying that 'Men are the heavens and women are the earth' to indicate their relative position within a spatial hierarchy. Different cultures imagine gender differences through a diversity of different metaphors that reveal hierarchy and subordination.

As a graduate student at Berkeley Maxine Kingston was active in the Free Speech movement of 1964, when moves to limit students' political activities sparked mass protests, and in the anti-war movement when the US began bombing North Vietnam in 1965. Two of her brothers and a sister's husband were drafted: "We had such hysterical worry, the only thing I knew was right was to join peace demonstrations." As a US general threatened to bomb China 'into the Stone Age' for arming the Vietcong, "Asian-Americans faced dilemmas similar to that posed by the jailed conscientious Mohammed Ali: 'No Vietcong ever called me a 'nigger'" (Jaggi in *The Guardian Review of Books*, 13 December 2003, p 22). In a chapter of the book *China men* (Kingston, 1981), one of the brothers, unable to take refuge in bravado about 'gooks', has nightmares about slicing up his own family. Often it is through dreams, fantasy and imagination that the unconscious *works through* unresolved emotional fears that we are as yet unable to name for ourselves.

Kingston came to Buddhism partly through the Beat poets, who, she says, went to Asia and brought Buddhism to the West. "Young writers were always gathering", she recalls of San Francisco at the time, "but there were no women; you couldn't participate as a woman". She recalls:

> I gradually became a Buddhist – maybe I was born that way. When I was a child the Chinese went to Methodist church, but my mother told us we weren't to be baptised; we're Confucian. She had mysterious ceremonies which, years later, I learned were an integration of Confucian, Daoism and Buddhism. (*The Guardian Review of Books*, 13 December 2003, p 22)

In *The woman warrior* (1976), Kingston wrestles with being a Chinese-American, half-ghost among ghosts, as white people were known in her community, while struggling to sift truth from invention in her mother's talk-stories. As Jaggi explains:

> Influenced by Hawthorn's portrayal in *The scarlet letter* of "women who stood out in a puritanical society", the book broke silences and secrets about the No Name Women – an aunt hounded to death for an illegitimate child – or women who have been made mad through cultural dislocation. Adopting the legend of Fa Mu Lan as a female avenger, she emerges from muteness into a voice. (*The Guardian Review of Books*, 13 December 2003, p 22)

Eva Hoffman, author of *Lost in translation* (Hoffman, 1991), recognised that *The woman warrior* (Kingston, 1976) broke new ground in that "US immigrant literature had been about an external journey towards success, or the vicissitudes of getting on in America; the psychological, emotional aspects hadn't been explored. In voicelessness – losing one's voice as one comes into a new language – Maxine was discovering a subject, giving it legitimacy" (p 22). Kingston recognised that:

> It may be a new kind of autobiography, where I tell dreams and fantasies of real people. Inventing a new language that could use the rhythms and tones of Chinese in English ... treating seriously myths of the old world I'd never seen. (p 22)

Kingston was not concerned with historical accuracy but with reimagining history for her own purposes. She insists that she is an improviser not an archivist:

> Those who accuse me of tampering with myth don't understand that a myth dies when it cannot help people in modern times. When the migrants left the old world and retold myths in a new place, they changed them. If stories don't change for new listeners in a new age, they die. (p 22)

In *China men* (1981), despite her father's reticence, she told four alternative tales of his passage to America: "Most of my parents' generation came illegally but they invented false stories for the immigration authorities." After the 1906 San Francisco earthquake and fire that destroyed public records, "an authentic citizen, then, had no more papers than an alien. Every China man was reborn out of that fire a citizen" (p 22). It was this moment of fire as transformation that through its destruction brought a sense of security to the community. Different ethnic groups will narrate their migrations in their own ways and they might find spaces in which to share their migrations, but there will often be silences if there are pressures to assimilate or if particular communities feel marginalised within available multicultural imaginations.

Further reading

Literature and social theory
For some helpful reflections on the relationship between literature and social theory see, for instance, George Steiner's *After Babel* (1975) and *Language and silence* (1967).

African–American history and culture
For some interesting historical and cultural reflections on African-American experience in the US see, for instance, Nell Irvin Painter (2006) *Creating black Americans*; Robin Kelly and Earl Lewis (2000) *To make our world anew*; James O. Horton and Louis E. Horton (2001) *Hard road to freedom*; Robin Kelly (2002) *Freedom dreams*; Tricia Rose (1994) *Black noise*; David Levering Lewis (2001) *W.E.B Du Bois*; Susan Willis (1987) *Specifying*; Robyn Wiegman (1995) *American anatomies*; June Jordan (1991) *Technical difficulties*; Alice Walker (1997) *Anything we love can be saved*.

African–American women
For some historical and cultural explorations of the changing situation for African-American women both in the south and in the cities of the north see, for instance, bell hooks' *Talking back* (1989), *All about love* (2000) and *Salvation* (2001).

Homi Bhabha
For some sense of Homi Bhabha's work and a sense of some of its leading themes to do with culture, history and displacement see, for instance, *Nation and narration* (Bhabha, 1993) and *The location of culture* (Bhabha, 1994).

Language and identity

Ien Ang offers an insightful discussion on the relationships between language, identity and belonging in *On not speaking Chinese* (2001). Furman develops arguments in relation to language and culture in (2005). See also bell hooks' (1992) *Black looks*;Vron Ware's (1992) *Beyond the pale*; and Ruth Frankenberg's (1993) *White women, race matters.*

EIGHT

Transformations: masculinities / choices / futures

This chapter looks at intergenerational transmissions, and explores issues around family, histories, tradition, culture and sexualities. It also explores the choices that individuals can make for themselves in circumstances when they feel torn between different pressures.

Language

John Berger's father served in the trenches during the First World War but it was not an experience that he discussed with his family (see Berger, 1991). As Berger says, "He didn't talk much about it. He couldn't. But I could feel it in him" The fact that his father did *not* talk about it did not mean that these traumatic wartime memories were not somehow 'present' in the family and shaped his identity with them. The fact that Berger's father never felt easy about sharing his wartime experiences might say something about the stoic masculinity with which he had been brought up to identify. He might have felt that it was somehow his duty as a father to *protect* his family *from* these memories. He may have thought that maintaining silence with his family was a way in which he could protect them and so feel that he was fulfilling the obligations of fatherhood. He may also have wanted to save himself from these memories, learning that silence could also be a form of self-protection (see also Chapter Seven). At some level he probably also realised that this strategy did not work, especially when he woke up in the middle of the night with terrible nightmares of wartime conflict.

John Berger's father was of a generation who learnt that, as men, one must *control* one's emotions and feelings and that it would be a sign of weakness (and so a threat to male identities) to share his feelings with his son. Rather than feeling that he owed it to his son to share his experiences, so allowing for continuity between the generations, he had learnt that he should never show 'weakness' in front of his son, to set a good example. He had to model a stoical masculinity through controlling his emotional life and had learnt to identify masculinity with this *self-control*. He would not have spoken about the war even if his son had asked him too. He may have wanted his son to feel proud of him but, within the terms of his generation, this meant sustaining his silence and keeping his emotions to himself.

The fact that he did not share his emotions in language did not mean that they did not exist, however. It is not, as a structuralist tradition might encourage us to think, through language alone that we can articulate experience. Within a **Saussurean linguistics** we learn that meaning is established through a system of signs, as if language alone is the bearer of meaning. This encourages the notion that meaning is *discursive*, that it can only be expressed through language, and the idea that there are no meanings that exist 'prior to' language (see also Hall, 1997; and Chapter Two). This tradition also shapes Lacan's vision of the unconscious as a language and the ways in which he thinks of emotions within the terms of mental life. In this, Lacan was following Freud who had, in turn, taken emotions and desires that had been located within the *body* by Kant, as forms of 'unfreedom' and determination, where freedom was identified with reason and *mind*. Freud repositioned emotions and feelings as *aspects of mind* through his vision of unconscious mental life which also allowed for an expression of emotions.

When John Berger says of his father's war experience, "He didn't talk much about it.... But I could feel it in him" he is acknowledging *how* these experiences made themselves present in the tension and unease that existed between them. These wartime experiences made themselves *felt*, even though they were not *talked about*. Reflecting back on his childhood John Berger can recognise them as part of the atmosphere in which he was growing up; they worked to establish an unspoken distance in his relationship with his father that was difficult to undo. For it was not that this was a single topic that everyone learned to avoid, but that his father's wartime experience somehow shaped who he could be both with himself and also with other people. He could not simply decide to hold back these painful experiences but share everything else; rather they helped shape the stoic masculinity that formed who he was and how he related to others.

Stephen Dobson says that this is "Not necessarily an indication that he lacked the words, perhaps more the case that he had of his own volition become incarcerated in himself" (2002, p 10). As Berger writes in another connection – in his short piece about prison life, 'A man of discernment' (1992) – "the aim of incarceration is to reduce all exchanges with the world to a minimum" (p 19). But we should be careful about this analogy because is also works to *undermine* the voluntarism that is otherwise suggested. It might be that Berger's father had not "of his own volition" become incarcerated in himself even though the effect could be to "reduce all exchanges with the world to a minimum". We might think that growing up to identify himself with the stoical masculinity expected of his generation and class made it difficult for him to choose otherwise, without being left feeling that he has somehow failed to be 'man enough'.

There might well have been moments when he wanted to reach out and express himself more with his family but felt that he *could not*. He did not know how to express himself differently even when he felt that he was somehow locked into his own history. He could not find a way of expressing more, even when he would have wanted to. It could have been difficult for him to reach out, although we could imagine a moment, for example when he was ill in hospital, when he might have reached out to take the hand of his son. Through this gesture he could have sought to renew a contact that he could not make in words. Like many working-class and middle-class men of his generation he felt that he could only sustain his authority as a father if he sustained a distance with his children. If he got close to them emotionally this would have somehow undermined his position as an authority figure, which would have been failing in his responsibilities as a father.

As noted above, men can experience themselves as somehow 'locked within' their inner lives. They can get too used to the silence and the sense of loneliness that they barely recognise it for what it is. Sometimes something happens within a family to break this pattern. For example, a working-class man who might have been more open and responsive while 'courting' his wife might withdraw once married, taking his partner for granted (even though he would deny this). In this, he is living out cultural expectations of **working-class masculinities** which suggest that, once married, a man can return his attention to proving himself within the sphere of work. But if his wife feels a deep sense of *disappointment* in the early days of married life having been led to expect a very different relationship, she could retaliate by giving him a 'bit of his own medicine', reflecting back his silence to him. This might well come as a shock to him and be enough to force him to recognise the ways he has interacted with her. He might have learnt his lesson and be determined not to lock himself away in his own silence, even though that tendency is still there, so entrenched is that behaviour in cultural expectation.

When people have grown up in families in which there is very little conversation they can learn to take silence for granted. They might have been taught that 'silence is golden' and that you should only express yourself when you have something to say. This has been a significant means of social control that has reinforced particular patterns of class dominance. Social relations of power work to reduce people to silence and so many people, even within democratic societies, are left feeling that they are *not* entitled to speak. Even though they might learn that everyone is entitled to have their own say, social relations work to undermine identities and reinforce silences.

Ethics and family histories

In a small piece about his mother, reprinted in a collection entitled *Keeping a rendezvous* (1991), Berger tells that throughout his childhood his mother was reluctant to explain things. As he says, she had "a secret loyalty to the enigmatic". When he asked her why she had been a vegetarian when young she replied simply "'Because I'm against killing.' She would say no more. Either I understood or I didn't. There was nothing more to be said." However, Dobson argues that it took Berger many years before he understood this. Berger himself says that, for he chose "to visit abattoirs in different cities of the world and to become something of an expert concerning the subject. The unspoken, the unfaceable beckoned me. I followed" (Berger, 1991).

Sometimes we find ourselves exploring emotional spaces that our parents would never have discussed. Berger's interest in abattoirs could have been some way of continuing a conversation with himself that he could not have with his mother. For her the matter was clear and you either agreed with her or you did not. But for her son there were questions that still needed to be raised and experiences that he needed to have before he could make an ethical decision for himself. He needed to put himself in a certain position *to open* himself to certain experiences that would have been forbidden; he needed to move towards the forbidden before being able to understand what could have led his mother to her decision. His mother would not give reasons herself and so he was left hanging without an explanation.

The unspoken, the unfaceable, often beckons us. I know from my own experience how many years it has taken for me to face my own family's traumatic histories of war and the impact this had on my own sense of identity and ways in which I could relate. My mother did not want to speak about her painful experiences in Vienna, especially around the death of her younger sister. Towards the end of her life when she was suffering from dementia her unresolved emotions returned, as if she had to experience the impact of a loss that had been locked away for so many years because she could not deal with it without feeling that her own life might somehow dis/integrate. It was as if she could not *move on* in her own process towards death until she had somehow come to terms with the death of her sister more honestly; as if she could now allow herself to feel some of the pain she could not feel all those years before because as the eldest she felt responsible for the safety of the family.

At some level she was always conscious of the fact that she had left her sister behind in the Jewish cemetery in Vienna when she had left to find refuge in London. It was as if my mother could never really *leave* Vienna knowing that her sister was left there. She wanted to put her painful experiences in Vienna behind her so that she could live in the present, but at the same time she did not want to abandon her sister. She owed it to her sister to remember her, but felt obliged to keep these memories to herself. Although she was willing to remember the better days before Hitler's troops marched into the city, she felt she could not *share* these memories with the family, or only very occasionally.[1] She did not want to bring the traumatic pain into the present and, like John Berger's father, felt an obligation to protect her children from these painful histories so that we had more chance of growing up to be 'normal'. She wanted us to feel that we could *belong* even if she could not herself. As children we felt that we owed this effort to her. She wanted us to 'speak properly' and took pride that we spoke without an accent; we could not be marked out through our language in a way that she always was. As soon as she spoke she knew that she was 'foreign' even though she had lived in England for over half a century.

My mother did not want her hurts to be carried by her children. She was ready to carry these hurts herself, especially if she felt she could protect her children from them. She felt that her children would only be *safe* if we could 'become English' which, for us, meant being 'like everyone else'. But at some level we continued to experience ourselves as different, as 'outsiders', even if we could not name this experience. If we had known more about where our parents had come from and if there had been more conversation between the generations, paradoxically, it might have made it easier to belong (see Seidler, 2000). This is an experience echoed in many different migrations where the younger generation, sometimes born in Britain, feel that they need to separate from their parents and the histories that they carry. They often learn to think that these histories have nothing to do with them, but silently carry the unspoken legacies and unresolved feelings that their parents have not worked through for themselves.

Journeys across racisms

In the film 'Bend it like Beckham' an Asian father talks about how he had been shamed when he attempted to join a cricket club when he moved to Britain. Rather than contest the racism, he felt that he needed to behave as if he was *not* hurt by it. He knew that the power was against him in those days and that things would just be worse for him if he took a stand against it. This motivates the fears that he has for his daughter, Jesminder, who wants to play football with a local girls' team: he does not want her to suffer the rejection and humiliation that he suffered. He is proud of her football skills, though, and as the film moves on he realises in some part of himself that if his daughter denies expression of this talent she will end up feeling bad about herself. His life has been haunted by this early rejection and he knows that he has suffered because he never again risked playing cricket. He withdrew into the family and into a traditional conception of himself as father.

When Jesminder is offered an opportunity to move to the US on a football scholarship he speaks up in her favour. He does not want to let her down, nor does he want her to make the same mistake that he made in his life. Even though it is not conventional for a girl to play football, he recognises her talent and feels a need to *support her* in the family even if it brings him into conflict. In the end he wants to feel that he is there for her. Although Jesminder does not expect her father to come through for her, he does, as he also redefines his responsibilities as a father.

There is a touching moment when Jesminder feels embarrassed to show the scars on her knee that were the result of an accident in the kitchen when she was left to prepare food for herself. She was discussing her fear of rejection with her young Irish coach who shared how hard it had been for him to endure the constant rejection by his father who felt that he was a 'loser' because he had to withdraw from the professional game due to injuries. He never felt loved or accepted by his family and as the film goes on Jesminder *learns to appreciate* the warmth and love that she receives from her family even if there are many restrictions on her as a woman. In the end her coach helps her to recognise that she will have to make decisions for herself, even if it means that she may earn the disapproval of her family. Her football is important for her and it is the way in which she is able to express herself, so she realises that if she denies herself the opportunity she will regret it for the rest of her life. This is a regret that her father has lived with and in the end he recognises too that this is not what he wants her to suffer.

In this film, it is not just that the father does not want his daughter to live with the kinds of *regrets* that he has had to live with – his first impulse is to protect her, because he does not want her to suffer the pain of rejection that comes with racism. He also recognises that his acceptance of his daughter's *choices* involves questioning traditional Hindu ethics which assume that daughters should fulfil obligations within the family and cannot expect to make decisions for themselves without bringing shame on the extended family; he was prepared to speak up and take a stand for his daughter even though he recognised this went against traditional culture. The film illustrates dilemmas felt by *second generation* young people who have been educated in British schools and so found their own compromises between the freedom offered by liberal 'Western' education and the family cultures and histories with which they can also identify. Sometimes this helps to produce *hybrid identities*, but often these *pressures* are gendered and individuals learn to share their own responses – supported by close friends – to what they can feel obliged to deny and conceal as they move across different spaces of identity.

Transformation/s

In the film 'Bend it like Beckham', there is a scene in which a friend of Jesminder who has not come out as gay to his family offers to marry her so that she can take up her scholarship. (Jesminder refuses this offer because she knows that, sweet as this gesture is, it is based on a dishonesty that she does not want to live with.) But, a young Asian gay man might feel that there is little space within traditional Asian culture for him to be honest about his sexuality and he is likely to live such a double life, with many of his friends not knowing about his sexual orientation (see also Chapter Two). He might feel that there are spaces that he can visit which allow him to feel more at ease with his sexuality but he knows that it is unlikely he will ever be able to talk openly with his family. Even if they suspect his gayness they will not want to talk about it, as if language offers it *a reality* that can be denied as long as it is not discussed openly. People might *know* but they will not *talk* about it.

For many people brought up within traditional religious cultures, however, there is a refusal to accept sexual diversities or to see this as a matter of discrimination against a sexual minority. Those who subscribe to this view insist that homosexualities are a perversion from a heterosexual norm and that it is sinful to involve yourself in homosexual behaviours even if you have such feelings. For example, within a dominant Christian discourse there is an emphasis on sexual renunciation, which states that people must exercise *control* over their sexual impulses. Even if they are allowed to accept their sexual orientation they should be discouraged from acting on their impulses. This is in line with Church teachings that refuse to question the idealisation of celibacy and the potential **demonisation** of sexuality as 'animal' and therefore no part of our existence as spiritual beings.

Diverse religious traditions make it difficult to think about notions of *self-acceptance* especially when it comes to issues of sexuality. Wittgenstein struggled with these feeling of guilt and self-torment for most of his life. As he wrote in his diary: "Am completely ensnared in pettiness. Am irritable, think of myself, that my life is wretched, and at the same time I have no idea of how wretched it is" (Monk, 1990, p 374). Often, traditions encourage people to think that they can change or transform themselves. As Wittgenstein reflected on Christianity in his diary on 4 September 1936:

> Christianity is not a doctrine, not, I mean, a theory about what has happened and will happen to the human soul, but a description of something that actually takes place in human life. For 'consciousness of sin' is a real event and so are the despair and salvation through faith. Those who speak of such things (Bunyan for instance) are simply describing what has happened to them, whatever gloss anyone may want to put on it. (quoted in Monk, 1990, p 376)

This can be difficult to relate to in today's secular consumer culture but, as Foucault also recognised, if we are to read and so make legible feelings of *insecurity* and *self-rejection* we need to understand how these theologies still shape the ways that people *feel about their bodies* and sexualities even when they rationalise that they should be feeling quite differently.

Ideas that gay and lesbian feelings were perverse and could be cured were pervasive within psychoanalytic theory, which presented a possible 'solution' through the medicalisation of sexual diversities. If homosexuality was an illness it meant that people could be 'cured'. It also meant that 'sufferers' could not be held responsible for their own feelings nor expected to accept them within a culture that denigrated homosexualities (see also Chapter Six). At some level this discourse is still pervasive, but now is more often framed around 'common-sense' notions of **social construction**, which suggest that identities are not 'given' in nature but are rather 'constructed' within the terms of culture, so that sexualities can be presented voluntaristically as a matter of individual freedom and choice. Sexual identities are therefore not *given* at birth, but *learned* in society, but sometimes this can make it harder for young people to accept their feelings and desires so be able to shape positive transgender or gay identities for themselves, while acknowledging the freedom that people have to shape their gendered and sexed identities as they also respond to shifts in their desires as they journey through different stages in their lives and want different things for themselves.

There are problems with thinking about identities in terms of 'social construction', or believing that identities are articulated through available discourses, even if there is a need to move away from thinking about identities in essentialist terms (as somehow given in nature). Not only does this constructionist approach tend to conceal the *tensions* that exist between language and experience, assuming that experience is always articulated through language, but it makes it difficult to value what people can *learn* from their own experience and the difficulties they may confront in *naming* their own experience. These are problems of which Wittgenstein was aware, as he framed ways of thinking about the relationships between identities, language and culture, possibly because of his ambivalent feelings at different times towards his own gay sexuality and Jewishness. He recognised a need to come to terms with diverse aspects of his own identity and knew that, if this was a matter of individual choice, it was also a necessity if he was to become more honest with himself and so be able to think and write more clearly (Monk, 1990).[2]

Cultural imaginations

While Wittgenstein was living in Rosro, Ireland, for a short while in late 1940, he appreciated that understanding music or understanding humour provides an analogy for philosophical understanding. What was needed was not the discovery of facts, nor the construction of theories. As he wrote about music: "Someone who understands music will listen differently (eg with a different expression on his face), he will talk differently, from one who does not" (quoted in Monk, 1990, p 530). Through exploring what it was to be unable to appreciate music he was thinking about what it means to be 'aspect-blind'. "What would a person who is blind towards these aspects be lacking?",Wittgenstein asks, and replies:"It is not absurd to answer: the power of imagination" (p 531). But the imagination of individuals, although necessary, is not sufficient, for what is further required is a *culture*.Wittgenstein asks:

> For how can it be explained what 'expressive playing' is? Certainly not by anything that accompanies the playing. – What is needed for the explanation? One might say: a culture. – If someone is brought up in a particular culture – and then reacts to music in such-and-such a way, you can teach him the use of the phrase 'expressive playing'. (quoted in Monk, 1990, p 532)

In the same series of remarks, exploring what it is to understand a joke,Wittgenstein asks:

> What is it like for people not to have the same sense of humour? They do not react properly to each other. It's as though there were a custom among certain people for one person to throw a ball which he is supposed to catch and throw back; but some people, instead of throwing it back, put it in their pocket. (quoted in Monk, 1990, p 533)

But more seriously:

> Humour is not a mood but a way of looking at the world. So if it is correct to say that humour was stamped out in Nazi Germany, this does not mean that people were not in good spirits, or anything of that sort, but something much deeper and more important. (quoted in Monk, 1990, p 530)

If it is true that the Nazis had stamped out humour, as Monk comments, it would have meant that:

> the Nazis had been successful in destroying a whole way of life, a way of looking at the world and a set of reactions and customs that go with it. (It would have meant that the Nazis had, so to speak, pocketed the ball.) (Monk, 1990, p 533)

Choices

People are not able to choose the predicaments they will face in their lives even if they can choose to deny or escape from confronting aspects of their own histories and experiences. People do not *choose* their sexualities, and at the same time they do not want to be controlled or fixed through sexual classifications. This is something Foucault felt strongly and is central in his discussion with Richard Sennett in their piece 'Sexuality and solitude' (Foucault with Sennet, 1981; see discussion in Chapter Four). Foucault became dissatisfied with his own thinking in *The history of sexuality, vol 1* (1976) and was looking for different ways of exploring a relationship between ethics and subjectivities, recognising that he needed to come to terms with diverse religious traditions within the West that still shaped identities within secular cultures. He felt a need to break with his own thinking about the relationship between knowledge and power, which could paradoxically work to 'fix' identities through thinking they are constituted through available discourses. If identities are constructed in this way, it leaves little space for people to *explore* their own identities, even if not in conditions of their own choosing.

Questioning **social constructionism** also helps to reveal complexities in thinking identities that Foucault's own dualistic ways of thinking helped to conceal. The relationship between nature and culture needed to be reassessed, where, as Freud recognised even if Foucault denied it, people recognise themselves as *both* part of nature and culture. This can help question the voluntarism that encourages people to believe that if identities are not *given* in nature, then they can be *created* within the sphere of culture. In his earlier work Foucault was against 'unification' in a way that can establish an unhelpful dualism. Learning from Nietzsche a method of genealogy that is not a search for the origin of a concept, in 'Nietzsche, genealogy, history' Foucault states:

> Where the soul pretends unification or the self fabricates a coherent identity, the genealogist sets out to study the beginning – numberless beginnings whose faint traces and hints of colour are readily seen by an historical eye. The analysis of descent permits the dissociation of the self, its recognition and displacement as an empty synthesis, in liberating a profusion of lost events. (Foucault, 1978, p 145)

This 'dissociation of the self' is not to be welcomed, even if we roughly accept the asocial vision that he wants to avoid. Rather, it is a condition that people know too well within a postmodern culture and it is a condition which Ronald Laing helps us to name. He knew the 'unreality' that so many people can feel within a culture in which people are encouraged to *displace* their emotions and feelings. This makes it difficult for people to face the conditions of their own everyday lives. This creates it's own 'displacement as an empty synthesis' (p 145). For Wittgenstein the only way through was in part a way back that recognised "a profusion of lost events" (quoted in Monk, 1990, p 533), which could not simply be acknowledged intellectually, but which people had to come to terms with emotionally if they were to establish a deeper connection and to live with more truthfulness in their own lives.

Foucault is often categorical in his thinking and frames oppositions that cannot be sustained in practice and which he later questions in his own thinking. Following on from the quote above, he goes on to state that:

> The purpose of history, guided by genealogy, is not to discover the roots of our identity but to commit itself to its dissipation. It does not seek to define our unique threshold of emergence, the homeland to which metaphysicians promise a return; it seeks to make visible all those discontinuities that cross us. (Foucault, 1978, p 162)

If it is appealing "to make visible all those discontinuities that cross us" we can still feel a need at different moments of our lives to come to terms with particular aspects and histories that, up to that time, seemed of little consequence to us.

When Foucault says that we are not concerned "to discover the roots of our identity" he is questioning a particular vision of that quest, as if the truth of our experience somehow lies waiting to be discovered in our childhood experience. This is often the direction that orthodox Freudian psychoanalysis takes, refusing to dwell on the predicaments we face, say in the break-up of a present relationship, but encouraging us back into the framework of past familial relationships where the causal explanations need to be sought. It can be a weakness in traditional psychoanalysis when compared with psychotherapies that they value the past in preference to the present. They can also *minimise* the hurts of class, 'race' and gender relations assuming that these are projections of childhood familial relationships to which one must constantly return.

Freud questions a linear vision of time, knowing how the past exists in the present, but the practice he develops often denies this insight (see Seidler, 1993, 2000).

Walter Benjamin was reaching for a similar insight when he questioned a historicist attitude that is satisfied with the causality of different historical moments. For Benjamin, a materialist historian, one should "stop telling the sequence of events like the beads of a rosary" (Benjamin, 1968, p 265). Instead he grasps the *constellation* that his own era has formed with a definite early one. Thus he establishes a conception of the present as 'the time of the now', which is shot through with chips of messianic time. This offers its own vision of genealogy where the focus is on 'the time of the now' that promises its own histories of the present. It is this focus on the *now* that alternative psychotherapies have also explored, recognising the difficulties of staying with present emotions rather than escaping into the past *or* the future.

Psychotherapies are also concerned with opening up possibilities in the present that can be potentially transformative. Sometimes this involves learning how to be more *self-accepting* in the present and can involve *naming* diverse negative messages that have been inherited from the past. For example, traditionally girls have not been allowed to 'Bend it like Beckham', nor have young gay men and women been encouraged to celebrate their own sexualities within a homophobic culture. Equally people do not want to be contained and fixed by their gay identities, but want also to be open to new opportunities in the present. As a friend said recently, "I am a lesbian who is currently having a loving relationship with a man." Often we cannot predict what opportunities will open up in the future, but we can be assured that it will be easier to accept them for what they are if we have learnt to face the diverse histories that we have inherited from the past. In facing the past we can also learn to face possible futures.

Endnotes

[1] For some insights into the Vienna that my mother was forced to leave when Hitler's army marched in to be overwhelmingly welcomed by the population (although this was to be systematically denied in the post-war years when Austria presented itself as the 'first victim' of Nazism rather than as a willing collaborator) see Clare (2007).

[2] Wittgenstein insisted on the importance of making a confession to friends to whom he might have formerly given the impression that he had less Jewish

inheritance than he did. This is explored by Ray Monk in his biography (1990), who hints that the confessions might also have referred to Wittgenstein's sexual identity. Wittgenstein insisted on the importance of self-scrutiny: "If anyone is unwilling to descend into himself, because this is too painful, he will remain superficial in his writing" (quoted in Monk, 1990, p 366).

Further reading

Wartime experiences
For some helpful reflections on the First World War and the ways that it affected soldiers who fought and who came home see, for instance, Pat Barker's trilogy (1998) and the historical accounts of Chris Hedges (2003) and Glenn Gray (1998).

Fatherhood
I have written about fatherhood and the ways that it has been framed differently in different cultures and generations in *Transforming masculinities* (Seidler, 2007). For an account of contemporary fatherhood see, for instance, Burgess (1997) *Fatherhood reclaimed* and Beck and Beck-Gernsheim (1995) *The normal chaos of love*.

Semiotics
For some reflections on semiotics as a theory of language and the influence that it has had in social theory, particularly in media and communications, see Stuart Hall's *Representation* (1997).

Working-class masculinities
For some helpful reflections on class masculinities and ways in which they have shifted across generations see, for instance, Hall (1991) *Hidden anxieties*; Morgan (1992) *Discovering men*; and Mangan and Walvin (1987) *Manliness and morality*.

Homosexualities
Explorations of homosexualities in the West and their relationship to Christianity are given in John Boswell's (1980) *Christianity, social tolerance and homosexuality*; reflections on homosexualities in diverse cultures and histories are given in Louis Crompton's *Homosexuality and civilisation* (2003).

Walter Benjamin

For some helpful explorations of Walter Benjamin's work that help place his ideas in historical and cultural context as well as giving a sense of their development and shifts over time see, for instance, Caygill (1998) and Benjamin and Osborne (1994). For a sense of Benjamin's own writings, see *One-way street and other writings* (1979) and *Illuminations* (1968).

NINE

Conflicts: complexity / cultures / youth

This chapter looks at complex race, ethnicity, sexed and gender identities formed by young people and the ways that they negotiate these complex identities across different spaces.

Complex identities

When asked who we are, we learn to introduce ourselves in different ways depending on the context. Many young people who have grown up with complex identities, for example young people from immigrant families or of mixed parentage, can be wary of being asked 'Where are you from?' and recognise that it is a 'mini-issue' whenever you are asked. These young people will be familiar with issues of 'belonging, yet not belonging' (see Chapters Seven and Eight). Sometimes it is possible to tell by *the way* the question is asked that the question is really about ethnicity, for example, 'Oh, *you look different*, where are you from?' The way people respond to such questions will depend on who's asking and how they ask. Younger generations learn to handle these questions in different ways and can be more attuned to the unspoken intentions of their questioner.

A focus on a person's ethnicity as a way of categorising identity is problematic for 'hyphenated' individuals who carry *diverse inheritances*, for example children of immigrant parents who have been brought up and educated in the UK. It can also indicate the impossibility of complete integration into the dominant culture because, as long as ethnicity is regarded as the yardstick by which one is deemed to belong or not belong, migrant communities will always fall short of that 'ideal'.

In the cover notes to his album 'Beyond Skin', Nitin Sawhney[1] introduces himself in the following way:

I am an Indian. To be more accurate, I was raised in England, but my parents came from India – land, people, government or self – 'Indian' – what does that mean? At this time, the government of India is testing nuclear weapons – Am I less Indian if I don't defend their actions? … Less Indian for being born and raised in Britain? – For not speaking Hindi? Am I not English because of my cultural heritage? Or the colour of my skin? Who decides? – 'History' tells me my heritage came from the 'Sub' continent – a 'third world' country, a 'developing' nation, a 'colonised' land – So what is history? – For me, just another arrogant Eurocentric term. … I learned only about Russian, European and American history in my school syllabus – India, Pakistan, Africa – these places were full of people whose history did not matter – the enslaved, the inferior. (Sawhney, 1999)

These are challenging questions that show the complexities of postmodern identities. As Nitin Sawhney asks, who decided? Does the fact that he does not speak Hindi make him less Indian? Is he not English because of his cultural heritage, although he was raised and schooled in England? Does the colour of his skin mean that he cannot really consider himself as English? England is where he learnt 'history' that taught him that there were places full of people who did not seem to have a history that mattered: "the enslaved, the inferior". Again, who decides?

A young man interviewed for a project on mixed Iranian-British identities says about being asked where he comes from:

"there are tricky terms for this, I guess the terms that I went by are quite derogatory, it was … uh … uh … 'half-caste'. But, uh, 'mixed-race'. Yeah, I guess Iranian-English. I guess British-Iranian. By nationality I … actually, by culture, I guess I have to be British."

If he is to decide for himself, does it matter how others treat him and think about him? How are we to think about these difficult questions once we have realised that there are not simply answers waiting to be discovered? This means that we will not necessarily resolve these questions in similar ways, since others might make quite *different* decisions for themselves.

There is a recognition for Sawhney that his relationship with England is somehow *tied up* with what is going on in India and also with how he relates to these events. He does not deny these connections, although it is not easy for him to think about them. His album, 'Beyond Skin', is so called because it marks an attempt to struggle with these complex realities, as he explains:

> This is an album with a time span that runs backwards – it begins with the Indian Prime Minister –Vajpayee – proudly announcing the testing of three nuclear bombs on Indian soil. Vajpayee is the leader of the BJP [Bharatiya Janata Party] – the '**Hindu fundamentalist**' party. These tests first took place in 1998. In 1945, two years before the Independence of India, Oppenheimer, creator of the atomic bomb, witnessed the first test of his creation. Afterwards he quoted the *Bhagavada Gita* – the Hindu 'Bible' – in condemnation of his own creation. His quote ends the album. He quotes Vishnu saying, 'Now I am become death, the destroyer of worlds', as he breaks down in tears.
>
> The western creator of the bomb condemning it in the name of Hinduism, the Hindu Prime-Minister testing it in the name of what? Progress? Should India be thanking the West for donating weapons of mass destruction? If I ever have children will they discover their heritage through BBC news bulletins about radiation sickness? – or nuclear war with Pakistan? I wonder.
>
> My mother and father are featured in this album – they speak with optimism of the future, while British Nazis like Combat 18 or the BNP [British National Party] rush to claim responsibility for nail bombing Asians in Brick Lane.
>
> BJP in India. The BNP in England. The first would define me by my religious heritage, the latter by the colour of my skin.
>
> I believe in Hindu philosophy. I am not religious. I am a pacifist. I am a British Asian.
>
> My identity and my history are defined only be myself – beyond politics, beyond nationality, beyond religion and Beyond Skin. (Sawhney, 1999)

Nitin Sawhney shares the clarity of his beliefs and he questions the notions of history and progress that, in England, he has grown up to take very much for granted. He rejects the claims of others to define his own reality and insists that "My identity and my history are defined only by myself." In different ways this reflects a postmodern sensibility in its suspicion of politics, nationality and organised religious practices. Within modernity politics, nationality and religion would seek to define identities that individuals would learn to *accept* as their own. Identities would be established through reason or they would be inherited through traditions that could not be questioned (see Bauman, 1994, 1995a, 1995b).

From Sawhney's reflections on the atomic bomb, I recall my own ethical and political questioning in the Campaign for Nuclear Disarmament (CND) in the late 1950s. There was an *intensity* of reflection within the CND because we knew that we were talking about an ultimate destruction against which values had to be *tested*. This was a generational moment of truth as we were determined to speak out against nuclear arms. In this sense our *values* were formative in relation to our identities. This **social movement** also questioned the traditional sovereignty of the nation state and the claims that it could make for its citizens; the state could no longer promise security in an age of mass destruction. At the same time there was a questioning of the superiority of the West, with Oppenheimer quoting the *Bhagavada Gita* as he recognises the nuclear bomb as the bringer of death and destroyer of worlds.

India is already firmly within the consciousness of the West so that it cannot be cast as some primitive 'other'. When it matters, India is called on to express horrors at what progress in the West has delivered. Are nuclear weapons supposed to be a *gift* for which India should feel grateful? Nitin Sawhney wonders whether, if he had children, they would "discover their heritage through BBC news bulletins about radiation sickness?" This would become part of their heritage, because the India that is developing in the current globalised economy is no longer the India of the past. Rather the difficulties of the present will become part of the heritage that will be passed on to the next generation. We might have wished it to be otherwise, but we cannot determine the shape of the world within which the next generation will have to shape their identities.

The fact that Nitin Sawhney can state so clearly: "I believe in Hindu philosophy. I am not religious. I am a pacifist. I am a British Asian", shows that beliefs are crucial in shaping his identity. These are beliefs for which he has had to struggle and had to test for himself, rather than being a faith that has been handed down as a matter of tradition. In this example reason and faith are not in conflict in the way that a rationalist modernity has tended to assume. But he insists on the authority of his *own beliefs* and the right to define his own identity. He is ready to learn from tradition, but he is also able to critique when he feels that the tradition is perpetuating forms of injustice.

Double lives / complex inheritances

The pressures of tradition are gendered and many young Asian women growing up in the UK can feel that they are denied an independence and autonomy that has been allowed to their older brothers. Sometimes they feel that they have been let down by their brothers who have failed to speak up on their behalf, but have readily taken sides with the patriarchal position of their fathers. They can feel forced to live a *double life* because of their desire to socialise like other young people, but their fear of being seen out with young men and being reported back to their parents. They have the burden of carrying the honour of the family, because if, for example, it is discovered that they have been seen in the cinema with a young man, they can be blamed for bringing shame on the whole family. Often the family puts a particular pressure on girls to consider their obligations to sustaining the future honour of the family. They can be constantly reminded that their future is not a matter of individual happiness alone, or of the freedom and autonomy they learn about in the West (see Wilson, 1978).

Young Asian women can therefore feel *torn* between the demands of traditional culture and the freedoms that they see other girls of the same age enjoying. Often they are not allowed to participate in parties and they can feel that this threatens their friendships. These pressures express themselves differently in diverse communities, partly depending on how integrated the family is within the Asian community. In the Gujarat community in London, for instance, there are widespread aspirations for higher education among both young men and young women. There are also significant shifts in gender relations with young men who continue to have traditional expectations for their partners who will often be expected to live in an extended family with their in-laws. Even if the young men promise greater freedom and equality, they can feel under the influence of their own mothers who demand that their partners give due honour and respect. This can create *tensions*, especially when women feel that their partners are not really supporting them but expecting them to conform to traditional expectations they have rejected for themselves.

Sometimes this means that young Asian women choose relationships with white men because they believe that there will be more freedom and recognition. They can feel restricted in their relationships with Asian men who they think have yet to challenge traditional notions of masculinity. They sense the pressures that come from family expectations and doubt whether Asian men will be prepared to resist *disappointing* their own parents. Young Asian men who have been brought up within white communities can feel as if they have little in common with Asian women who have been brought up more traditionally. They can feel as if there is a distance and unease, especially when young women are encouraged to be subservient. This can make *communication* difficult across genders, especially when you are dealing with larger familial expectations. Since Asian men have also been 'feminised' within discourses of popular racism, they can feel a pressure to prove their masculinities. They also know they have to be able to defend themselves against racist attacks on the streets. This response can produce its own 'toughening up', which can make it difficult to *show* vulnerability and openness within relationships. Men can feel trapped within the male identities they have organised for themselves, unable to reach out (see also Chapter Six). Often this is a vulnerability that their fathers never had to learn, when gender relationships were traditionally segregated with women's roles confined to domesticity and childcare.

These tensions cannot be theorised simply as a conflict of values between Asian tradition and Western modernity. There are complex processes at work that have partly to do with creating new British Asian identities but are also related to pressures to assimilate into a dominant culture that was so irreverently portrayed in the TV comedy programme 'Goodness Gracious Me'. We have to be careful to explore relationships between cultures and identities so we can *recognise* the very different power that Asian women have been able to draw on. In many ways they remain the spiritual centres of the family with a strong influence over their children. Hindu tradition acknowledges the power of the feminine in a way that Western culture can find it difficult to acknowledge.

These traditional sources can help shape a different order of gender relations. It can be part of the continuing appeal of Hindu philosophy, as Nitin Sawhney acknowledges. But there are also tensions between a secular materialism that is expressed within a postmodern West and diverse Hindu and Moslem spiritual traditions. There are important castes, religious and ethnic divides that show themselves in diverse British Asian identities. These communities carry very different traditions and expectations that are also mediated by class relationships and levels of education. The tensions between different generations are modulated in different ways and there are complex patterns of loyalty that need to be carefully explored through their transformations (see Modood, 1992; Baubock, 1994; Back, 1996).

Black youth cultures

Even though some people in the Asian community identified themselves politically as 'black' in the 1980s, they have more recently sought different identifications that reflect the complex interrelations between African-Caribbean and Asian youth. In 2000, Tony Sewell, a Leeds University lecturer, claimed that his community was 'not interested' in intellectual activity and blamed black youth culture for the poor school record of African-Caribbean boys and girls. His inquiry into levels of exclusion from a south-east London school claims that too much concern with money and consumer goods was almost as damaging to black pupils' chances as racism: "What we have now is … not only the pressure of racism, but black peer grouping [which] has become another pressure almost as big as institutional racism was" (quoted in *The Observer*, 20 August 2000, p 1).

We must be careful about interpreting these claims, especially as they set up different pressures as if they were independent of each other. They also appear to gloss over significant gender differences. He acknowledges that black children have gained much needed self-*esteem* from black youth culture becoming part of the mainstream but says

> that culture is not one that, for example, is interested in being a great chess player, or intellectual activity. It is actually to do with propping up a big commercial culture to do with selling trainers, selling magazines, rap music and so on. (quoted in *The Observer*, 20 August 2000, p 1)

Again we have to be careful to discern the diverse strains within black youth culture while being critical of the homophobia and misogyny that has recently taken hold in black music cultures (Gilroy, 1993). We must acknowledge how music systems are working to question these tendencies, while also recognising the pressures of institutional racism that is still very much part of a present reality. It is not surprising that Sewell's comments, which were taken up on the front page of *The Observer*, ignited an acrimonious debate about the real causes of underachievement in British schools. Sewell has been accused of encouraging a 'blame the victim' culture in the face of official figures that showed African-Caribbean pupils were *four times* more likely to be excluded by head teachers than white pupils.

In his book *Black masculinities and schooling*, Tony Sewell claims that "there are both positive and negative aspects in relation to boy peer group culture particularly in schools where black boys' masculinities are represented as a negative force" (1996, p 2). But he also insists "black people are facing racist attacks and suffering discrimination" (p 140) and that young black boys "experience a disproportionate amount of punishment in our schools compared to all other ethnic groupings" (p 1). Lee Jasper, who acted as an adviser to former London mayor Ken Livingstone on race relations, said:

> Tony Sewell … is somebody who gets attention for saying the things that well-meaning white liberals would naturally agree with. [While Sewell argues in the same article that he is telling a truth that liberal white researchers dare not.] I don't believe that any community can suffer the levels of unemployment and missed education that we have had without suffering the kind of problems that are now apparent. It is a 'blame the victim' culture yet again – if it's not the Government saying it's lone mothers that are the problem, it's the aggressive nature of black kids. (quoted in *The Observer*, 20 August 2000, p 1)

Jasper would explain the underachievement of black children by saying that British schools are suffering a 'race crisis', particularly over exclusions: "There is a raft of evidence that white female teachers find black boys intimidating, difficult to deal with. They have an expectation about their behaviour which tends to dictate the quality of teaching" (*The Observer*, 20 August 2000, pp 1-2). But is this simply shifting blame, as if it is a matter of blaming teachers' expectations rather than asking more difficult questions? For example, Ofsted has realised it is boys who make a good start in primary schools but who seem to go into marked decline when it comes to the early years of secondary school. These are often difficult times for boys who have to deal with difficult questions of sexual and masculine identities as they become aware of *how they are perceived* in the larger culture. It can also be a time when issues of racial identity come into focus in more intense ways (Frosh et al, 2002).

Maxie Hayles, Chair of the Birmingham Racial Attacks Monitoring Unit, said in his submission to the UN that black children "are often labelled by teachers as disruptive and less intelligent than white pupils", creating a self-fulfilling prophesy:

> It would be daft to think that all social exclusions are based around institutional racism.… But I would never attack

black culture.... Black youth need something: they feel debased, they need something to identify with. (quoted in *The Observer*, 20 August 2000, p 2)

We should also think about black youth cultures, in part at least, as a response to institutional racisms.

Trevor Phillips, current head of the Equality and Human Rights Commission, also contributed to this debate. As a successful black journalist and political candidate he was challenged for not being in touch with youths on the street because he was educated and middle class. He discerns "a new kind of bondage – a subtle psychological entrapment that the late Bob Marley called 'mental slavery'. The horror is that this time we are willingly turning the key on ourselves and our children" (Philips, 2000, p 31). Some will object that this betrays what Bob Marley was about and that his defence misses the point that, "After all, the roots of this country's black community lie in a group of ambitious immigrants who washed their hands of the colonial Caribbean backwaters so that their children *could* be middle-class lawyers, doctors, teachers and accountants" (Philips, 2000, p 31).

What Philips is talking about are individual solutions that can also isolate you from the community you have grown up with. There is a complex dynamic at work here, which seems particularly connected to black masculinities, as explored by bell hooks (1991, 1995). Many white working-class boys are also struck by the realisation that in an increasingly competitive school culture, if you *never really try* then you cannot really be marked as having failed. There might be a genuine desire for achievement, but a rejection of the means and a fear of failure. Sometimes it can seem preferable not to try.

As Phillips has it, "Coming from 'the street' is the latest test of authenticity for us. We are only genuinely black if we speak Jamaican, wear expensive designer clothes and reject anything that resembles formal education or scholarship" (Phillips, 2000, p 31). As far as he is concerned this kind of 'authenticity' is nothing but a pernicious racist trap and he rejects

the new legend – that in a racist society, the only true representative of 'black' culture is to be found on the streets of the ghetto. Anything else is infected by the racism of white society, and any black person who refuses to conform is obviously an Uncle Tom. (Phillips, 2000, p 31)

Rejecting this language of authenticity, which too often refuses the complexity of lived black identities and which has its own inglorious history, Phillips reminds us "There has never been a time when there wasn't a myth about what defined a 'real' black man: our instinctual rhythm, our unbridled sexual potency, our uncontrollable rage, stupendous athleticism – oh and yes, our unrivalled propensity to fail" (Phillips, 2000, p 31). Phillips insists that we need to honour a *complexity* that recognises that there are as many different kinds of blacks as there are whites:

> It's time for everyone to wake up to the fact that the major thing that black people share, whatever their age, beliefs and station in life, is the way they are treated by white people. Wherever we are, we are still likely to meet prejudice and discrimination. (p 31)

You can sense the different pressures pushing Phillips in different directions, but you can also recognise them as the contradictions that those who have achieved success will experience within a racist society. We cannot forget the aspirations and achievements of the young Stephen Lawrence who was brutally murdered. He knew from his own experience that black people were as varied as any other group, but he also tragically experienced the realities of race hatred (see Chapter Eight). Phillips is right to insist that "there is no one way of being black, and there is no single 'authentic' black experience" (Phillips, 2000, p 31). But this could as well mean there are a *diversity* of authentic ways of being black and of shaping black identities in the face of a dominant white culture. There are spaces of resistance that young people have created for themselves in which they can feel a greater sense of freedom and self-expression.

But, within black communities, there is also sexism and homophobia that can make it difficult for people to explore more complex identities. As black gay men and lesbians explore the contradictions they live with, they shape new identities for themselves and develop different strategies to live their identities within the different cultural settings they move across. They can often feel *isolated* and *alone*, until they realise that there are alternative communities that are able to sustain their complex identities. They might become used to living out different identities with different groups of friends and in different spheres of life, but attitudes are also changing as a younger generation becomes accustomed to living with differences and negotiating their desires and needs within mixed relationships. Within urban multicultures young people learn to move across spaces of difference more successfully than previous generations and often learn to respect the individual choices that people have made for themselves.

White masculinities

'Laddish' white youth cultures have also been blamed for the developing 'gender gap' that has been reflected in recent school achievements. The main factor behind the improvement of results has been the better performance by girls, while the figures for boys remain relatively unchanged. David Aaronovitch, who has watched the effects of the gender revolution over the past 20 years in changing the country, says:

> It has been fascinating to watch, one by one, the citadels fall. First girls did better than boys at primary schools, and then fell behind in secondary schools. The explanation for this was that boys lagged till puberty, and then 'naturally' overtook girls. Breasts grow, brain shrinks. Then girls did better at O-levels and at GCSE levels, but boys were ahead at A-levels. (Aaronovitch, 2000, p 3)

The trend has continued with girls now outperforming boys in most A-level subjects. As Aaronovitch has it:

> What we've seen is a rapid social evolution as girls have become aware of the possibilities of careers, have been shown role models, as their own mothers have behaved differently from their own mothers, and been exposed to a world where they can no longer depend on men. The intellectual ability of girls and women was, as feminists argued all along, latent. It was awaiting social permission to emerge. (p 3)

On publication of the A-level results in 2000 the then Education Minister Baroness Blackstone said, what many people recognise, that girls work harder than boys and are more conscientious. The head of the head-teachers' union, David Hart, blamed this on "laddish culture, that despises academic achievement and [which] is tolerated by too many parents" (quoted in Aaronovitch, 2000, p 3). He concluded that boys often come to school unwilling to learn and convinced that they can succeed without application.

It is important to appreciate that in many ways the changes in school achievement have been a matter of girls doing better, rather than boys doing worse. But we should be concerned about what is happening for boys. This is not simply a matter of what the schools can do to help boys along but as Aaronovitch acknowledged:

> We have to change for boys what we changed for girls: the way they are treated within the family, and the way that the culture deals with them. All this daft preoccupation with sport and dangerous hobbies … the notion that a footballer is the best role model. The continual portrayal of young men as useless, violent, sexually inadequate lame-brains. (2000, p 3)

The figures which showed that girls for the first time achieved more A grades at A-level, followed the publication of statistics revealing that young men between the ages of 15 and 24 are three times more likely to commit suicide than young women of the same age.

Boys can find it difficult to have to compete directly with girls. Whenever girls do well in a given field, that field can be instantly discredited in the eyes of boys. The 'feminisation' of education produces its own threats to male identities because, as Emma Brockes points out in her article for *The Guardian*:

> It is competition corrupted by the lingering belief that a boy who comes second to a girl has not only lost the race, but something much more profound; something that involves his gender and his dignity as a man. With stakes so high, many boys would rather drop out of the game altogether than risk trying and failing. (Brockes, 2000, p 4)

Adrienne Katz, head of the charity Young Voice, says her research which interviewed 1,400 male teenagers aged 13-19 "showed that this type of news about girls' A-level success can make boys go, 'Well, if girls do so much better then why should we bother to try'" (quoted in Brockes, 2000, p 4). This shows that boys take very seriously the idea that girls should, by their very natures, do considerably less well than boys. The so-called 'overachieving' of girls appears to be having an impact on boys' self-esteem. Somehow boys are not being rewarded in the way they should be, or so they often assume. This is linked to a more general disorientation which Susan Faludi explored in *Stiffed* (Faludi, 2000). The men Faludi interviewed often felt that the values they were brought up to assume had been systematically discredited. They had often learnt from their fathers at least that if they abided by certain codes of behaviour their dominance in the home and in the world would be assured. As Andrew Samuels argues:

> If men turned away from softness, play, emotional connection, all the so-called feminine attributes society would reward the traditional man, if not with material wealth and political prominence, then at least with dominion over his wife and children. Men did all that, but the reward did not come. (1993, p 5)

If this frames the issues too starkly, without acknowledging the growth of diverse masculinities, Samuels is still right to think, "Boys are finding that the old ways of doing things don't work and perhaps they have yet to find new ways" (p 5).

In interviews with three 16-year-old white, working-class youths (Brockes, 2000), Scott says

> "You don't need qualifications these days. I've done my GCSEs and I've already had loads of jobs. That's without doing my A levels. I'm working for a printing company at the moment but I don't know what I want to do when I am older yet. I don't feel that girls are doing better than boys at school. I left school because I hated it, not because I wasn't any good at it." (p 5)

His friend, Terry, left school with no qualifications. He was working in the markets at the time of his interview but looking for work:

> "I do worry about the future because I don't want to end up like a bum, so I know that it's important to get a job and save some money.... Some of the girls I know are doing better than the boys but some just waste their lives by smoking all the time. The boys do that too but they can handle that better." (p 5)

Lee stayed on at school to do A-levels. His views are no less complex:

> "It is good to have qualifications behind you. But I do think as long as you've got ambitions in life you can do anything

you want. If you want it you should go for it. I talk to my
mates about any problems I have but there are less boys
around me at school – the girls around here are staying in
education longer than the boys. They like it more. I think
school's a good laugh but I don't do much work there." (p 5)

Even if Lee has to work hard to succeed at his A levels, it can be difficult
to acknowledge this in front of others. It is the girls who have to do
the work; it is important for boys to *show* that they do not really need
to make the effort. This becomes a mark of their superiority, or at least
of their difference.

Sharing social worlds

There are many crossovers between black and white youth cultures
and in some areas it can be difficult to draw sharp boundaries because
young people share cultural influences and have formed strong
relationships across differences within the routine masculinities that
they have grown up to take very much for granted in different urban
spaces. We might also have to be more sensitive to gender differences
that have been often overlooked as socially constructed. Alan Smithers
believes that the gender gap, which goes across race and ethnicities,
has its roots in innate but relatively small *differences* between boys and
girls that are exaggerated in our education system which insists on
formal education at a much earlier age than other European countries.
A return to single-sex classes in mixed secondary schools would be far
too little too late, according to Smithers. He refuses to blame laddish
culture on its own, but insists that we need to re-vision the education
of children:

> the system seems to exaggerate the small difference in verbal
> ability, so you get a significant difference in English results
> between boys and girls at the age of seven, which opens up
> into a massive gap at GCSE. (quoted in *Evening Standard*,
> 24 August 2000, p 16)

The system has found ways of compensating for the difference in
numerical and spatial ability, because girls are about level with boys
in maths and science. The huge differences in subjects which depend
on verbal skills, are, according to Smithers, the consequence of an
educational system that expects children to read and write before
they can speak. This appears to disadvantage boys particularly. The

government policy of setting 'goals' for very young children – for instance to be able to count up to 10 and write their own name – could be forcing young children to perform in ways for which they are not ready. He says:

> Other countries teach children what the number four means. We just teach children to write it down. The government ought to put in place an 'early years' curriculum based on the ability to talk, and cut back learning to read and write until the age of six, so when they are physically able to draw shapes on bits of paper they actually know what they mean. (quoted in *Evening Standard*, 24 August 2000, p 2)

The testing regimes for pupils that have been put in place are so often justified in terms of the ability to identify children who are having difficulties, but they create a culture of failure that places pressure on young children when they should be free to explore and create. It echoes an emphasis in postmodern culture on individual achievement and success that conceives childhood as a *series of hurdles* that children must learn to overcome. Not only does it make children feel uneasy with themselves, but it produces a competitive culture with an intense fear of failure. Often this will play out differently with boys who feel that they have much to *lose* if their male identities are threatened. With the decline of traditional industries that have sustained working-class masculinities and the questioning of gender relations, boys can often feel that they only have their embodied male identities to sustain them in a threatened sense of self-worth.

An intensification of competitive school cultures also influences children differently, depending on their class, gender, 'race' and ethnic backgrounds. Official educational discourses appear to be *blind to* the complex issues of identity that children at different ages must manage and the emotional traumas of separation and loss which affect so many families. Often, as teachers know too well, children's learning is regularly affected by emotional issues they have in the rest of their lives. Education is not a space apart but inevitably reflects issues of class exploitation, racial and sexual oppression within wider society.

Policy makers and educators have been concerned to understand the 'underachievement' of boys, but they resisted thinking critically about issues of masculinity and male identities. Instead they have remained tied into an aspirational liberal rhetoric that wants to identify boys who might need extra provision, but does not aim to understand how larger changes in the labour process affect boys in particular. Until recently it has been easy to blame laddish culture, but the higher suicide rates for young men tell a different, more tragic story, that should encourage us to really understand what was happening for young men.

Endnote

[1] Nitin Sawhney has produced a number of influential albums and worked across a variety of diverse art forms. His work also included a collaboration with Nirmal Puwar, 'Noise of the past', which brought Asian memories of loss into Coventry Cathedral so creating a diverse space in which to remember differently the Second World War.

Further reading

Migrant communities

For historically and culturally sensitive studies of the migration of different communities into Britain, particularly Islamic communities, and ways that different generations have adapted to Britain as a multicultural society see, for instance, Modood (1992) *Not easy being British*; Back (1996) *New ethnicities and urban culture*; Baubock (1994) *From aliens to citizens*.

Postmodern identities

For some helpful reflections on the nature of postmodern theories and ways it frames understandings of identities see, for instance, Zygmunt Bauman's *Intimations of postmodernity* (1994), *Life in fragments* (1995a) and *Postmodern ethics* (1995). His more recent writings mark a shift away from a postmodern framing since he questions some of the assumptions postmodern theorists make. See, for instance, *Liquid modernity* (2000) in which he prefers to think about different kinds of modernity.

Hindu fundamentalist

For a helpful exploration of the sources of Hindu fundamentalism and ways it has spread in the sub-continent see Bhatt (2001) *Hindu nationalism*; Varshney (2001) *Ethnic conflict civil life*; Jaffrelot (1996) *The Hindu Nationalist movement and Indian politics 1925 to 1990s*.

CND

For some historical reflections on the CND movement in Britain and how it helped shape a challenge to traditional politics see Frank Parkin (1968) *Middle class radicalism: The social bases of the British Campaign for Nuclear Disarmament*. See also more recent work on social movements, including Beverly Skeggs' *Formation of class and gender* (1997); Ken Plummer's *Telling sexual stories* (1995) and Zygmunt Bauman's *Life in fragments* (1995a).

Black music cultures

For some reflections on black music cultures see, for instance, Paul Gilroy's *Small acts* (1993). For a sense of the interrelation between black and Asian music cultures over time and in different urban spaces, see Sharma (2004). The culture of African-Caribbean sound systems has also been well written about by Lez Henry (2006).

Underachievement in British schools

For some discussions about the underachievement of people from diverse ethnic and racial backgrounds in British schools see, for instance, Epstein et al (eds) (1998) *Failing boys?*; Thorn (1993) *Gender play*; Mahoney (1985) *School for boys?*; Lloyd (1990) *Work with boys*; Frosh et al (2002) *Young masculinities*.

Discussions of the experiences of African-Caribbean students in schools in Britain and their differential experiences when compared with other groups are explored in Connolly (1998) *Racism, gender identities and young people*; Gilroy (1987) *There ain't no black in the Union Jack*; Mac an Ghail (1994) *The making of men*.

Black masculinities

For some of bell hooks' reflections on black masculinities see, for instance, *Yearning* (1990a) and *Black looks* (1992). See also Audre Lorde's *Sister outsider* (1980) and Toni Morrison's *Playing in the dark* (1993).

TEN

Rejections: shame / fear / hatred

This chapter explores the limits of a rationalist modernity to illuminate the psychosocial dynamics of rejection, shame, fear and hatred, and the ways in which they make themselves felt across the borders of inner emotional life and the rage against 'others'.

Modernity and shame

Within an Enlightenment vision of modernity that has been shaped through a secular Protestant tradition (see Chapters One and Two) there is a particular relationship between 'inner' and 'outer' that influences how we think and feel about identities, and the distinctions we make between private and public spheres. These are modulated differently within diverse cultural and historical settings. Within a Protestant tradition there is a suspicion that others cannot really know who I am, for the 'true self' is not what I show to others, but that which remains hidden as an 'inner self'. It is this inner self which has a relationship with God, a relationship which in a Protestant tradition is unmediated. It is therefore to God alone that I am accountable and God alone can recognise who I am in my individuality. This tradition results in a strong sense of interiority, in which we learn to accept that others can only gaze at what we present to them in our public presentations of self, but cannot see who we *truly are* (Marcuse, 1967; Taylor, 1979).

This sense of interiority is already fraught with uncertainties because the same Protestant tradition teaches that our inner natures are 'animal' and so the source of sin and transgression. We learn that we cannot *trust* our natures and that we must actively suppress our own impulses so that they cannot lead us astray. It is through a notion of reason, which in Kantian ethics is radically separated from nature, that we can supposedly discern the *moral law* and so what is required of us as a matter of obligation. So it is that *reason* comes to have a transcendental character as it takes up the position formerly occupied by *faith*. It is through reason that we can discern the moral law and so act out of a sense of duty. We inherit an identification between reason, morality and freedom. It is as rational moral agents that we can know freedom and autonomy (see Kant, 1986).

A liberal moral culture inherits from this Protestant tradition particular notions of freedom and autonomy that are projected as impartial and universal. It is through a **Durkheimian tradition** in social theory that we can watch the transformation of these Kantian assumptions as reason comes to be identified with society and the moral law with the social rules and norms that a society legislates for itself. This captures a crucial aspect of a Kantian inheritance and its ambiguous relationship with freedom. Kant argues that individuals are free to legislate for themselves so that, rather than experiencing the moral law as *constraining*, it has been *freely chosen* by autonomous moral agents. However, at the same time, it is through reason that they discern a moral law, which is, at some level, already given and waiting to be discerned and recognised in its obligatory nature.

If Kant accepts that individuals will pursue their own diverse wants and desires, which will give them happiness, he does not think that these endeavours have any moral worth. In some way happiness is separated from any connection with morality. It is through acting out of a pure will and doing what is *obligated* that we learn to act against our 'animal' natures. This legitimates the notion that individuals *cannot* really know what is good for them, because they are constantly led astray by their own inclinations. It is only through a technology of suppression that they can learn to *silence* their inclinations and can begin to hear the voice of reason. As they gradually learn to identify with this voice and so discern the dictates of the moral law, so they develop their individualities.

With Durkheim it is made clear that society presents individuals with a 'higher' sense of themselves through social rules and regulations. It clarifies an instrumental relationship with self that is often implicit within a Kantian ethical tradition. Left to their own devices individuals are egoistic and selfish, following their own conceptions of happiness. It is only through the constraining force of social rules that individuals are forced to reconsider their egoism and accept the 'higher' vision of themselves that they can realise by conforming to social norms and moral regulations. It is through conforming to social rules that individuals can draw the strength to resist the temptations offered by their animal natures. In this way Durkheim has fostered a tradition of **normalisation**, in which social theory has tended to legitimate the prevailing social rules, identities and disciplines and so is often still thought about in terms of socialisation – how people learn to adopt the norms and values of a particular culture and society. Those who refuse to conform or to assimilate into the dominant culture are considered 'abnormal' and 'pathological'. The fear of being thought 'abnormal' has continued to be very powerful in Britain in the post-war period. There has been a *fear* of difference, which has also been part of a Kantian rationalism as culture and history were deemed to be forms of 'unfreedom' and determination, as we have explored in Chapter Six. If you were different you learnt to conceal it (see Seidler, 1991a).

Fear and difference

Growing up in a culture of assimilation (as discussed in Chapters Three and Nine) you learn to show aspects of yourself that accord with the dominant culture. I experienced this myself growing up as Jewish within post-war Britain: I learned to be careful about which aspects of myself I showed to others. In similar situations, people often learn to minimise the significance of differences as they learn to behave 'like everyone else'. Not knowing what was really expected of us since we could not learn this from our refugee parents, my brothers and I learnt to observe others and often to *imitate* their behaviours, hoping that the appropriate feelings would somehow follow. We wanted to be English and we learned to think that we were English because we were born here, but we did not really know what this meant or feel any confidence in it. At some level we learnt to fear our difference, because it threatened to expose us.

As a Protestant culture taught people to fear the revelations of their 'animal' natures, so it produced anxieties in the public sphere where people did not want to be *betrayed* by their desires. This has further fostered an image of masculine identities that have been closely identified with 'self-control', meaning a relationship of dominance over 'animal' natures. For me, as a boy I was concerned to be 'accepted' for who I was, but this worked in subtle ways to shame my Jewishness. Within a culture of liberal tolerance, Jewishness was to be tolerated in a way that meant that it was not really allowed to count against you, but it was not to be celebrated either because difference was deemed to be *threatening*. Rather we learnt to keep quiet about it as we learnt not to be 'too Jewish'. We learned to deflect attention away from ourselves and in different ways to become *less visible* so as to minimise possibilities of *rejection*. We developed strategies that would be familiar to other children of refugees and migrants.

Through Enlightenment rationalism, liberal moral culture assumed that 'Jewishness', like 'blackness' or 'Asianness', was an incidental historical determination which did not have to define 'who' you were. As we learn to be individuals in our own right, so we learn to think that we are 'persons like everyone else', and want to be judged on the basis of our personal and individual characteristics rather than on the basis of our class, religious or ethnic backgrounds: 'Judge me for who I am, not on the basis of my class, gender, "race" or ethnic background' becomes a strategy of self-defence. A liberal moral culture encourages us to want to be evaluated on the basis of achievements due to individual talents, capacities and abilities. In its own way, this produces a competitive culture of individual achievement and success in which individuals must constantly *prove* their adequacy (see Weber, 1930).

This drive towards endless activity has been tied to a dominant form of masculinity through a Protestant ethic. So, for example, you could really do well in your exams but find yourself focused on the marks that you did not gain. This can make it difficult to feel the satisfaction in your achievements, to experience a well-deserved feeling of fulfilment. It is this sense of inner nourishment that is often forsaken in a postmodern culture. People often live in intense activities in which time has been accelerated and it becomes difficult to take time and space for themselves (Seidler, 1991b).

Spaces of exploration

A **poststructuralist sexual politics** has often assumed the fragmentation of identities in ways that sustain the idea that identities are somehow provided for people through prevailing discourses, so that in different spaces people learn to assume different identities. There is suspicion of any singular notion of identity that seems to be inevitably tied to essentialist ideas of *authenticity*. Social theory has become wary of any idea of an inner emotional life assuming that it means an identity waiting to be discovered, and has argued instead that identities are 'socially and historically constructed', even if it is often difficult to articulate what this means.

However, these theories of subjectivity, although they often draw on psychoanalysis, can lose touch with the importance of *spaces of exploration*, which were acknowledged within sexual politics, and which allowed people time and space to explore tensions between, for example, what their parents and teachers expected of them within the terms of the dominant culture and what they wanted and needed for themselves. This has meant, for example, critically evaluating inherited gender identities and contesting the subordination of women or the identification of a woman's happiness with their partner's and children's happiness. A younger generation is shaped through different subjectivities, for example supposedly absorbing notions of 'gender equality' as part of a postmodern 'common sense', without somehow needing to engage in practices of consciousness-raising (Walter, 1999). They are framed through a different sense of *entitlement*, although their anxieties and insecurities more often show in relation to bodies and feeling about food that, as Freud recognises, so often also relate to sexualities and desires.

As an example of spaces of exploration, a young man might feel at ease about discovering his gay sexual orientation, but feel that he cannot really share it with his parents. Even when he is depressed, going through a difficult time at school, he cannot really share it with them. He worries that his high voice might betray him, and he is careful about what he is willing to share in his school friendships. He seeks protection in his intellectuality and gains a class position of respect through being prepared to question the teachers. He becomes aware of school as a *dangerous space* in which he must protect himself. There is little discussion of gay identities, although he tries to bring gay issues into his A-level sociology project. He asks questions about homosexualities, even within his family, but continues to protect his own identity. It is only on leaving school that he feels able to 'come out' to his parents and friends.

Later reflecting on this experience, he can understand how an earlier generation of gay men and lesbians could feel shamed about their sexualities and feel that they are 'abnormal', but he also resists the idea that his sexuality rests only within the *limited space* of sexual desire and that otherwise he is 'like everyone else'. He questions this liberal construction and is eager to be able to acknowledge the significance of sexuality as a sensibility that informs particular ways of thinking and feeling about other things.

In part, this young man wants to be defined by his sexuality. This is contrary to Foucault with Sennett (1981), who questioned the ideas of gay liberation and wanted to resist the idea that your sexuality can somehow define 'who' you are, because there are many other equally significant aspects of your self-identity. Foucault and Sennett find it hard to explore a middle ground that does not give way to a form of sexual liberalism that makes sexual orientation merely incidental (Caplan, 1987; Miller, 1992).

The assumption that identities are 'given' and thereby waiting to be discovered, fosters a kind of essentialism which would limit the possibilities open to, say, women who reject the option of motherhood for themselves. The notion of identities as 'socially and historically constructed' can then be useful, if it is carefully handled. Often **social constructionism** can, at the opposite extreme, minimise expressive notions of identity that open us to narratives of embodied personal emotions and feelings which can be too quickly labelled as 'essentialist' because they seem to assume a 'nature' that needs to be expressed. But, if this questions the notion of a shared collective nature, it can still be important to realise *how* identities can be *shamed* and people left unable to express aspects of their natures. For example, a person might be in a job that is wrong for them, even though it is well paid and seems a rational choice, but if they are not open to discovering what they need for themselves, it can be difficult to appreciate that they are doing something that does not allow them to grow and use their particular energies appropriately.

For example, a man shares his experience of living in South Africa before the end of the apartheid regime. He felt what was going on there was quite wrong and inhumane. He felt that he could not breathe there and realised that he would soon have to leave to live in a different country. But he was struck by how many people colluded with the regime and did not question its legitimacy. The white population was doing well and lived privileged lives they did not want to disturb. He felt differently to a lot of the people he met.

This experience helped him to realise that you cannot live your individual life without understanding how your identity is being shaped and influenced by larger political forces. Many young people in South Africa were growing up to take for granted an unjust and oppressive system that they did not question, for it was the 'reality' that they knew.

White supremacy has long been part of a European colonialist inheritance and, as well as supporting an oppressive system like that which existed in South Africa, it has shaped gender identities that assume superiority over colonised 'others' (Middleton, 1992; Lundqvist, 1996).

As individuals gain greater clarity about their individual needs and desires they can also feel at odds with the larger structure of capitalist social relations they grow up to take very much for granted. Individualism has taken on new consumer forms that can encourage people to evaluate themselves through the goods they possess and the money they earn *as if* these are measures of their value (see Giddens, 1990; Featherstone, 1991). However, some people question the consumerist identities that they are encouraged to adopt and wonder about the labour conditions that produce the branded goods of Nike and other corporations. They learn to ask more fundamental questions both about the lives they want for themselves and the structures of power and domination within the larger society.

Within a postmodern culture it is easy to assume that individuals are free to create their own identities, so they really only have themselves to blame if they do not succeed in finding happiness. But this can also reinforce the distinctions between private and public, between personal life and politics, which sexual politics sought to question. Women today can be encouraged to think that they have realised an equality that an earlier generation could only dream about. This intensifies the pressure, as anxieties are internalised and women feel that they *should* be able to compete on equal terms with men and that they are to blame if they fail (see also Chapter Five). This works to reinforce a renewed privatisation of experience, in which people conceal their private doubts and anxieties making sure that they have a competent image in public.

In the 1990s the private realm became an arena of style over which you exerted control, as the consumer culture encouraged both young women and young men to believe that they could remake their identities; that what mattered was how you presented yourself and *performed* your identities in public (see Chapter Eleven). Work remained central in the making of identities and this resulted in an intensified dependency on work for both men and women. There is often a compulsive quality in people's relationships with work that reveals itself in how they shape their bodily tensions and somatic experience and the little balance they have with other areas of life. Often people are locked into an intense competition with themselves, unable to take time and space for themselves. So, although in postmodern culture there is a greater acceptance of difference, there is also an intensified fear of individual failure (Sennett, 1998, 2004) and a sharpening of the distinction between self-control in public and unspoken anxieties and insecurities in private. But there are also darker forms that can suddenly erupt and disturb, as if without warning. This can reveal itself as self-harming or anorexia, but also more publicly as hatred of 'others'.

Fear and hatred

When David Copeland was convicted for the nail-bombing campaign in London in April 1999, which killed three people and injured 139 others, the jury had decided that he was 'bad' not 'mad'. He had claimed that his actions marked the start of a racist and homophobic war and that he was a righteous messenger from God. The jury heard evidence that he was a lonely, sad individual who was worried that his penis was too small and that people might think that he was a homosexual. His anger was channelled into virulent right-wing extremism and he finally vented his hatred on black, Asian and gay communities in 13 days of carefully planned outrage.

As the judge Michael Hyam, QC, sentenced him he rejected his pleas of manslaughter on the grounds of diminished responsibility:

> The evidence shows you were motivated by virulent hatred and pitiless contempt for other people. You set out to kill and maim and terrorise the community. As a result of your wicked intentions you have left three families bereaved. You alone are accountable for ruining their lives. Nothing can excuse or justify the evil you have done. (reported in *The Guardian*, 1 July 2000, p 1)

Gary Reid, who lost a leg in the Soho blast, said that Copeland's victims felt a "deep sense of relief and gratitude" following the verdict: "The fear, loathing, hatred and ignorance culminating in the bombings is a warning to society and the world as a whole that racism, prejudice and homophobia – and the fear of difference – is out there" (quoted in *The Guardian*, 1 July 2000, p 1). Martin, the brother of Nick Moore who died in the Soho bombing added:

> This case clearly illustrates the harm that may be done by the failure to recognise, accept and nurture the sexuality of our offspring. It can, at best, cause misery and personality disorder, and at worst turn a child into a murderer. We must learn from it. (quoted in *The Guardian*, 1 July 2000, p 1)

This insightful statement calls us to appreciate the significance of an *ethics and politics of recognition* as a way of re-visioning the connections between the personal and the political. At some level it resonates with insights Bert Hellinger (1997) has developed into family systems. Hellinger talks about the significance of "an early interrupted reaching out movement towards one of the parents, usually the mother" (1997, p 62):

> If a child is sent away very early or separated for some reason, then the movement towards the mother is interrupted. At that moment, the child very often experiences despair or

anger, and that's just the other side of love. The *interrupted* love turns towards hate or rage or despair. Very often the child makes a decision at that point that it won't come near to its mother anymore. That basic decision is very often transferred later onto other persons as well, and as adults they don't dare to come closer. When such a person wants to be intimate with someone else, he or she reaches that point where the body remembers the early interruption, and instead of going forward, they make a sideways movement. They make a circular, sideways movement coming back to the same point again and again. (p 62)

This helps identify the psychological processes which Hellinger links to what he regards as the other source of unhappiness or suffering in families, which is when "there is something to be brought into order within the family system" (p 62).

David Copeland's defence relied on the evidence of six psychiatrists who argued that he was suffering from paranoid schizophrenic illness at the time of the bombings and so had acted 'like a robot' who was incapable of taking full responsibility for his actions. But a prosecution expert, Philip Joseph, said Copeland "had overwhelming anxiety over his sexual orientation and intense rage and hatred of others that led to extreme views and a desire to destroy" (reported in *The Guardian*, 1 July 2000, p 1). Joseph concluded that Copeland was not suffering from schizophrenia, but had a less serious personality disorder. Concerns that some psychiatrists had exaggerated the condition were heightened when it was revealed that in letters Copeland had written to Bernard O'Mahoney, a writer who was posing as a female pen-friend he named 'Patsy Scanlon' (and who later sold the letters to *The Mirror* for a substantial sum), Copeland boasted that he could not believe he had fooled so many experts over his illness.

When Copeland was finally arrested and the police knocked on the door of a semi-detached house in Sunybank Road, Cove, he opened the door half-dressed, as if half-expecting the visit. He rubbed his eyes and mumbled, "Yeah, they were all down to me. I did them on my own" (as reported in *The Guardian*, 1 July 2000, p 2):

Any doubts the officers may have had disappeared when Copeland led them upstairs to his bedroom. Two Nazi flags were hanging on the wall, alongside a macabre collage of photos and newspaper stories. The theme was bomb blasts. There were pictures of victims from the explosions in

Omagh and at the Olympics in Atlanta – and in the middle
of this homage to bloodshed was a poster of Hitler. (*The
Guardian*, 1 July 2000, p 2)

Copeland was very eager to give detectives a detailed account of how
he made and planted the three devices, but it was harder to explain
why he did it, which became the crux of the trial at the Old Bailey.
His mother said that David was the quietest of her boys: "He was very,
very gentle, and out of all my children, the most sensitive, loving and
caring. He was never naughty" (quoted in *The Guardian*, 1 July 2000,
p 2). After the trial she said

> We, least of all, understand. Something was going on in his
> head, and he must have been so lost and unhappy to have
> done as he's done.... I can't forgive him. But I can't change
> it and, at the end of the day, he's my son, my baby. I wish
> I knew why he's done this but I don't think we will ever
> know. I don't even think he knows himself. (quoted in *The
> Guardian*, 1 July 2000, p 1)

Copeland studied at Yately comprehensive, in a fairly affluent area to
which the family had moved when he was 10. His friends remembered
him as a little introverted but not as aggressive or racist. He is small –
5ft 3in – and was occasionally pushed around by other pupils but he
was not bullied. One contemporary, Richard Travers, said: "He seemed
harmless. He didn't seem to have a problem with any of the black kids
in our year. He didn't show any sort of violent behaviour" (quoted in
The Guardian, 1 July 2000, p 2).

His father suggested that the turning point in his life came later,
when, aged 19, Copeland's mother walked out (after a row with his
father) and never returned. The following morning he told his sons.
"Maybe this triggered his mental illness. Immediately afterwards, he
became very angry and very drunk. He never talked about her leaving
him and he wouldn't see her" (quoted in *The Guardian*, 1 July 2000,
p 2). Copeland's mother countered that her ex-husband blamed her
because he was still bitter about their divorce.

There is obviously a difficult family history here which cannot
be resolved by shifting blame and responsibility, although, within
modernity, this is often how we learn to deal with emotional issues –
if there is always a person to be blamed and if we can prove who it is
then we do not have to explore how we may have also been implicated
in what went on. It is not clear how much it helps when his mother

says, "On a prison visit, I asked David if my leaving affected him, and he said 'No, mum'." She added:

> There was no reason for him to hate people. He didn't know any one, as far as I am aware, who was homosexual. There weren't many black people at his school. All I can think is that, when he finally left home to live in London something must have happened. (quoted in *The Guardian*, 1 July 2000, p 2)

We need to be aware of how a search for reasons can so easily lead us astray. Often we are concerned to clear ourselves of any responsibility through *projecting onto others*. But Freud questions such displacements and the assumptions of a modernity shaped within the terms of a Protestant tradition that fosters an idea that *if* we can prove that others are to blame, then we can conclude that we are blameless ourselves. Often it is painful to acknowledge the responsibilities we also carry in creating and sustaining emotional relationships. This relates to the fact that we rarely learn, especially as men, about the *emotional work* that is involved in sustaining a relationship. It is only when things begin to go wrong that we can detect a 'problem' that requires some kind of 'solution'. Often the patterns are more deeply embedded than our rationalist culture is yet to acknowledge. The increasing turn to counselling and the acceptance of therapeutic notions can be personally helpful, but can in itself be a form of denial if it marks a refusal to ask questions about the formation of personal and social identities (Seidler, 2000).

To return to Copeland, he never mentioned his parents' divorce as having any significance; it seems as if his phobias set root earlier. He told the police that his hatred of gay men stemmed from childhood and was a reaction to his parents thinking that he was homosexual. According to *The Guardian* report, "He recalled how when he was 13 they sang the theme tune of 'The Flintstones', and seemed to emphasise the lyrics, 'we'll have a gay old time'" (*The Guardian*, 1 July 2000, p 2). He was appalled that his mother had then asked him if he wanted to confide any secrets. His parents say that the episode is a figment of his imagination. Copeland's father recalled an occasion when his son, then 19, was challenged about his sexuality by his grandmother: "She asked him: 'What's up with you, David? Do you like boys because you haven't got a girlfriend?' That was the only time the subject of his sexuality was raised. Copeland vowed never to speak to his grandmother again" (*The Guardian*, 1 July 2000, p 2).

We see here the same 'cutting off' that happened between Copeland and his mother after she left, which can be interpreted as a form of punishment. But we also see a culture of denial in which his parents refer to a 'figment of his imagination'. After his arrest, Copeland claimed he had been having violent and sadistic dreams from the age of 12. He had thought about killing his classmates and had wanted to be reincarnated as an SS officer surrounded by sexual slaves. Later, he said he read biographies of Hitler and became obsessed with the idea of becoming famous. This demonstrates how it is possible to be drawn to *impersonal* sources to shape a *personal* life and to make identifications that help form your experience.

The explosion in Centennial Park during the Atlanta Olympics in 1996 seems to have also been significant for Copeland. As he watched news reports from the scene he wondered why nobody had bombed the Notting Hill Carnival. According to *The Guardian* report he could not get the idea out of his head and woke up months later vowing to do it himself: "'I am the first domino', he said to one psychiatrist, 'Everything else will fall'" (*The Guardian*, 1 July 2000, p 2). Four months after joining the BNP he cancelled his subscription because they refused to countenance a 'paramilitary struggle'. A year later he joined the National Socialist Movement, thought to be the political wing of Combat 18 (a violent British neo-Nazi organisation).

When Copeland turned up in Brixton in a taxi after having taken a train to Waterloo station with a primed bomb taped to the inside of a new sports bag he had never been to Brixton before. He walked up and down the high street, scouting around its stores and markets. He was surprised so many white people lived there. The explosion stunned Scotland Yard's anti-terrorist branch. Two days later anonymous calls arrived claiming the explosion was the work of Combat 18, the English National Party and the little known White Wolves: "Tension grew when threatening letters signed WW were sent to high profile black and Asian community leaders, including MP Oona King, Copeland later criticised the 'thugs who were trying to steal his glory'" (*The Guardian*, 1 July 2000, p 3).

When Copeland's bomb ripped through the Admiral Duncan pub four people were killed and 79 injured. Later he admitted to the police that he felt "sick" about the death of Andrea Dykes who was four months pregnant with her first child. Jeevan Vasager suggested that:

> Perhaps Copeland, surprised as he was by the presence of
> so many white people in Brixton, thought it inconceivable
> for a straight couple to have been drinking at the Admiral

Duncan. With the personal hatred he felt for gay men, he would have found it even more astonishing that a straight couple could have chosen John Light, a gay man, as the best man at their wedding, and as the godfather of their child. (*The Guardian*, 1 July 2000, p 2)

John Light had been delighted to be a godparent and had brought the tickets for the Abba musical 'Mamma Mia!' to celebrate; they were having a drink together in the pub before a night out at the theatre.

Conclusion

As we think about the different ways in which people can be shamed because of their class, 'race' or ethnic background or because of their sexualities, we learn to think across the boundaries of the personal and the political, as well as the different levels of people's experience that often remain unspoken and unexplored. Although poststructuralist traditions have proved vitally significant in shaping a sense of fluidity and fragmentation of identities, they have helped to produce their own rationalist distancing and externalise relationships to embodied identities.

Relying on the capacities of discourses to articulate experience and identities, they have often treated bodies as objects of discursive practice so displacing the formative processes of lived emotional lives. Fearful at some level of the 'personal' and the 'emotional', they avoid these spaces and so are often unable to frame analyses that can journey across the borders of the 'psycho', the 'social' and the 'political'. Embodying identities involves *opening up* those very emotional spaces to explore sources of violence and rage, and learn how to heal, feel and think across these boundaries.

Further reading

Interiority

Herbert Marcuse in *Reason and revolution* (1967) has some interesting discussions about the ways a sense of interiority is framed through a Protestant tradition and the implications for inherited senses of identities and politics. There is also helpful discussion in Charles Taylor's *Hegel and modern society* (1979) and in his more recent *Sources of the self* (1989). Taylor points out: "What Weber called 'disenchantment', the dissipation of our sense of the cosmos as a meaningful order, has allegedly destroyed the horizons in which people previously lived their spiritual lives" (1989, p 17).

Kantian ethics

In *Kant, respect and injustice* (Seidler, 1986) I explore some of the implications of the identification we are encouraged to make through Kant between reason, freedom and morality for the rationalist senses of identity we inherit and the difficulties of recognising emotions and feelings and sources of human dignity and respect. I have explored some of the implications of an identification of reason with morality and ways that it is framed through diverse Christian traditions in *The moral limits of modernity* (Seidler, 1991a).

Durkheimian tradition

For a helpful introduction to Durkheim's social theory see, for instance, Anthony Giddens' *Capitalism and modern social theory* (1971) and his shorter *Durkheim* (1978). See also, Steven Lukes, *Emile Durkheim* (1983).

Poststructuralist sexual politics

Issues around sexual identities and tensions with liberal moral and political theory are explored in contributions by Weeks, Seidler and others to Pat Caplan's edited collection *The cultural construction of sexuality* (1987). See also Miller (1992) *Out in the world* and Mangan and Walvin (1987) *Manliness and morality*.

I have explored the ways that Protestant moral culture has helped shape the inner lives and performances of dominant masculinities and the unspoken tensions between men and the masculinities they feel destined to live up to in *Recreating sexual politics* (Seidler, 1991b). See also Elliot (2008).

Gay identities

For some helpful discussions about young gay identities and processes of 'coming out' see, for instance, Jeffrey Weeks, *Coming out* (1977) and *Inventing moralities* (1995), and Weeks and Porter (eds) *Between the acts* (1998).

Colonialist inheritance

For some helpful reflections on different colonial inheritances and ways they shape gendered identities of superiority see, for instance, Lundqvist (1999) *Exterminate all the brutes*; Middleton (1992) *The inward gaze*; Steyn (2001) *"Whiteness just isn't what it used to be"*; Mbembe (2001) *On the postcolony*.

Consumer culture

Explorations of the changing nature of consumption within late capitalism and the relationships shaped through a consumer culture are given in Anthony Giddens' *The consequences of modernity* (1990); Croucher, *Globalization and belonging* (2004); Niezen, *A world beyond difference* (2004); Tomlinson, *Globalization and culture* (1999); Slater and Tonkiss, *Market society* (2000); and Mike Featherstone, *Consumer culture and postmodernism* (1991).

Relationships with work

For some reflections on the changing nature of work identities in the new capitalism and how this helps shape a particular relationship with space and time see, for instance, Sennett's *The corrosion of character* (1998) and *Respect* (2004); Skeggs' *Class, self, culture* (2004); du Gay and Pryke's edited volume *Cultural economy* (2002); Lash and Urry's *Economies of signs and space* (1994); and Keat and Abercrombie's *Enterprise culture* (1991).

ELEVEN

Postmodernities: individualisms / performances / sexualities

This chapter looks at postmodern individualisms and the reshaping of communities. It uses the BSE crisis to explore relationships between animal and human, nature and culture, nature and technology. It also discusses gender as 'performative' and the ambivalences of gender and sexual identities.

Postmodern individualisms

Within the competitive cultures of postmodernity young women and men increasingly learn to identify themselves with their individual successes and ambitions. Cultures of neo-liberalism and of a globalised new capitalism have helped to shape their 'common-sense' belief that motivation is all and that if you really want something then you simply have to 'go for it'. This is a notion that Prime Minister Margaret Thatcher fostered in Britain during the 1980s and 1990s, while President Ronald Reagan did the same in the US, and it has been influential in shifting class, 'racial' and ethnic identifications. This individualistic culture has led to a weakening of group identifications, especially in relation to class, as has the development of new service sectors and the decline in Western industrialised societies of trades unions. There is now a more *instrumental* relationship to work and relationships, which is part of a 'new realism' that helps shape contemporary cultures. Consumerism and celebrity cultures that are framed through a new significance for global brands and logos help shape new identifications and perform new notions of self-worth and identity.

Despite these postmodern individualisms, people often want to form relationships with others but they do not really have the time and space for them in their lives. They dream of intimate relationships but in actual fact they often prefer a single lifestyle to which they have become accustomed. They do not want to risk vulnerability; they feel that they have more control over their own lives as individuals. Robert

Putnam has argued in *Bowling alone* (2000) that Americans have seen a collapse in honesty and trust. The system of social capitalism – in which all citizens benefit from shared networks and reliance on one another – is in crisis. Putnam's image of the individual who now goes 'bowling alone' rather than with friends has found a striking resonance. He argues that people spend far less time playing team sports and they eat on the move or in McDonalds, rather than with friends and family in traditional restaurants. Putnam argues that a post-war generation, which was brought up as a 'civic generation' with shared values and a readiness to sacrifice for the community, has given way to a crude individualism. America has become a more isolated and terrified nation than ever before. There is no longer a widespread belief, as Putnam has it, that:

> Members of a community that follow the principle of reciprocity – raking your leaves before they blow on your neighbour's yard, lending a dime to a stranger for a parking meter, buying a round of drinks during the week you earn overtime – find that their self-interest is served. (Putnam, quoted in *The Observer*, 20 August 2000, p 20)

In Britain too we are witnessing the growth of singular identities. The solitary activities of gym membership and running are replacing team sports for adults who take active exercise. In a recent national poll of volunteers a mere one in ten young people cited helping their community as a reason for doing unpaid work. The most compelling attraction for them was the opportunity to acquire marketable skills or to add to their CVs. Putnam would see this as further evidence of a 'de-socialising' society. Another symptom of a withdrawal from community is disengagement from the democratic political process. May 1997 saw the lowest turnout in any general election in the UK since 1945, and this has continued to decline in both national and local elections. But Lisa Harker, research director at the Institute of Public Policy Research, warns against drawing quick conclusions:

> There may be some worrying signs of disengagement, but we're not certain it's true. Choosing to live alone doesn't mean that you don't want to be part of the community. You may just be living differently, with as many outside contacts as you would have had before. (Harker, quoted in *The Observer*, 20 August 2000, p 20)

There are also trends towards individualisation within families, who today rarely eat together and operate as individuals on different routines, and in which 68% of British 14 year olds now have music systems in their bedrooms and 80% have their own television sets. Despite this, Harker suggests that "We might well be different from America. We've had shared values for generations about things like the health service. It may well be that those shared values can extend to other areas as well" (quoted in *The Observer*, 20 August 2000, p 20). This could be wishful thinking, since postmodern culture has been characterised by a breakdown in shared values, with people much less clear about the basis of their beliefs and values. With the growth of secular values, religious traditions have been obliged to give up their absolutist claims and recognise themselves as but one of a number of 'faith communities'.

According to Will Hutton:

> The moral imperative in a humanist, secular age is to improve the human condition in the here and now; nor can there be any legitimate constraint on permitting scientists to follow where their ingenuity and logic leads them.... That does not mean that there are not fundamental moral questions raised by where science is leading, but religion is not going to be able to provide the answers. We have to find answers ourselves. (Hutton, 2000, p 29)

He continues:

> For the trajectory of Roman Catholicism being the moral authority that underpinned every aspect of society – from the monarch's divine right to rule to the rules over divorce – to its current standing alongside the Church of England and Islam as another faith community exactly mirrors the rise of science and its humanistic project to extend man's power over nature. (p 29, and see below)

At the same time Hutton readily admits that many people would love to create 'moral anchors' such as those our ancestors possessed, which he connects to the growing interest in environmentalism and natural remedies. His rationalism does not allow him to appreciate the nature of the *challenges* these movements make to a rationalist modernity. Hutton assumes an Enlightenment identification between science, reason and progress, even though he must also be aware of the destruction that science has wrought. He does not look to diverse spiritual traditions as potential sources of *value* within a postmodern culture. Rather, he states that

> we are damned by our knowledge and the frontiers that science opens up as it continues the quest to explore and control nature. At the same time we are making our own ethical judgements as we progress. We are human beings. We can do no other. This is not a crisis for science. It is a crisis for religion, whose moral importance before the march of the rational is again so crudely exposed. (p 29)

But it is this very Enlightenment rationalism which has shaped the common sense of modernity that is itself in crisis (see Giddens, 1991; Flax, 1993; Bauman, 1997, 2003). It depends on a vision of reason as an autonomous and independent faculty radically separated from nature, which has fostered its own instrumental relationship with nature, and which has conceived of progress in terms of the control and domination of nature. This is a vision that Hutton refuses to question, tied as he is to the notion of the rational self that underpins a dominant white, heterosexual masculinity. This is not to question *reason*, but it is to question the *particular vision of reason* that we have inherited and the ways in which this Enlightenment view has legitimated particular dominant masculine identities while silencing the voices of others who were deemed to be 'irrational' and 'unreasonable' because they were deemed to be 'closer to nature' (see Chapter One).

Within a postmodern culture there is a sense that new technologies have further undermined shared moral values. With the decline in traditional religious beliefs there was recognition that moral values could be discerned through reason alone. But this faith in the progressive character of reason has been undermined as the relationships with nature that it assumed have been brought into question. With an ecological postmodernism there has been a widespread movement, especially in the face of the crisis of global warming, to question prevailing relationships between humans and nature. There has been a growing awareness of the ways in which new technologies work to sustain prevailing relationships with nature.

Nature and technology

Treating nature as a disenchanted resource that is waiting to be exploited by human beings can no longer be justified. The idea that the distinctions between different species were somehow arbitrary, waiting to be transcended through scientific progress, was dramatically challenged in the UK by the BSE crisis of the late 1990s and early 2000s. When the cattle disease bovine spongiform encephalopathy (BSE) first emerged in 1986, government advisors dismissed any threat to people. They were forced to admit that feeding practices in dairy farms, where cows' diets included the grounded remains of other cattle and sheep, probably sent the disease into its catastrophic spiral; natural boundaries had been crossed and nature could be seen to be getting its revenge. After years during which warnings about potential death to humans through eating infected meat met public scorn, the fatalities began in March 1995. The first victim to die of the human variant Creutzfeldt Jakob disease (vCJD) was Stephen Churchill aged 19. It was a year later, in March 1996, before scientists made the first connections between BSE and vCJD. People were then forced to acknowledge that the food we absorb into our bodies could be contaminated, and to recognise that they lived in a new **risk society** which encouraged new fears. As James Meikle reported:

> The revelation that BSE and its human form may be able to jump the species barrier and be highly infective even when a person or animal with the disease shows no signs of it, appears to confirm some of the worst fears scientists have about the fatal condition. (Meikle, 2000, p 6)

The repeated argument that there was 'no scientific proof' established for a connection between eating infected meat and vCJD came to have a bitter ring. It reflected a failure in prevailing scientific methodologies and technologies to have anticipated the dangers in refusing to respect species boundaries. As Meikle put it, there was a widespread assumption "that a species barrier between humans and the animals they eat would cut the number of people who might succumb to BSE" (p 6).

This widespread assumption was based on a notion of social constructionism that imagined distinctions between culture and nature to be arbitrary constructions that could be transformed with few consequences (also see Chapter Eight). It encourages us to revise basic conceptions of 'the human' and so to rethink relations between 'the human' and 'the animal'. This served to question fundamental notions of human identity within a modernity that assumes *reason* as an independent faculty, radically separated from *nature*. Rationality set human beings apart with a fundamental differentiation of superiority over animals. Not only were human beings radically different from other animals in that they alone had reason but they were superior, having dominion over the rest of nature. As we challenge this superiority and rethink human beings' treatment of, and attitudes towards, animals (see Ryder, 2000; Dunayer, 2004), so we must re-vision relationships with nature and thereby challenge an Enlightenment modernity, which has assumed that progress involved the control and domination of nature. In this way ecology allows for a fundamental challenge to traditional forms of social theory, including poststructuralisms that silence nature by treating it as a 'construction' of culture.

The BSE crisis helped to produce a shift in public attitudes and a greater sensitivity to what people eat. This increased perception of risk has made people suspicious about genetically modified crops, resulting in many people in government initially rejecting approval for GM crops to be grown in the UK. It was not felt that the risks were worth taking. People were concerned about the genetic engineering of foods as they framed an alternative sense of life politics. In part this connects to a transformation of values within a postmodern culture, particularly in the West, where there has been a growing interest in alternative forms of healthcare, such as traditional and complementary medicine, in organic food and even in 'growing your own'. There is a sense that the capitalist exploitation of nature has created dangers that a dominant culture had been unable to anticipate. There is a widespread questioning of the assumption that progress lies in the domination of nature, especially with regard to the dangers of global warming, and a new openness to the idea that people must *re-vision* their identities by developing a different relationship with nature.

As the dominant identity of individuals as rational selves gives way to a more holistic vision in which people increasingly begin to recognise themselves as embodied emotional and spiritual beings in the wider world, so they question instrumental and disenchanted relationships with the self that characterised an Enlightenment vision of modernity. There is a developing awareness of *quality* of life and quality of relationships and so of different aspects of being. As people within new work cultures feel less able to predict their futures at work and become more aware of the risks and uncertainties they face (see Chapter Six), so they are also more aware of the different ways in which people can be harmed, abused and undermined. This has produced a complex vision of identity that goes beyond a postmodernism that would insist that there is no single subject/rational self in the Cartesian image to an understanding of the self that is made up of fragmented, multilayered, complex, fluid, embodied identities.

This also questions a postmodern denial of different levels and depths of experience, which assumes that everything is to be seen on the surface at the level of appearances. If people can celebrate diversity they also want to acknowledge the fears and anxieties of being torn between diverse cultural traditions as they shape hybrid identities. If postmodern theories aim to restore to people a sense of their own agency, as authors of their own embodied identities, there is also a need to 'come to terms' with the complex histories and inheritances and traumatic experiences we carry both individually and collectively. This can involve questioning an essentialism that tends to *fix* people in given, pre-established categories and identities, so curtailing opportunities for people to create their own identities (see Chapter Three). At the same time we can feel a need to respect individualities as people learn to *define* what they want and need for themselves at any given moment in their lives. If people learn to frame their experience externally, they may form an **externalised relationship** with themselves. For example, if a young person decides to pursue the subjects in which they performed well in exams rather than choosing subjects that they enjoy or about which they have a positive *feeling* they will often find themselves on the wrong track, unable to establish a deeper relationship with themselves (see Chapter Twelve).

Identity / performance

Judith Butler's notion of gender as *performative* (1990) has drawn on J.L. Austin's theory of 'performative utterances', which he developed in *How to do things with words* (Austin, 1975; see also Searle, 1969). Austin was concerned to question a generalised vision of language as *descriptive* and the correspondent theory of 'truth': words do not only describe, they are also part of *doing* an action. For example, the idea of saying 'I do' as part of a traditional marriage ceremony is to enter into a contract of marriage. The words help seal the contract and are part of *performing* a marriage. This helps Austin to question an assumption that philosophers had made for too long "that the business of a 'statement' can only be to 'describe' some state of affairs, or to 'state some fact', which it must do either truly or falsely" (Austin, 1975, p 1).

At the same time marriage can be seen as performative in a different sense, as people are aiming to live out idealised cultural images of what is expected of them. People have questioned the traditional subordination expected of women as expressed in their vows to 'obey' their husbands and have sought more egalitarian formulations. While some feminists have sought to challenge the institution of marriage itself, others have sought to remake it. Some have sought to create their own ceremonies and have found their own words in which to express their commitment to each other, in both heterosexual and gay relationships. For some it has meant conforming to a tradition they have inherited, while for others it means *creating* new cultural forms in which they feel able to express their identities, love and trust in their relationship.

If women are 'gendered' by social processes from birth to adulthood they are likely to carry certain symbolic images of marriage they have inherited from family and culture. Young women may have to confront difficult emotions within themselves, as they question expectations that they have been brought up to take for granted. They might want to perform their femininity in different ways, but realise that this will bring them into conflict with significant others in their families. But there are also generational shifts with a 21st-century post-feminist generation turning again towards the large, public wedding ceremonies that their parents' generation had rejected. This is not a voluntaristic vision in which women and men are free to choose their gender identities and commitments but there are cultural shifts marked by a return to ritual and the public performance of marriage vows, in both straight and gay relationships, that an older generation might never have anticipated. People might have to try new ways of behaving which in the beginning can feel awkward as they try to embody new gendered or sexed identities, but which they get used to as they repeatedly perform these behaviours. We might discover *how* feelings follow behaviour as people learn to relate differently both with themselves and with others.

This is a complexity that Butler finds hard to illuminate, even though she wants to explore the implications of Simone de Beauvoir's insight that "one is not born a woman" but *becomes* a woman. It is this process of *becoming* that is not caught in the notion of gender as performative, of gender being achieved through a constant iteration, although a sense of the difficulties people can face in choosing to live their gender identities differently is expressed when Butler says that:

> performativity ... is not a singular 'act' or event, but a ritualised production, a ritual reiterated under and through constraint, under and through the force of prohibition and taboo, with the threat of ostracism and even death controlling and compelling the shape of the production, but not, I will insist, determining it fully in advance. (Butler, 1990, p 95)

The ways in which boys and girls learn to 'do gender' involves more than a process of conscious learning and instruction. Often, what is expected of them is never put into words, but they somehow learn what gender expectations others carry for them. The fact that traditionally girls are expected to help their mothers in the kitchen to prepare food, while boys are allowed to go out to play marks out gender differences that can still be taken for granted. This gendered division of labour does not need to be explained, as men learn that the kitchen is 'not their place'; that they traditionally have no business in this space. If girls question this order of things, they might be punished for asking questions that cannot be tolerated. They might be told that they are 'rude', 'naughty' or even 'evil' for voicing such a question, since it proves they do not know their place.

When Butler discusses how the subject, as she frames it, engages in 'gender as performance', she draws on an impersonalised language. She gives an account of the 'girling' of a new-born baby when its gender is declared by the doctor and suggests we should "ask after the conditions of (the subject's) emergence and operation":

> Consider the medical interpellation which … shifts an infant from an 'it' to a 'she' or a 'he', and in that naming; the girl is 'girled', brought into a domain of language and kinship through the interpellation of gender. But that 'girling' of the girl does not end there. (Butler, 1990, p 7)

With different family relations it can mean quite *different* things for girls to be 'brought into a domain of language and kinship' and quite different expectations can follow within different cultural settings. When Butler says that "Subjected to gender, but subjectivated by gender, the 'I' neither precedes nor follows the process of this gendering, but emerges only within and as the matrix of gender relations themselves" (p 7) we must be careful about the instrumental form of the process of language. We can welcome the insight that the 'I' does not precede nor follow the process of this gendering, but emerges only within, but remain sceptical about "the matrix of gender relations themselves". Often, new parents, especially those who have assumed that gender is 'socially constructed', are surprised to discover how much their children bring with them at birth. Of course children are shaped by parental and cultural expectations and by how they are treated and related to, but there is a significant sense in which they come with personalities of their own, and early parenting involves learning how to develop a responsive relationship with another being who is also gendered (see Benjamin, 1990, 1998).

These are difficult notions that help us to question the dichotomy that gender is either given or else is socially constructed. Often parents of first children are so identified with them that it can be difficult to appreciate the qualities they bring themselves. It is when parents realise how different a second child is, that they can be forced to question cultural assumptions that separate too categorically and completely 'nature' from 'nurture'. Social theory has found it difficult to engage effectively with psychoanalysis, partly because it has classically been tied to this sharp Enlightenment distinction between nature and culture. It is not enough to acknowledge differences of temperament and personality, we must also appreciate the *qualities* that children need the freedom to express in their lives. This is part of realising that we must respect others in their individuality, not simply in Kantian terms as rational selves.

As our daughter Lily was born and named by the midwives as a girl we were struck that the names that we had prepared for her did not seem to fit. This is not as unusual an experience as it sounds if you interview other new parents. It took many days for us to settle on the appropriate name and this partly involved 'getting to know' *who* Lily was through developing a relationship with her. This is a personal naming that Butler does not appear to address because it involves a process of recognition of personal qualities that cannot be illuminated in the impersonal/rationalist language she invokes. We need a recognition of identity as a process that can recognise that the 'I' does not precede nor follow the process of gendering, but should also acknowledge tensions between the cultural interpellations of gender and the emotional, mental and spiritual needs of children themselves.

Psychoanalytic theory teaches us about the different stages that infants go through in forming a sense of 'I', and Freud illuminates the relationship between bodily emotions and the formation of an 'ego' (Freud, 1977). This is part of a development process that can be disturbed in diverse ways. Gender is part of this process, but it does not exist separately. When babies are born with an unclear gender identity, doctors have traditionally operated to ensure that they can define themselves as either male or female according to their sexual organs. At Great Ormond Street Hospital in London, around 15 operations on children born with both male and female sexual organs are carried out annually. At birth, such infants' external genitalia usually look ambiguous: "not really female and definitely not male". According to Dr Peter Hindmarsh, deciding on the gender in which to raise an intersex child is problematic: "It depends on what's inside: you usually find a uterus, fallopian tube and an overy, so it's usually easier to rear the infant as a girl" (quoted in the *Jewish Chronicle*, 4 August 2000, p 25).

To illustrate the cultural complexities of unclear gender identities, we turn to the story of Sarah-Jane Brookes who was born a hermaphrodite – a chomosomal mix-up gave her one ovary and one testicle, neither of which has ever worked. As others have made her painfully aware, her overall appearance sends out conflicting messages too. She challenges us to imagine what it feels to be hermaphrodite:

> How would you feel if you had been born like me? How would you feel if you were ridiculed, hated, abused even, for something over which you have no control? I just wish people would try to understand. I am a human being too. (quoted in the *Jewish Chronicle*, 4 August 2000, p 25)

She explains her own feelings thus:

> As far as I'm concerned, I am a woman and always will be but, at the same time, I know that I have a masculine appearance. I want to behave as a normal woman and wear short skirts but, because of the looks I get, I don't. Most of the time, I hide beneath a baggy sweatshirt and jeans, even that prompts curiosity. (p 25)

Within a patriarchal culture that can be fearful of gender and sexual ambivalence and uncertainty there is often an insistence on a dualism between male and female. Transgender identities become difficult to recognise and acknowledge, and the decisions that young people might want to make about their transgender lives are often taken away from them. This fear may be projected as blame and rejection on the abjected other who does not fit into the categories that we learn to take for granted. This is not simply a matter of Butler's 'gender as performance'. As Sarah-Jane explains, "Sometimes it just gets too much. Occasionally, I just can't get up in the morning, and there was a time when I used to cover all my mirrors so I wouldn't have to physically confront myself" (p 25).

Having a sexually ambiguous appearance is made even more complex because her chromosomal balance affects, as Karen Glaser puts it, "not just the shell, but the very core of her being". As Sarah-Jane describes it:

I have a male way of thinking and a female way of thinking. It's a chemical imbalance which means I'm at constant war with myself. The female side is much stronger, but sometimes it can be knocked sideways be maleness. (p 25)

She is concerned to distinguish her condition from that of the transsexual, where the person emotionally feels himself or herself to belong to the opposite sex: "As dreadful as being transsexual must be, you can at least have a sex change and bring your body in line with your mind" (p 25).

Explaining how her own confusion manifests itself, wanting to help people understand her situation she says:

I am a woman who longs to be with a man and, for example, if a female friend is hurt, I become very protective towards her, as any other woman might. But, as I seek to protect and comfort her, my male side can rush to the surface and my feelings for my friend transmute into sexual attraction. It's a horrendous feeling and, even though I always manage to control my male impulses, every time it happens I feel sick. (p 25)

Recently, her mother, who had been a rather distant figure, told her daughter that she was Jewish. Although initially shocked, Sarah-Jane's Judaism has become an important part of her identity and illustrates the importance of acknowledging the complexity of embodying identities. As she puts it: "This religion is my life-preserver. Because of the way I was born, I used to find it difficult to believe in God, but not any more" (p 25). Rabbi Mark Solomon hopes that she will find acceptance and respect as the courageous woman she has proven herself to be. As he explains in the article:

In the modern world, many of us have to struggle with ourselves and our society to establish a religious, cultural or sexual identity, but Sarah-Jane's struggle is exceptional and more difficult than most. At every turn, she has had to contend with mistaken assumptions, misunderstandings and prejudice. (p 25)

After identities

As poststructuralisms lose their grip and we recognise a need to rework a relationship between language and experience, we also recognise the limits of language as we learn to *listen* to different layers and levels of embodied experience. This creates a different sense of human agency as people learn to trust their own embodied identities. As we more fully recognise how feminisms and ecology have fundamentally questioned an Enlightenment modernity and the forms of social theory that have been formed through categorical distinctions between nature and culture, we learn to think across those boundaries. We learn how to recognise emotions and feelings as forms of embodied knowledge and how to name the histories and cultural inheritances that we need to come to terms with if they are not to produce future hauntings. We shape understanding of embodying and complex identities and how they are variously distributed across time and space.

Further reading

Globalised new capitalism

For some reflections on how a post-1989 world has been shaped through globalisation and market relationships that has begun to be challenged in the emergence of a multi-polar world with the rise of China, India and Brazil see, for instance, Zygmunt Bauman's *Globalization* (1998); Alberto Melucci, *The playing self* (1996a); Richard Sennett's *Uses of disorder* (1996); and Paul Heelas, Scott Lash and Paul Morris, *Detraditionalization* (1996).

Robert Putnam's *Bowling alone* (2001) has provoked widespread discussion about shifts in the moral culture of new capitalism. For other reflections on the changing nature and appeal of collective actions, see Alberto Melucci (1996b) *Challenging codes* and Jeremy Seabrook (1988) *The race for riches.*

Secular values, religious traditions

For some interesting discussions on the changing relationship between the secular and the religious that has been framed within a post-9/11 world see, for instance, An-Na'im (1992) *Human rights in cross-cultural perspectives*; Barber (1995) *Jihad vs McWorld*; Borradori (2003) *Philosophy in a time of terror*; Seidler (2007b) *Urban fears and global terrors.*

Relationships between humans and nature

Historical investigations into the relationships between humans and nature and their implications for gender relations of power and subordination are offered by Caroline Merchant (1982) *The death of nature*;Victor Seidler (1993) *Unreasonable men*;Val Plumwood (1993) *Feminism and the mastery of nature.*

Risk society

For some helpful reflections on risks and the ways they influence and shape contemporary identities and produce cultures of fear see, for instance, Ulrich Beck's *The risk society* (1992) and *The brave new world of work* (2000);Appadurai's *Modernity at large* (1996) and his edited *Globalization* (2001).

Control and domination of nature

Reflections on notions of progress as involving the control and domination of nature and the ways this has shaped notions of identity in relation to nature are developed in Brian Easlea's *Science and sexual oppression* (1981); S. Clarke's *The nature of the beast* (1982); Mary Midgeley's *Beast and man* (1979) and *Animals and why they matter* (1983); and Peter Dickens' *Society and nature* (2004). See also Merchant (1982), Naess (1989), Haraway (1991), Mies and Shiva (1993) and Franklin (2002).

Externalised relationship

I have explored how a Protestant moral culture can work paradoxically to encourage people to establish an externalised relationship with self in *Recreating sexual politics* (Seidler, 1991b).

TWELVE

Spaces: virtual worlds / technologies / globalisation

This chapter looks at how identities are shaped through new technologies and virtual spaces, so framing anew forms of embodied experience and possible forms of resistance. Engaging with globalised new capitalisms, it explores anxieties and possibilities for global change and personal transformation.

Virtual spaces

People today growing up with new technologies learn to take virtual spaces for granted. These become spaces in which they can explore various identities and test emotions and feelings. They are spaces in which people can explore fantasies and assume diverse identities that they might never be able to articulate within their normal everyday lives. For example, a young woman working in e-commerce might decide to present herself as a hospital consultant as she engages in a relationship with a woman who presents herself as an American. This is one of the plot lines in the BBC television programme 'Attachments', which imaginatively explored life and relationships in an e-commerce company. In the world of 'Attachments' to be 30 is already to be 'past it' and allegiances *shift* as people present themselves as loyal to the current grouping while at the same time being constantly on the look out for promotions and better stock options.

The young woman in 'Attachments' involves herself in a virtual relationship in which she can explore and take initiatives in her lesbian desire. They engage in cyber-sex as a distraction in the office, although she also insists on a certain level of privacy for the relationship; she only reveals what she is ready to let others know. This is a relationship that has become sexualised and explicit so there are ways that these women come to know each other. It comes as a shock when, later, the American woman is in town and asks for a meeting; anxieties come to the surface as she discovers that she is about to meet a woman in a bar whom she has 'had sex with', but whom she has never met face to face. They have had a personal relationship but it has taken place in a *virtual space*. When they meet, the American woman admits that she was not from America but assumed that identity to protect her current relationship in England. She felt safer exploring a new sexual relationship as an American. As they decide to embark on their sexual relationship in person, both women have to admit that they are not who they claimed to be after all. At some level the fantasies give way to a reality that can be difficult to deal with.

When the two women arranged to meet they were entering from one reality into another. In virtual space where you are able to move with ease across diverse boundaries of space and identities there appears to be little distinction between truth and falsehood, and identities can be performed as a matter of will. It was generally acknowledged that within the postmodern culture of the office in 'Attachments' there was little space for morality and that morals were something that you readily manipulated for your own advantage. This provided opportunity for yet another means of experimentation in virtual space where you might well escape the demand of traditional moralities. Morality becomes a matter of *self-presentation* in which you can readily change your views; identity becomes something that you manipulate and change in particular situations. Integrity is again something that is not fixed in relation to given identities, but becomes an aspect of identity that you can assume if it fits with your purposes.

At some level, this presentation of life in 'Attachments' portrays relationships as conditional since you can never trust anyone but yourself. There are people whom you have to trust to achieve a particular task, but the relationship remains conditional. You might have old friends with whom you share some history, but otherwise you feel that you must be constantly on your guard. You are careful not to reveal too much to others. It is easier if you do not have any deep commitments that might get in the way and threaten identities that you have to produce for the moment. Rather, you learn, as Baudrillard puts it, to 'live on the surface', always ready to *shift* your image so that it is appropriate to the situation in which you find yourself. This requires a constant willingness to change and adapt to prevailing fashions. In the new capitalism and celebrity culture you learn to judge people according to the property and power they have; the image you sustain seems to matter above all.

It is in virtual spaces that you can test out new identities and also where you might be able to explore ideas and emotions that you are no longer able to express in everyday life. The internet can provide a kind of virtual unconscious in which you can move across boundaries and explore desires and fears. This is living in a different reality, like when the lights go down in the cinema and you can explore unconscious fantasies through the figures on the screen. As darkness falls in the cinema so you can enter a different world in which you can identify with lives you could not know yourself. Within these unconscious spaces of fantasy you can imagine diverse possibilities and feel diverse fears.

Families / new connections

In the West young people today have grown up in a different, more globalised world than the world their parents knew. This can make them feel estranged from the ways their parents think and feel. In part this is related to the changing place of technologies in people's lives, with computers and the internet working as sources of knowledge and virtual spaces in which new identities and relationships are shaped. These new technologies challenge traditional authorities and their claims to exclusive knowledge as people gain access through the internet to knowledges that would not have previously been accessible to them. This can offer people a sense of control through the information that they can find for themselves without having to rely on the authority of particular expertise. For instance, the internet has challenged traditional medical power as patients no longer feel the same deference to doctors and will often come to consultations having already searched for information pertaining to their conditions. Not only does this mean that people can be more informed themselves but it encourages them to *question authorities* in ways their parents might never have done. Of course, with so much information there is a risk that people might misinterpret what they have read or provide it with a context that is not relevant, and this can create new difficulties in communication with people in positions of expertise and authority, such as doctors.

Young people in particular can feel empowered by the information that is available to them on the internet and the speed with which new forms of knowledge are made available. But this can also create its own *disconnection* between what they can know as information and, say, what they can do for themselves in their own basic reading and writing. This can lead to frustration because they have grown accustomed to information being immediately available to them. As computers have become faster there is greater immediacy and less of a time lag between questions and answers. Young people increasingly expect that answers will flow automatically and they can feel tense and uneasy when they confront questions of value that cannot be so easily settled. Because of this, some young people have become disillusioned with technology and what it has to offer and by their early teenage years turn towards philosophy and questions of value and aesthetics that engage them in different ways. The rise in popularity of philosophy since the turn of the millennium has been a global phenomenon that may indicate a search for deeper values and relationship with self than postmodern theories that dispense with notions of self as 'constructions' will allow.

The disjunction young people can feel between the power offered by the internet and the ease of communication on social networks such as Facebook and the powerlessness and lack of communication they can still experience at home and at school can be difficult to tolerate. Children who have grown up in prosperous suburbs, particularly those with working parents, might feel as if their parents have provided for their material needs but at the cost of absenting themselves from their children's lives (Hochschild, 1997). Often children are told that they have 'everything they could possibly want', which makes it difficult for children to *name* their need for more loving contact with their parents, but this is what they are denied in families in which both partners are heavily identified with their work. Sometimes the home is considered a space of emotional chaos and disorder that both parents long to escape for the ordered routines of the workplace. Children are not satisfied with the 'quality time' they are offered because they want more time than their parents are able to give, but they can be made to feel selfish and ungrateful if they make these time demands as if they should appreciate that their parents are only working these long hours to provide for their families.

Middle-class children can feel that their lives are being *administered* as they are shifted from one after-school activity to the next. They are left with relatively little time for themselves to explore their own needs and desires, even if they are offered choices between different possible activities. They are either looked after by poor women, often migrants from the global South, or else left for hours with the TV as their childminder. They become hooked on TV programmes that create their own forms of dependency. It is hardly surprising when young people grow up to hate television and turn to the internet as a world that they can at least shape in their own image. They escape into a virtual world that their parents know little about and in this way can express the silent rage they so often feel for their parents' absence in their lives. While parents 'escape' into work, so young people escape into virtual worlds of their own. To understand the different levels of unexpressed feelings and emotions in modern family life we need new social theories that can illuminate different levels of experience and move beyond the terms of social construction.

Often different family members live in quite distinct and separate worlds that rarely overlap with each other. People have different schedules so families rarely meet around the dinner table, and parents and children heat up their individualised meals in the microwave. As people rarely eat together, the family ceases to come together on a daily basis. Rather the family becomes individualised, as it becomes fragmented and people realise that they know relatively little about what is going on in the lives of others. This might be why the rituals around Thanksgiving and Christmas in the US assume such significance. They reinvent the myth of family life that has long disappeared in reality. This idealisation of the 'American family' remains a powerful cultural myth that conceals the reality of widespread divorce and separation. It refuses to recognise the processes of individualisation that leave many people choosing to live alone (see also Chapter Eleven).

Children become accustomed to these dishonesties as they recognise just how identified their parents can be with their work lives. It is not that family has ceased to be important to them, but it is easier for their parents if they can live administered lives at home. Parents are often so tired coming home from work that they do not want to have to deal with their children's feelings of isolation or depression. Having become used to their own feelings of aloneness within the family, they can find it difficult to respond to their children's demands for more contact. They can insist that their children 'have no reason' to feel lonely or depressed thereby invalidating their experience as they silence them. Children will often be made to feel that they are being 'selfish' or 'ungrateful' so will learn to keep their own counsel. They will look for other sources of contact, possibly through social network sites on the internet, or through chat rooms in which they can share more of their experience with other young people. They might connect to their friends on MSN so creating a supportive world for themselves in new technological spaces outside of the family.

Conflict and violence

Michael Moore's film 'Bowling for Columbine' explores the mid-West United States, where, in 1999, a major school shooting took place that shocked the country. Two young students came into school fully armed and shot and killed 12 school students and one teacher. One girl tells how she begged them not to shoot her as they shot a friend close to her. She also said how they shot someone just because they were black. In his film, Moore does not focus on the family lives of these young people because he does not want to pathologise them as individuals, rather he is concerned to show how this violence reflects a larger history and culture of violence in the US. He is struck by how the shootings at Columbine took place only hours after one of the heaviest US bombings in Kosovo; he also makes a connection with the local armaments factories where many people are employed. He wonders why there is comparatively little gun violence in Canada even though there are also many guns. He concludes that, lacking global power, Canadians have a history of encouraging negotiation when there are situations of conflict. In the US there appears to be a culture of shooting first and asking questions later. If there is conflict there is always an enemy who needs to be destroyed so that good can supposedly prevail.[1]

As noted above, within modern family life it can be difficult to name the sources of conflict. Instead there is often an elaborated psychological language that is available for parents and children to talk themselves out of conflict. People *talk about* the need to be respectful of one another and to give time to one another, at the same time as their work schedules mean they have no time to make themselves available. Somehow the language can work to silence and smooth over conflicts that are rarely identified and talked about openly, rather there is a belief that all conflict is 'negative' and so to be avoided at any cost. Children are told not to raise their voices and can be taught that anger is a 'negative' emotion. Therapeutic language has shaped a common-sense culture in the US that has paradoxically worked to make it harder to identify and deal with sources of conflict.

Possibly it is this tension, which cannot otherwise be expressed, that explodes from underneath every so often. Young people, having withdrawn from contact within their families, can sometimes shape oppositional identities in virtual realities that can sustain them also in school. The two boys who were responsible for the shootings at Columbine, Eric and Dylan, had assumed Goth identities and wore long trenchcoats to school. They were loners who used to listen to Marilyn Manson music; they kept themselves apart from other young people at the school who did not seem to know them. It was as if they were rejected for being freaks – for *being different* – within a culture that supposedly appreciates individual differences but which also forces a sharp sense of conformity. It is only certain kinds of differences that are deemed acceptable; you are expected to accept the norms of the school community and, in the case of Columbine, the hegemony of the sporting elites who were officially honoured. Eric and Dylan felt rejected by the prevailing school culture and grew to hate the school jocks who patronised and disdained them. Somehow, the school jocks came to represent what the school stood for to Eric and Dylan, so everyone at the school was deemed equally responsible for sustaining this regime. It was evil and it needed to be destroyed.

As President Bush was to famously declare in the aftermath of 9/11 when talking about the relationship of the US with other countries 'you are with us or against us' in this 'war against terrorism'. To ask questions about the possible causes of terrorism or to seek questions about the sources of a particular tendency within radical Islam, let alone to question why the US could be so hated that people were prepared to take such violent actions against the country, was already to be defined as 'soft on terrorism'. It was to put you beyond the pale of acceptable discussion. For months after 9/11, anyone asking questions was considered 'suspect' and you were to be approached with caution. Somehow this enemy had to be named and war had to be declared against it for this was supposedly the only way that the 'enemy could be defeated'.

Although it might seem strange to make the connection between Columbine and 9/11, it is this dualistic vision – 'you are with us or against us' – that was also at work in these young people's minds. They had also grown up with a culture of violence in which you cannot hope to reason with your enemy because violence has become the only language that people can understand. Somehow, in the paranoid perception of these young minds, their fellow school pupils had become the 'enemy' that needed to be destroyed, even if they would have to kill themselves in the process. And they had come to believe that the price was worth paying. They also knew that they would be assured fame within a celebrity culture that has come to value fame almost above any other value. They would prove that they were not 'good-for-nothing nobodies', but that they counted for something. The world would know their names.

In Britain there are related issues concerning young men and schooling, raised in the gendered arguments about the underachievement and exclusion of working-class boys in school (as discussed in Chapter Nine; see also Seidler, 2006). Here, issues of class have come together with issues of gender, 'race' and ethnicities. But, we must also acknowledge and understand how boys learn to shape their language through the control of emotions they feel unable to share with others. Often boys carry psychic pain they feel *unable* to express because it will further diminish their masculinity in their own eyes. They grow up feeling that they should be able to control their emotions and that it is a sign of weakness to talk about their fears and depression (see also Chapter Eight). They do not want to be a burden on others and they assume that others will just not be able to understand what they are going through. They learn to be careful about what aspects of themselves they can show and often they do not want to know what they are feeling themselves. Often there is an uneasy silence as boys *withdraw* into themselves, unable to reach out for the support that they need. It is hard enough knowing that you are depressed, much worse if you talk about it because you just risk further rejection from your friends.

New technologies of communication

Young men from diverse backgrounds often pride themselves in their skills in relation to computers and new technologies. It can provide them with a sense of competence that they can feel missing in other areas of their lives. Often they will use their mobile phones as a way of showing to others the *control* they have over their lives, whereas for young girls mobile phones are more often used as a means of staying in contact with each other. Since boys grow up feeling they should not need contact and that is a sign of weakness, they often identify with the notion they could contact others, *if* they wanted to. Rather, the mobile phone can represent their control over time, since it shows that there is always something that you need to do; it shows you are in demand.

In other ways mobile phones can also threaten a young man's feeling of independence and self-sufficiency, for it can seem as if your parents can always contact you wherever you are. As adults, on the one hand, men who have traditionally withdrawn into 'male spaces' such as the pub, can feel that a mobile phone means that at any moment their partners can call to find out where they are and when they are getting home. This can make it more difficult for men to create spaces of their own, in which they can remain undisturbed. They may feel as if they are always at the 'beck and call' of their partners. On the other hand, the mobile phone can encourage men to develop new habits of staying in touch with their families. They might discover that they enjoy communication that they had formerly avoided.

Sometimes it is in 'face to face' contact that men can find it difficult to express their emotions and feelings to others. They can feel uneasy with more direct forms of communication, partly because they have grown up to believe that it is fine for women to have emotions but that men are not supposed to have them, so that expressing emotions somehow *proves* their inadequacy. Men can sometimes feel that they have to *conceal* their inner emotional lives, even from themselves (see Chapter Eight). They often learn to silence their emotions because they can feel threatened by their fears and vulnerability. They learn to keep their silence and thereby keep their 'cool'.

This explains why some men find it easier to communicate on the internet than in person. The large number of cyber-suicide spaces shows that young men can often express themselves emotionally when they do not have to speak directly. Evidence from the Samaritans shows that young men often feel more comfortable about sending an email that expresses very directly their depressive and suicidal feelings, emotions that they would find it very hard to express over the phone. As you write an email you are not faced with a personal interaction in which others can also see or hear your reactions. Instead you are sitting alone in front of the screen and, in some way, this can be like being alone with yourself even though you are engaged in communicating with others. It can be the very *impersonality* of the contact with the screen that allows for a more personal expression. The screen can provide an equivalent to the silence of the analyst within the analytical encounter. People feel free to express some of their loneliness and suicidal feelings that they would never be able to express to their family, or even their friends. They might give voice to a desperation they feel they have to hide from their mates, because it would threaten their male identities.

Somehow giving voice and *speaking* your distress to others, even over the phone, seems to carry a different weight than writing an email and then sending it off. You do not have to connect personally so there can appear to be much less at stake. It can also give you a sense of freedom allowing you to explore emotions, even if you are uncertain about them, which could feel much too *risky* when you are facing others, or speaking to them on the phone. On the computer, however, there is a different ordering of experience, as you communicate with others who cannot *see* who you are.

Sometimes technology can be enabling by providing a seemingly neutral space in which people can explore their emotional lives. In chat rooms they can find people who are dealing with similar issues, say, drugs problems or eating disorders. This can help break an isolation which leaves many young men (and young women) feeling that others can only know the front which they give to the world, not what they are suffering in silence emotionally. Often there is a sharp discontinuity between the masculinities which young men learn to present in public and what they are feeling internally, which they often cannot even *name* for themselves. Sometimes men want to believe that the front, the performance, is the reality of their identities and that the insecurities they live with emotionally are weaknesses that they have to master. They cannot allow others to *know* about their inner emotional lives because it would give them a reason to reject them and they would be left feeling even more lost and alone.

Mobile phones can allow young men to present an image of themselves as being in contact with others; you are never alone with your phone, because at any moment you could choose to contact someone. In this way the phone can serve as a form of emotional reassurance for young men who might otherwise fear isolation and loneliness. Even if they rarely do contact others, they know that they *could*. Often, as they speak on the phone, they enter a 'different space' as there is a privatisation of otherwise public space. Young men can be turned into themselves as they can bodily reject the social world around them, even if only for a moment. They can show to the world that they have friends and that their lives are meaningful. In this way technologies can help young men to *perform* their masculinities and so sustain an image of male identity in front of their peers. Sometimes it can play a different role in their lives as they often learn to use their new technologies in gendered ways to affirm their male identities.

Media and power

Dennis Potter once explained that he wrote for TV rather than the theatre because only television offered the possibility of a 'common culture'. It provided a common space in which people of all classes and generations experienced the same event simultaneously and could talk about it the next morning. But technological developments in transmission are expected to undermine this aspiration as viewing becomes a more fragmented and isolated experience. In this envisaged world individuals will increasingly be able to choose what they want to see and when. It will only be the dramatic news event – the sudden death of a princess, 9/11 or the London bombings for example – which will have the power to unite an audience.

However, Nick Bateman's confrontation for breaking the rules in the first series of 'Big Brother', Channel 4's house-share elimination programme, the internet – frequently predicted as the killer of the common culture – offered a shared viewing experience that gripped a vast national population. According to Mark Lawson's piece 'So, where were you when Nasty Nick was kicked out of "Big Brother"?':

People in homes and offices unable to receive broadcasts on the internet kept up with developments in the house through email and mobile phones. Technology expected to divide and isolate was unifying people around the media phenomenon of the summer of 2000. (Lawson, 2000, p 2)

Through use of the live web transmission, a significant moment of popular television – the rumbling of Nick Bateman – was remarkable for being the first of the television's high points not actually to have occurred on TV. As Lawson has it:

It is the first television hit in which the scheduled transmission is almost incidental to the effect.... By the time Nick's departure is seen in conventional form – on Friday's edition of Big Brother – it will seem second-hand to many viewers. This is a remarkable change in the nature of what it means to watch TV. (pp 2-3)

We also need to recognise the limits of technology because, as Lawson reminds us:

Nick's ostracism could have marked the coming of age of Internet broadcasting, but in the event, this was not the case. Like an impotent bridegroom, the world-wide web is always let down at the potentially sweetest moments by the equipment. The infuriating message 'web congestion'... frequently interrupted coverage. (p 3)

Putting the event in some perspective, Lawson recognises that:

The shaming of Bateman wasn't remotely equivalent in cultural significance to the shooting of Kennedy or the death of Diana, but it marks a stage in the technology of television revelation. JFK died on amateur celluloid. Diana died on live 24-hour television, Nasty Nick was nixed on the net, a day before you'll see it on the set. (p 3)

Kathryn Flett, in her piece 'TV's theatre of cruelty', attempted to place the appeal of Channel 4's Big Brother in context by arguing that it had all the lurid appeal of a ghastly car crash when we cannot resist looking back even though we have decided not too. According to Flett:

It has been a cruel summer, a season of media witch hunts and the opportunistic exploitation of 'ordinary people', of fake intimacy and knee jerk emotional outpourings: emotional porn. The empathetic coverage that accompanied the death of Sarah Payne turned swiftly to troubling old-fashioned retribution; the casually curious, channel-hopping Big Brother viewers turned into a placard-waving mob. Perhaps in a cynical society that doesn't quite know what to believe in anymore, where 'truth' so often comes loaded with spin, Reality TV is simply, inevitably, further blurring the boundaries between life and the game show. (*The Observer*, 20 August 2000, p 15)

If there is some truth in this assessment there is also a tendency towards generalisation. We have to recognise how people are looking towards the media in part to reflect the tensions and uncertainties in their own lives. If it is true that there is a widespread uncertainty in relation to values, there is also a questioning of traditional values that have been handed down. Within the terms of new democratic cultures and with the *circulation* of images and knowledges that have historically been carefully controlled by authorities, people feel more entitled to have their voices heard. They have access to communication through new technologies that have radically transformed the relationships that people can have with one another. The ways in which people's identities are entwined within these new technologies is a central concern within postmodern cultures. In part what we are witnessing is the development of new democratic identities that are searching for new forms of expression.

New media and imagination

Almost 20 years ago, British scientist Tim Berners-Lee wrote the electronic code that enables computers across the world to 'talk' to each other down a telephone line. From a single website, the worldwide web has grown to transform the ways we can live and relate. Interviewed on the tenth anniversary of the creation of the internet, Berners-Lee commented that we are "just scratching the surface" of what the internet can do: "The web is far from done. Just imagine that you were back in the Middle Ages and somebody asked 'Given the full impact that paper is going to have, where will we be?' That's where we are" (quoted in *The Observer*, 8 October 2000, p 15).

Berners-Lee also dismissed fears over paedophiles targeting youngsters in web chat rooms and racist sites on the internet. Although he agrees that illegal material like child pornography and 'video nasties' should remain illegal, Berners-Lee believes that you cannot banish technology or regulate content:

> Regulation is censorship – one grown up telling another what they can and cannot do or see. For me, the idea is horrific. Universality is the key. You must be able to represent anything on the web … the world is a diverse place and we should trust people, not try to police them.… There are many cultures and they are continually changing.… So any attempt to make a global centralised standard is going to be unbelievably contentious. You can't do that. (quoted in *The Observer*, 8 October 2000, p 15)

Tim Berners-Lees argues that instead of regulation it is up to parents to 'catch up' so that they can teach young people how to use the web safely: "They need to catch up so they can teach their children what to see and what to avoid" (p 15).

We must be careful, however, about the confusion we often make within a postmodern culture between *information* and *knowledge*. The fact that children have so much information available to them does not mean that they are more knowledgeable or more creative. The rush to computerise education could result in stunting children's intelligence, creativity and social skills, and these are the very competences that a postmodern culture relies on. The Alliance for Childhood in the United States produced a research paper 'Fool's gold: A critical look at computers in childhood' (Alliance for Childhood, 2000), which was particularly damning of software packages marketed for very young children. According to Bob McCannon, a US literacy expert: "Reading involves concentration, attention span, enjoyment of detail and some level of inspiration. To this date we haven't seen any software that accelerates that and there is a tremendous amount that detracts from it" (quoted in *The Observer*, 24 September 2000, p 14).

Within a postmodern culture there is an acceleration of experience that can affect capacities for attention. Some might argue that what is lost in attention is gained in a capacity to switch between different sources of information. My children's generation seem to consider switching between channels on the television as a kind of second nature and they can stretch their attentions across a range of different internet sites at the same time. They seem to be able to switch attention almost immediately; often they can even be watching more than one programme at once. But the capacity to give your attention to what you are reading is crucial to comprehension. It can allow you to delve into the text or the subject, rather than skim over the surface.

Again, we must be careful about generalisations. <u>Simone Weil</u> (1952) values *attention* and recognises the time it takes for children to develop their attention and so develop capacities to absorb whatever texts they are reading. Iris Murdoch (1970) was influenced by Weil's concerns with attention and this helped shape her moral thinking about how we learn to give attention to people in relationships with them. She learns from Weil to recognise the ways we 'read' people in moral relations and so the conditions necessary for *developing* certain moral capacities and relationships.

We need to think about how an early exposure to computers can work to undermine a capacity for attention. According to Ewout Van Manen, special education coordinator and teacher in Forest Row, West Sussex:

> Computers are marvellous, but we don't need to bring children to them. Childhood takes time and each development stage happens at a specific time. You cannot rush it by putting a child in front of what is essentially a tool made for adults. Earlier is not necessarily better. (quoted in *The Observer*, 24 September 2000, p 14)

Recent educational reforms that have stressed the measurement of capacities at each stage of development have tended to ignore crucial differences between children. Each child has its own time and, as a parent, you can recognise that. Rather than fostering individuality and self-worth, we are reducing children to bearers of universal abilities. This marks a return to an Enlightenment rationalism that a Romantic tradition has long challenged in its appreciation that thinking *cannot be* separated from feeling, minds from bodies, reason from emotion. We tend to overlook the relational aspects of learning which Van Manen reminds us of when he states, "There is an aspect to education which disappears with computers – the connection between adults and children. A child learns best from a teacher, not a machine – that is the way they are designed" (quoted in *The Observer*, 24 September 2000, p 14).

Van Manen believes that computers may 'jump-start' analytical thinking prematurely, although this is a notion that we have lost in an educational culture too ready to assume that earlier has to mean better. As he explains:

> A small child needs physical action, direct experience, to develop the imagination and senses of space and time. If you give a child a mechanical digger, then all they can do is dig – if you give a child a cardboard box, they have to bring in their own imagination to finish the story and make out of it what they will. (p 14)

This is a challenging notion because it appreciates *how* senses of time and space are not given as Kantian categories, but must themselves develop through bodily experience and relationships. There is a recognition, to repeat, that "If you give a child a cardboard box, they have to bring in their own imagination. That's what computers can damage" (Van Manen, quoted in *The Observer*, 24 September 2000, p 14).

The emphasis on standards in English schools has tended to marginalise imagination and creativity, as if they have no connection with intellectual development. Young children have had their childhoods threatened as they are being tested within the educational system and marked as failures from the age of seven. Not only are young children being sent into formal education much earlier than in other European countries but they also have to deal with the *anxieties* of being constantly tested. A recent OECD report on childhood showed that children in Britain are the most tested in Europe, and are some of the unhappiest children in Europe. They are introduced to formal schooling at four years of age and education quickly becomes a series of hurdles they need to overcome. This can help shape an externalised relationship to learning and education so that later, at universities, students see their courses as a series of discrete tests they have to pass and can have little integrated sense of their disciplines.

Imagination

Prevailing modes of educational achievement often treat intellectual learning as if it were an independent and autonomous process. There is little sense of the connections between learning and imagination, knowledge and creativity. This tends to reduce the space in which children can explore their identities and develop a sense of self-worth and emotional security. There are ways in which creativity and imagination are the very qualities that are increasingly being acknowledged as crucial within globalisation, even though their values have been marginalised within state schooling in Britain.

In contrast, Singapore, for example, has recognised that it will need to reform the city's state educational culture if it is to help transform a nation of cautious followers into a nation of technophile, creative entrepreneurs (McNulty, 2000). Schools are aiming to develop more creative students who might eventually be able to take risks involved in the new globalised economy. Universities are also changing as they take account not only of tests but also student project work and interests in their admission procedures. The Singaporean government also hopes to transform the culture of work, through, for instance, encouraging people to take courses in how to solve problems creatively. It subsidises in order to prepare people at every level of industry for the new globalised economy in which creativity and initiative will be necessary qualities.

We can watch the transformation of educational systems in order to relate to the skills and capacities demanded by the new globalised economy. This has opened up new opportunities but it has also created new globalised relationships of power and subordination. Along with this has grown a transnational anti-globalisation resistance to the power of corporations, as we have witnessed in Seattle, London and Prague. There is a refusal to accept, as politicians in Britain have tended to do, that globalisation is a reality we have to live with. With this is a demand that we reflect on possibilities of new economic relationships that allow for a sustainable relationship with nature and which offer a sense of greater global justice between the global North and South.

Globalisation, power and new media

In a post-9/11 world, which fears radical Islamist groups and the potency of their threats to civilian populations, given their willingness to use terrorist methods to kill innocent citizens, there have been governments who have been ready to sacrifice human rights and democratic freedoms to protect their populations. After the bombings in Bali, Madrid and London, new landscapes of urban fear developed that threatened to curb freedoms of movement that people had taken for granted. There were also new restrictions on migrations across national borders imposed at the same time as citizens of the new Europe were able to travel more freely. As people began to *shape* new transnational identities and come to terms with their diverse inheritances and traumatic histories, they were also finding it difficult to defend multicultural politics that were being widely challenged and somehow held responsible for the alienation of young people prepared to attack their fellow citizens.

The emergence of the internet has provided a globalised space in which those who have access can communicate freely with each other. This has helped to shape new transnational identities and cosmopolitan identities, for it has allowed people to sustain contact across different global spaces. There was a hope that more democratic politics would be sustained as people had the opportunity to join in a global conversation. For a while at least the internet seemed free of the kinds of legal and business pressures that restrict more mainstream and broadcast media. But as Douglas Rushkoff has argued:

> The emergence of a new, interactive media space offers us an opportunity to redefine the very language of power. Sadly, our readiness to accept the tools we are given, in the form they are given, as well as the rules they come with, reduces our role to passive consumption, and threatens to end the digital revolution before it has even begun. (Rushkoff, 2000, p 14)

For a long time, the content and context of the media has served to maintain the *status quo* in each country. This explains why media centres have been the focus of revolutions in Eastern Europe in 1988 and in Belgrade in October 2000 and was at the centre of the attack on Baghdad that opened the war in Iraq in 2004. Struggles to control the media and new forms of communication were also central to the demonstrations that followed the disputed Iranian election in June 2009. The ability to dictate what we think about has been controlled to some extent by the people who decide the content of our media – which headlines will be printed and which stories will be covered. They have the power to influence *how* we think even if we may resist the overt meanings they seek to communicate. Those who have had power over the media could make it difficult for alternative voices to be heard and for different images to be seen.

Interactive media – from computers to camcorders, YouTube and mobile phones – have posed a threat to traditional media hegemonies. They have given people the ability to fill newspapers, web pages and even cable television channels with their own different stories, images and ideas; they have been able to send images and messages through mobile phones. Those worried about censorship of the new media have focused on government as the main threat to progress. They thwarted early efforts at limiting the spread of 'objectionable' content and sought to declare the internet beyond the province of any government agency. However, as Rushkoff recognises, "The problem with suppressing the role of government is that it gives business free reign.... As a result, the internet becomes a privatised zone, and altogether more insidious forms of censorship emerge" (2000, p 14).

Fears about hackers and internet porn encouraged a mass migration towards the internet safe havens with people believing that using a corporate branded ISP, such as BT or America Online, as their access provider somehow protects them from computer viruses. These users have simply succeeded in protecting themselves from the kinds of content that unseen corporate censors feel is dangerous. The conversion of a public telecommunications infrastructure into a privately controlled direct marketing platform transforms it into a territory where the only meaningful currency is money. As Rushkoff explains, "Ideas spread based on their ability to generate revenue, more than interest or thought" (2000, p 14). We can still value alternative spaces of resistance and question Rushkoff's pessimism when he states that "most forms of online activism concern issues of market" (2000, p 15). If Napster users were fighting, at least for a while until the site was closed down, for their right to distribute data that one of them has paid for, we must still think through the significance of such a consumer revolt before we conclude with Rushkoff: "It's a business angle, and the more it's fought for, the more like business people its advocates become" (2000, p 15).

However, Rushkoff is right to remind us that:

> On an even more fundamental level, the tools we use to navigate and even create the landscape of new media make many assumptions for us, of which we are increasingly unaware. The Internet's functional standards are set by companies like Microsoft, through processes that are anything but transparent.... Lest we forget, the Internet was a mediaspace before it was a marketplace. Now that monetary values are assigned to our online activities, there's much less room for alternative value systems to be entertained. (p 15)

Rushkoff is concerned that we realise that when artists use programmes like Adobe Photoshop to create graphics or Dreamweaver to design web pages they are indirectly censoring themselves. He reminds us that "computers are modelling systems, and that the market-driven internet is just one of the models they can create" (2000, p 15). We have to realise that the current media landscape has been assembled quite arbitrarily and it does not have to be this way and that many groups are working to create open access and new forms of open communication.

In *The age of access*, Jeremy Rifkin (2000) has argued that, with the spread of the internet and e-commerce, markets and lifestyles in the Western world are accelerating to such an extent that they are triggering a fundamental change in global capitalism. The ownership of physical property that was once the bulwark of capitalism is giving way as businesses are finding there is less of a profit margin in selling things. Rather than a one-off transaction lasting minutes, they want to establish a lifelong relationship with you, providing the car, the computer, or the house on a lease basis as an introductory transaction in a long stream of related goods and services: "Ford would rather never sell you a car again", Rifkin argues, "It would rather have you in its network, so that you continually buy the experience of driving rather than buying the vehicle. And the proof is in the pudding. The renewal rate on leasing is 54%. The renewal rate in market-based transactions is 25%" (quoted in *The Guardian 2*, 29 September 2000, p 4).

Julian Borger reports that 80% of US companies are now leasing some or all equipment rather than investing in ownership:

> Whereas old-style companies, such as General Motors, owned a lot of solid assets, the new industrial icons, such as Nike, own hardly anything in physical terms.... Its production is 'outsourced' – carried out by 'partners' in the developing world. Rifkin describes it as a 'virtual company'. Its assets are almost entirely cerebral – it is selling a concept and a lifestyle. (2000, p 4)

As Rifkin explains to Borger:

> eventually the nature of this technological revolution is leading us into an era where, by the mid part of the 21st century, market capitalism will have virtually disappeared. It will be there, but it will be only an appendage to a new network-based economy with access relations replacing property relations. (quoted in Borger, 2000, p 5)

At the same time we should not forget the young, mainly female, workers who are being paid exploitative wages to produce goods for companies such as Nike. Even if buyers and sellers do not come together to exchange property, it is the access that Nike offers to a globalised market that remains vital. We must be careful in thinking through the relations between 'property' and 'access' in a way that does not render invisible continuing relationships of exploitation of labour within a globalised economy. The fact that production takes place in China makes Nike no less responsible for the production relationships they rely on. Corporations can welcome a language of networks because they seem to shift issues of power and responsibility.

In words that may remind us of Marx's discussion of commodification in the early chapters of *Capital*, Rifkin explains that with all this packaging of lifestyles and experiences, everyday experiences once rooted in family and community, become a commodity that is sold back to us:

> You find virtually every activity you engage inside the family and outside the family is a paid-for commercial activity. We are commodified. We're moving from commodifying goods and services to commodifying culture. (quoted in Borger, 2000, p 5)

While corporations in the 19th and 20th centuries scoured the earth for mineral wealth and cash crops, mega-corporations like AOL-Time Warner search for cultures to 'mine' and turn into easily digestible experiences for their users to access. Thus 'ethnic' music is fused with rock to turn it into 'fusion', making it accessible while tearing it from its cultural roots:

> One of the messages here is that it's just as possible to deplete cultural diversity as it is biological diversity and physical resources. When you take a culture and homogenise it, transform it, package it and sell it back to people as a paid-for experience, then it is just as possible to deplete cultural diversity as biodiversity. And when you lose a culture to extinction it's just as final, you cannot get it back. (quoted in Borger, 2000, p 5)

There is an implicit challenge here to a kind of crude materialism, when Rifkin insists, somewhat starkly, that "commerce never precedes culture, culture always precedes commerce" (p 5). This is part of his challenge to third way politics that "thinks that if you can build a healthy economy which is compassionate, you'll build a healthy society". At some level this is also a critique of their acceptance of globalisation that has such disastrous effects on the integrity of cultures. In the face of the global financial crisis in 2009, governments have been forced to rethink their positions in relation to deregulated neo-liberal globalisation. They can hopefully listen to these concerns about democratic control and accountability as well as about cultural diversity and identities.

As Julian Borger explains, "Rifkin's remedy is to pay more attention to fostering culture, by promoting community-based education in an attempt to provide children with a deeper understanding of the world than computer screens alone can provide" (2000, p 5). This means encouraging forms of education that can also help young people appreciate the cultural identities they inherit. It is partly through honouring the pasts they carry into the present, that greater freedom can be created in the present. In part this involves developing a *critical* relationship with cultural traditions, say, where they sustain patriarchal and homophobic attitudes, as well as ecologically damaging capitalist developments. This also means questioning a rationalist modernity that assumes that it is through reason alone that progress can be assured as the control and domination of nature. We also need to create space for spiritual traditions as we revision relationships between nature and culture, identity and power. This involves appreciating what opportunities technologies have to bring, while also being ready to question the part they play in the education of transnational citizenship within a postmodern world and the reproduction of global inequalities and injustices.

As young people today feel empowered to create their own identities and can use the internet to explore diverse forms of transgender and sexed identities and use new technologies to find sources of support that might not be immediately available to them in their families or local communities, so they can shape new solidarities and points of resistance. People learn to live *across the boundaries* of different real and virtual spaces and they make connections that can sustain their identities and hopefully strengthen their engagements to transform the world into a more just and equal global space. However, there are also pressures of a neo-liberal globalised capitalism that can create its own insecurities and uncertainties about what the future might bring. Hopefully able to support each other emotionally a younger generation that assumes gender equality and a post-'race' liberal tolerance might be more literate emotionally while at the same time less able to contextualise their individual experiences, fears and uncertainties within the larger structural frameworks of global power and inequality.

As people learn to question some of their inherited rationalist traditions so they can also validate emotions and feelings as sources of knowledge and shape embodied identities for themselves. They might resist temptations to constantly 'speed up' when they can recognise that it makes their relationships with themselves and others more superficial than they would want them to be. This calls for an ecological postmodernism that remains sensitive to continuing inequalities and global injustices and which allows people to appreciate how their identities are formed across the boundaries of nature and culture, histories and futures, thinking and feeling.

Endnote

[1] See also Michael Moore's *Downsize this!* (1996) and *Stupid white men ... and other sorry excuses for the state of the nation!* (2002).

Further reading

New technologies

For some investigations into the ways new wired technologies are shaping new terms of consumer culture see, for instance, Michael Bull, *Sounds in the city* (2003); David Bell and Gill Valentine (eds) (1995) *Mapping desire*; and Nancy Duncan (ed) (1996) *Bodyspace*.

New capitalism

An interesting exploration of the pressures within new capitalism to remain fluid and adaptive and so wary of deeper beliefs and moral commitments that might stand in the way of winning the approval of those in the hierarchy who can make a difference to your future promotions is given in Richard Sennett's *The corrosion of character* (1998). See also reflections about personal life and ethics in Beck and Beck-Gersheim (1995) *The normal chaos of love*, and Thrift (2007) *Non-representational theory*.

Working parents

For some helpful reflections on the pressures of working parents within new capitalism and their desires to escape the chaos of home and family life for the relative order and control of office life see Arlie Hochschild (1997) *The time bind* and Hochschild and Machung (1998) *The second shift*.

Modern family life

For some helpful reflections on the changing nature and organisations of family and intimate relations see, for instance, Judith Stacey, *Brave new families* (1990) and *In the name of the family* (1996); Rubin (1994) *Families on the faultline*; Nardi (ed) (1999) *Gay men's friendship*; Probyn (1990) *Sexing the self*; and Bell (1999) *Belonging and perfomativity*.

9/11

For some helpful reflections on the impact of 9/11 on the US and its relationships with the rest of the world see, for instance, Butler (2004); and Seidler (2007b).

New democratic identities

For some interesting exploration of new democratic identities that are taking form within postmodern consumer cultures within a globalised world see, for instance, Seyla Benhabib (1996) *Democracy and difference*; Michael Keith (2006) *After cosmopolitanism*; Paul Gilroy (2005) *After empire*; Anne Phillips' *Democracy and difference* (1993) and *The politics of presence* (1995); and Iris Marion Young's *Justice and the politics of difference* (1990).

Simone Weil

Some of Simone Weil's thoughts on themes of 'reading' and 'attention' are provided in the collection from her notebooks entitled *Gravity and grace* (1952). For work that places Simone Weil's work in historical and cultural context and shows the development of her thinking over time, see Blum and Seidler (1991) *A truer liberty*. A sense of Iris Murdoch's moral thinking can be gained from *The sovereignty of good* (1970).

Urban fear

I have explored the new landscapes of urban fear and terror in relation to the London bombings in July 2005 in *Urban fears and global terrors* (2007b). See also Jessica Stern (2003) *Terror in the name of god*; Malise Ruthven (2002) *A fury for god* and his more recent comparative analysis of various fundamentalisms *Fundamentalisms* (2004); Jason Burke (2007) *Al-Qaieda: The True Story of Radical Islam* and *On the road to Kandahar* (2006b); Mary Habeck (2005) *Knowing the enemy*; Jean Baudrillard (2002) *The spirit of terrorism*; and Slavoj Zizek (2002) *Welcome to the desert of the real*.

Transnational identities

To explore some of the possibilities for imagining diverse identities within a globalised world and the ways in which the internet and social network sites allow for transnational identifications see, for instance, Kris Olds and Nigel Thrift,'Cultures on the brink' and other essays in Ong and Collier (eds) (2005) *Global assemblages*; Aiha Ong (1999) *Flexible citizenship* and Chris Berry, Fran Martin and Audrey Yue (eds) (2003) *Mobile cultures.*

For some interesting explorations on the complexity of sex/gender relations across different boundaries see, for instance, Arnaldo Cruz-Malave and Martin F. Manalansan (eds) (2002) *Queer globalization* and Lenore Manderson and Mararet Jolly (eds) (1997) *Sites of desire, economies of pleasure.*

Jeremy Rifkin

Jeremy Rifkin's helpful explorations into the changing global and intimate relationships of new capitalism are developed in *The age of access* (2000). See also his *The end of work* (1995); Bill Ryan (1992) *Making capital from culture* and Mary Douglas and Baron Isherwood (1979) *The world of goods.*

Gender, Westernisation and post-colonial politics

For an interesting exploration of sex/gender in relation to the interaction of 'Westernisation' and post-colonial politics see Uma Narayan (1997) *Dislocating cultures.* She explores some of the implications of feminisms being viewed within certain circles as foreign, Western and a betrayal of community.

THIRTEEN

Conclusion: Embodied identities: experience, power, difference/s and social theory

Identities and social theory

The idea that people can create their own identities and at the same time respect their complex inheritances, histories and memories suggests that identities are not 'fixed' or 'given' nor are they simply 'socially and culturally constructed'. We need new languages in which to explore identity-making as a creative and embodied process within a globalised postmodern world. Not only do we need to engage critically with the terms of classical social theories but we need to be able to imagine *how* people create their own complex sense of identities. That often embody diverse inheritances and stretch across transnational borders.

There might be a freedom to imagine your identity in the present, as existentialisms insist, partly through a wilful forgetting and disavowing of the past. But there are also processes of self-acceptance that can involve coming to terms with histories that can be *traumatic* for a parental generation to recall as well as familial experiences of migration that a younger generation might know relatively little about. Often parents who have migrated from different lands and carry histories of loss have wanted to conceal these painful histories to give their children more opportunity to belong. They want the movements across space to allow a freedom from histories and memories for their children. There are cultural and historical 'forgettings' that younger people also welcome, not wanting to be reminded of shamed histories and identities that potentially mark them out as different, particularly when still at school or at work where they might be anxious, even within multicultural spaces, to be 'like everyone else'.

People may have more freedom and choice in relation to their identities, but they may also have been born into circumstances of inequalities and oppressions, whether of class, gender, sexuality or 'race', religion and ethnicity, against which they have been obliged to struggle and to affirm themselves. As well as acknowledging that people can make their own histories, as Marx appreciated, this may not be 'in circumstances of their own choosing'. People also respond quite differently as individuals with their own qualities and abilities to these challenges and it can be difficult to predict who might respond in what way, even within the same family. Of course, opportunity partly depends on education: a young person may be lucky to have a chance encounter with a teacher who shows some belief in their capacity, but the odds can be overwhelmingly stacked against some, for instance young carers who have taken on responsibility for a parent ill at home.

Within a liberal moral culture, the ways that freedom has been presented as *autonomy* within a Kantian rationalist modernity has made it often difficult to understand how the relations of class, 'race', gender and sexed relations of power and subordination work to undermine a person's sense of self-worth and can demean a person in their own eyes as they learn to see themselves and frame identities through the terms of a dominant culture (Seidler, 1986). Within the terms of a Kantian rationalism, which has shaped powerful traditions in social theory emerging from Durkheim and Weber, we have learned to treat history and culture as forms of *unfreedom*, so that it is only through separating and disowning class, gender, 'racial' and ethnic histories and traditions that people can supposedly exist as 'free and equal' individuals in their own right.

A notion of the *disembodied* rational self has informed these rationalist traditions of social theory that have tended to *discount* the significance of bodies and emotional lives in the creation of identities. At the same time, inherited cultural histories and traditions have been forgotten or disavowed, so that people can take their place as rational selves, free to give whatever meanings they choose to their experience or to adapt to social rules that regulate civilised behaviours within a homogenised vision of society. It is assumed that, left to their own devices, individuals will be selfish and egoistic and that it is only through the disciplines and regulations of society that they learn morality and so can realise higher visions of their selves, as argued by Durkheim.

If Marx allows for the significance of people exploring their identities through the labour with which they engage and so for processes of becoming, he tends to give priority to work as a site of human emancipation, so neglecting other areas of human experience. Feminisms and gay liberation movements reminded us not only that 'the personal is political' but that bodies, sexualities and emotional lives are crucial sources of human identity and self-worth, and that if people are to create their own identities they have to be able to give due *recognition* to what the dominant culture shames and defines as pathological. This questions the distinction between the 'normal' and the 'pathological' that was defining for Durkheim's social theory and has been so vital for the widespread acceptance of *functionalist traditions* across sociology, social policy and social work.

Experience and identities

Movements for black consciousness, emerging from the civil rights movements in the US, inspired feminisms and sexual politics in the 1970s opening up questions about the *racialisation* of modernity. It began a process of questioning the Eurocentric character of classical social theories and the ways that Europe had, for so long, the power to create the world in its own image. This helped to illuminate a critical relationship between modernity as a project of a dominant European masculinity and the feminisation of colonial *others* who were assumed to be unable to make a transition from nature to culture without the external intervention of colonial powers. Visions of modernity were shaped through a European imaginary so that colonised others were defined as 'backward' and 'un/civilised'.

It was believed to be only through willingly accepting subordination to the colonial powers that they could hope to make a transition from 'tradition' to 'modernity'; it was only through serving the will of the coloniser that they could eventually leave their 'childish' conditions and assume the responsibilities of an 'adult' independence and democracy. Otherwise their identities were defined as 'lacking'. These were the shamed inheritances that were often unconsciously carried by generations of migrants who were encouraged to come to Britain in the 1950s, 1960s and 1970s, and were to shape the silences within families that a second generation were often to inherit.

Hegel's *Phenomenology of mind* (1807) set out a dialectic of master and slave that showed that the master was crucially dependent on the slave within a relationship of power. It was through the negation of the conditions of slavery that the slaves could find freedom and emancipation. But this relational insight into the creation of identities can be difficult to sustain within radically constructivist and historicist accounts, such as Rorty's in *Contingency, irony and solidarity* (1989), that tend to treat experience and personhood as exclusively discursive. For Rorty, since "everything is a social construct" there is no point in distinguishing between the 'natural' and the 'merely cultural'. Rather the task of social theory is in contesting 'metaphysical' claims that there exist realities, truths or moral principles beyond our descriptions of them:

> socialization, and thus historical circumstances, goes all the
> way down – that there is nothing 'beneath' socialization or
> prior to history which is definatory of the human. (p xiii)

> the self, the human subject is simply whatever acculturation
> makes of it. (p 64)[1]

This is a view challenged by Isaiah Berlin, himself a critic of
Enlightenment rationalism, who remarked that "the number of ends
that human beings can pursue is not infinite ... in practice human
beings would not be human if that were so" (quoted in Lukes, 2003,
p 113).[2]

As Sonia Kruks (2001) argues, for Rorty there is nothing 'intrinsically
abominable' about the subordination of women. Since there are
only descriptions and redescriptions, there is no point from which
we could make such an affirmation. As Kruks describes Rorty's
position, "Feminists must drop the claim that they act in the name
of principles: they simply struggle to redescribe and to create a new
social construct"(2001, p 134). As Rorty frames it, the proper project
of feminism is not to try to "express" women's lives but rather to
"create" women anew through "the production of a better set of social
constructs" (p 134).

As Kruks readily acknowledges, "language is never a neutral medium
through which we can capture previously unvoiced experience, and
experience is indeed altered in acts of linguistic formulation" (p 134).
Although I might put this slightly differently, the danger is clearly that
personhood "becomes an attribute of linguistic competence and is
denied to the silent or silenced" (p 134). Rorty makes clear that not
all human beings share equally in personhood. Since human beings
do not have "a central and inviolable core surrounded by culturally
conditioned beliefs and desires" (1991a, p 249) personhood is never
an "intrinsic attribute" of all members of the species but rather an
'acquisition', and some – those with the greater power of language –
acquire more of it than others. Personhood, Rorty claims, is:

> something that slaves typically have less of than their masters
> ... because of the masters' control over the language spoken
> by slaves – their ability to make the slave think of his or her
> pain as fated.... [There is] no deep reality which reposes
> unrecognised beneath the superficial appearances. (p 244)

As Kruks neatly frames it, this means that "Where oppression is not voiced, in short, it does not exist" (2001, p 134). Since Rorty wants more people to attain full personhood, he argues that since:

> There is no such thing as the 'voice of the oppressed' or the 'language of the victims'.... So the job of putting their situation into language is going to have to be done for them by somebody else. (1989, p 94)

This radical constructionism has encouraged social theorists to be sceptical about 'identity politics' that seem to assume notions of fixed or given identities and fostered a desire to think 'beyond race' and 'beyond gender'. Since they have learnt to accept that experience is articulated through discourse alone and that identities necessarily carry with them a sense of fixity, social theorists have often been tempted into thinking this can only be escaped through thinking of gender, 'race' and sexualities as categorisations that allow us to order the social world in certain ways. Against this, I argue that victims of racial or sexual abuse, violation and oppression 'know' what they have experienced, even though they might as yet have no way of putting it into words. Often it is only when people are prepared to listen to what they have to say, that they find the words to voice their sufferings.

In *Black skin, white mask*, Frantz Fanon (1986) draws on the Sartrean problem of authenticity and Sonia Kruks recognises a need to revise the English translation at some points, since it loses Fanon's use of explicitly Sartrean terminology. In a footnote she reminds us that Fanon

> repeatedly emphasises that black neurosis cannot be explained through conventional Western psychoanalytic frameworks. He insists, for example, that Oedipus complex rarely exists in the Antilles, adding wryly that psychoanalysts such as "Dr Lacan" will be "reluctant to share my view"(Fanon, 1986, p 152). It is not familial history but racialised social interaction that produces pathology in blacks: "A normal Negro child, having grown up within a normal family, will become abnormal on the slightest contact with the white world" (p 143). (Kruks, 2001, fn p 99)

As Fanon argues, most black men at the time of his writing were not capable of an "authentic upheaval" (1986, p 8) since they were the victims of a socially produced situation of inferiority that they had internalised. For Fanon they suffer from a "psycho-existential complex" (p 12) that inhibits them from engaging in self- or social transformation. As Fanon shares his own experience:

> Shame. Shame and self-contempt. Nausea. When people like me, they tell me it is in spite of my colour. When they dislike me, they point out it is not because of my colour. Either way I am locked into the infernal circle. (p 116)

As with **Simone de Beauvoir**, shame is here identified as the paradigmatic experience of inferiorised otherness. Although de Beauvoir's women and Fanon's black men both experience shame in a relationship to oneself constituted through the objectifying look of the other:

> Fanon's (male) black is constituted as an active, animal sexuality in the white male imagination, Beauvoir's (white) women as 'prey' or passive nature. (Kruks, 2001, fn p 99)

Learning from Sartre's discussion of anti-Semitism in *Anti-semite and jew* (1948) Fanon recognises that while the Jew can sometimes be anonymous, the black man is always visible as such. Taking up Sartre's notion of the "overdetermined" otherness of the Jew for his own purposes, Fanon writes "I am overdetermined from without. I am the slave not of the 'idea' that others have of me but of my own appearance" (1986, p 99).

To imagine 'the human' in newly global and postcolonial ways we need to re-vision relationships with nature and so question ideas that nature has become 'artificial' as distinctions between 'nature' and 'culture' have become undone through advances in techno-sciences. We still need ways to engage critically with the violation and abuses of nature so we still need to reconsider relations between the 'human' and the 'animal' without slipping into a technological rationalism that so often gets lost in its own rhetoric. We need to be wary of a dis/embodied rationalism that all too often takes shape in a frozen bodily identity unable to feel contact or engage emotionally.

Within an ecological postmodernism we can imagine and create different identities that can keep open tensions between 'nature' and 'culture' without resorting to an essentialism that fixes either category or which reduces nature to a 'cultural construction' as if it were the only way to grasp its historical transformations. But this is to create identities that question the insatiability of human desires that has so often underpinned classical forms of social theory and allows for a sense of human nourishment and fulfilment. Notions of sufficiency can help question the infinite desires of consumer and celebrity culture. This can allow people in the global North to live with less more responsibly, in ways that not only allow for the reduction in inequalities between global North and South, but also for the planet to be protected from the dangers of global catastrophe.

As people create their identities with a commitment to such global visions of social justice so they learn to question neo-liberal agendas and the kinds of identities they help to create. Learning to be hospitable to aspects of self that rationalist identities have long sought to deny or forget allows us to be responsible for ourselves as well as *responsive* to the sufferings and vulnerabilities of others. For Jacques Derrida the future of the political becomes the future of friends, the possibility of a radically new friendship (I would add, both with yourself and others), and so for a deeper and more inclusive democracy.

Global ecological humanism refuses to think in terms of the 'human' in contrast to the 'animal' but recognises how much is shared by all who inhabit the planet, as well as how different peoples and cultures can learn to create and sustain their hybrid identities with integrity. It values how people can learn from difference/s rather than be threatened by them, how they can learn to live together by sharing the world's resources in sustainable ways, and recognises the connections between local and global social movements.

Of course we should be wary of a knee-jerk romanticism which presents the poor as always good and generous while the rich are crabby, frightened and racist. The richer minorities in the South have often bought into the global market, into the brands and images of 'the West' that so often for a younger globalised generation represent 'modernity' and 'the future'. As Amarnata Wright (2005) argues, the rich often have less of a relationship these days with their own country than with some global identity, where capital flows across borders and productivity and markets rule. In a review of Wright's book, Angus Macqueen shares that he found himself reflecting that, in this post-Soviet world, when the ideology of socialism is almost an embarrassment, the book is:

> constantly searching for a language or a structure with which to describe these fundamental issues, which have not simply disappeared with the fall of the wall.... Today the left has no language, and the multinationals do. They want us to believe that free market democracy is the answer to everything.... Multinationals, for all their cool rhetoric of

change and mobility, will do nothing to challenge that social fabric, particularly when the disenfranchised poor provide a workforce grateful to be paid a dollar for a 12-hour day. (*The Guardian Review*, 28 May 2005, p 14)

The age-old dilemmas of class and exploitation have not disappeared but have been organised on a global scale that makes them difficult to illuminate within traditional social theories. When Wright returned to London from her travels in Latin America she was told by a charity sponsored by Levi's in Hoxton that "branding is the language of youth. They only understand through brands" (p 14). If this is true, as Macqueen comments, "We are already lost". Hopefully, through the explorations in this book, I show that not only is it only part of the story, but that if you listen to young people themselves, also in times of global financial crisis, you can witness them creating identities that reflect different values and global commitments. Often they are more aware than ruling political elites about the need to relate with insight and compassion to the powerless and dispossessed as they struggle for human dignity and global justice. They seek transformations in the terms of trade between rich and poor nations in the global North and South. If we are to meet the urgent challenges of global warming we need to revision the relationships between culture and nature, and between technologies and the human, as eco-social theories and embodied philosophies challenge the consumer materialisms that so often provide meaning and value. As we learn to live sustainable and just lives so we form embodied identities that connect us to diverse others with renewed feelings for global responsibility.

Endnotes

[1] This form of 'social constructionism' is defended by Richard Rorty in *Contingency, irony and solidarity* (1989). In his *Essays on Heidegger and others* (1991) he insists "we must avoid the embarrassment of the universalist claim that 'human being' ... names an unchanging essence, an ahistorical natural kind with a permanent set of intrinsic features".

[2] In 'An unfashionable fox', Steven Lukes (2001) explores Berlin's relationship as a critic of Enlightenment rationalism who

firmly believed in the place of reason in ethics and in the objectivity of values ... [and yet] showed no sympathy for those contemporary post-Nietzschean, post modernist foxes who have taken the notion of incommensurability far farther than he ever did, as when Lyotard says that 'to speak is to fight' and suggests that there is an irreducible incommensurability across discourses and narratives since these "define what has the right to be said and done in the culture in question, and since they are themselves a part of that culture, they are legitimated thereby". (pp 55-6)

Further reading

Frantz Fanon

To place Franz Fanon's work in a historical and anti-colonial context see, for instance, David Macey (2001) *Franz Fanon: A biography* and Paul Gilroy (1993) *The black Atlantic.*

Simone de Beauvoir

For a sense of the development of Simone de Beauvoir's feminism see *The second sex* (1968). A discussion of the very different influences her work had on diverse feminist theories may be found in Benhabib et al (1995). For a discussion that articulates the postmodern impasse for white feminism that deconstruction's destabilising of the category 'woman' has generated through a reading of Ellen Glasgow, Zora Neale Hurston and Elizabeth Bishop see Susan Lurie's *Unsettled subjects* (1997).

Bibliography

Aaronovitch, D. (2000) 'Why are people alarmed by the success of girls?', *The Independent*, 18 August, p 3.

Adam, B. (1990) *Time and social theory*, Cambridge: Polity Press.

Adkins, L. (2002) *Revisions: Gender and sexuality in late modernity*, Milton Keynes: Open University Press.

Adorno T.H. (1974) *Aspects of sociology*, London: Heinemann.

Adorno T.H. and Horkheimer, M. (1973) *Dialectic of enlightenment*, trans J. Cumming, London: Allen Lane.

Agamben, G. (1993) *The coming community*, Minneapolis, MN: University of Minnesota Press.

Agamben, G. (1998) *Homo Sacer: Sovereign power and bare life*, Stanford, CA: Stanford University Press.

Ahmed, S. (2000) *Strange emotions: Embodied others and post-coloniality*, Edinburgh: Edinburgh University Press.

Ahmed, S. (2004) *The cultural politics of emotion*, Edinburgh: Edinburgh University Press.

Alderman, G. (1983) The Jewish community in British politics, Oxford University Press.

Allen, T. (1994) *The invention of the white race*, London: Verso.

Alliance for Childhood (2000) *Fool's gold: A critical look at computers in childhood*, College Park, MD: Alliance for Childhood.

Althusser, L. (1970) *For Marx*, London: Verso.

Altman, D. (1982) *The homosexualisation of America*, Boston, MA: Beacon.

Anderson, B. (1991) *Imagined communities: Reflections on the origin and spread of nationalism*, London: Verso.

An Na'im, A. (ed) (1992) *Human rights in cross-cultural perspective: A quest for consensus*, Philadelphia, PA: University of Pennsylvania Press.

Ang, I. (2001) *On not speaking Chinese: Living between Asia and the West*, London: Routledge.

Anzaluda, G. (1987) *Borderlands – La Frontera: The new Mestiza*, San Francisco, CA: Spinsters/Aunt Lute.

Anzaluda, G. (ed) (1990) *Making face, making soul*, San Francisco, CA: Spinsters/Aunt Lute.

Appadurai, A. (1996) *Modernity at large: Cultural dimensions of globalization*, Minneapolis, MN: University of Minnesota Press.

Appadurai, A. (ed) (2001) *Globalization*, Durham, NC: Duke University Press.

Arendt, H. (1951) *The origins of totalitarianism*, London: Random House/Schocken.

Arendt, H. (1982) *Lectures on Kant's political philosophy*, ed by R. Beiner, Chicago, IL: University of Chicago Press.

Askew, S. and Ross, C. (1988) *Boys don't cry: Boys and sexism in education*, Milton Keynes: Open University Press.

Assiter, A. (1996) *Enlightenment women: Modernist feminism in a postmodern age*, London: Routledge.

Austin, J.L. (1975) *How to do things with words*, 2nd edn, Cambridge, MA: Harvard University Press.

Back, L. (1996) *New ethnicities and urban culture*, London: UCL Press.

Back, L. (2007) *The art of listening*, Oxford: Berg.

Barber, B. (1995) *Jihad vs McWorld*, New York: Random House.

Barker, P. (1998) *The Regeneration Trilogy: 'Regeneration', 'Eye in the door', 'Ghost road'*, London; Penguin.

Baron, S. (1957) *A social and religious history of the Jews*, New York: Columbia University Press.

Bartov, O. (2000) *Mirrors of destruction: War, genocide and modern identity*, Oxford: Oxford University Press.

Battersby C. (1998) *The phenomenal woman: Feminist metaphysics and the patterns of identity*, Cambridge: Polity Press.

Baubock, R. (1994a) *Transnational citizenship: Membership and rights in international migration*, Aldershot: Edward Elgar.

Baubock, R. (ed) (1994b) *From aliens to citizens: Redefining the status of citizens in Europe*, Aldershot: Avebury.

Baubock, R., Heller, A. and Zolberg, A. (eds) *The challenge of diversity: Integration and pluralism in societies of immigration*, Aldershot: Avebury.

Baudrillard, J. (2002) *The spirit of terrorism*, London: Verso.

Bauman, Z. (1990) *Modernity and the holocaust*, Cambridge: Polity Press.

Bauman, Z. (1991) *Modernity and ambivalence*, Cambridge: Polity Press.

Bauman, Z. (1994) *Intimations of postmodernity*, London: Routledge.

Bauman, Z. (1995a) *Life in fragments*, Oxford: Blackwells.

Bauman, Z. (1995b) *Postmodern ethics*, Cambridge: Polity Press.

Bauman, Z. (1997) *Postmodernity and its discontents*, Cambridge: Polity Press.

Bauman, Z. (1998) *Globalization: The human consequences*, Cambridge: Polity Press.

Bauman, Z. (2000) *Liquid modernity*, Cambridge: Polity Press.

Bauman, Z. (2001) *The individualized society*, Cambridge: Polity Press.

Bauman, Z. (2003) *Liquid love*, Cambridge: Polity Press.

Bauman, Z. (2004) *Identity: Conversations with Benedetto Vecchi*, Cambridge: Polity Press.

Bauman, Z. (2007) *Liquid times: Living in an age of uncertainty*, Cambridge: Polity Press.

Beck, U. (1992) *The risk society:Towards a new modernity*, London:Sage.

Beck, U. (2000) *The brave new world of work*, Cambridge: Polity Press.

Beck, U. and Beck-Gernsheim, E. (1995) *The normal chaos of love*, Cambridge: Polity Press.

Beck, U. and Beck-Gernsheim, E. (2002) *Individualization: Institutionalized individualism and its social and political consequences*, London: Sage.

Beck, U., Giddens, A. and Lash, S. (1995) *Reflexive modernization: Politics, tradition and aesthetics in the modern social order*, Stanford, CA: Stanford University Press.

Beetham, D. (1985) *Max Weber and the theory of modern politics*, Oxford: Polity Press.

Beetham, D. (1991) *The legitimation of power*, London: Macmillan.

Bell, D. and Valentine, V. (eds) (1995) *Mapping desire: Geographies of sexualities*, London: Routledge.

Bell, V. (ed) (1999) *Performativity and belonging*, London: Sage.

Bellamy, R. (1999) *Liberalism and pluralism:Towards a politics of compromise*, London: Routledge.

Benevenuto, B. and Kennedy, R. (1996) *The works of Jaques Lacan*, London: Free Association Books.

Benhabib, S. (1996) *Democracy and difference: Contesting the boundaries of the political*, Princeton, NJ: Princeton University Press.

Benhabib, S. (1997) *Situating the self*, Cambridge: Polity Press.

Benhabib, S., Butler, J., Cornell, D. and Fraser, N. (1995) *Feminist contentions: A philosophical exchange*, New York: Routledge.

Benjamin, A. and Osborne, P. (eds) (1994) *Walter Benjamin's philosophy: Destruction and experience*, London: Routledge.

Benjamin, J. (1990) *Bonds of love*, London: Virago.

Benjamin, J. (1998) *Shadow of the other: Intersubjectivity and gender in psychoanalysis*, New York: Routledge.

Benjamin, W. (1968) *Illuminations: Essays and reflections*, trans. H. Zohn, London: Collins/Fontana.

Benjamin, W. (1979) *One-way street and other writings*, London: New Left Books.

Berger, J. (1991) *Keeping a rendevous*, New York: Vintage.

Berger, J. (1992) 'A man of discernment', *Race & Class*, vol 34, no 2, pp 19-21.

Berger, M., Wallis, B. and Watson, S. (eds) (1995) *Constructing masculinity*, New York: Routledge.

Berlin, I. (1969) *Four essays on liberty*, Oxford: Oxford University Press.

Berlin, I. (1976) *Vico and Herder*, New York: Random House

Berlin, I. (1979) *The age of enlightenment*, Oxford: Oxford University Press.

Berlin, I. (1981) *The essays collected as 'Against the current'*, Oxford: Oxford University Press.

Berry, C., Martin, F. and Yue, A. (eds) (2003) *Mobile cultures: New media in queer Asia*, Durham, NC: Duke University Press.

Bettleheim, B. (1991) *Freud and man's soul*, London: Fontana.

Bhabha, H.K. (ed) (1993) *Nation and narration*, London: Routledge.

Bhabha, H.K. (1994) *The location of culture*, London: Routledge.

Bhatt, C. (2001) *Hindu nationalism: Origins, ideologies and modern myths*, Oxford: Berg.

Biale, D. (1992) *Eros and the Jews: From Biblical Israel to contemporary America*, New York: Basic Books.

Blackman, L. (2008) *The body*, Oxford: Berg.

Blum, L. (2001) *I'm not a racist but.... The moral quandary of race*, Ithaca, NY: Cornell University Press.

Blum, L. and Seidler, V.J.J. (1991) *A truer liberty: Simone Weil and Marxism*, New York: Routledge.

Bly, R. (1990) *Iron John*, New York: Addison-Wesley.

Bock, G. and James, S. (eds) (1992) *Beyond equality and difference: Citizenship, feminist politics and female subjectivity*, London: Routeldge.

Boellstorff, T. (2005) *The gay archipelago: Sexuality and nation in Indonesia*, Princeton, NJ: Princeton University Press.

Bologh, R. W. (1990) *Love or greatness: Max Weber and masculine thinking*, London: Unwin Hyman.

Bordo, S. (1993) *Unbearable weight: Feminism, Western culture, and the body*, Berkeley, CA: University of California Press.

Bordo, S. (1999) *The male body: A new look at men in public and in private*, New York: Farrar, Straus and Giroux.

Borger, J. (2000) 'This leading American business guru claims these trainers could spell the end of capitalism. Can he be serious?', *The Guardian*, 29 September, p 4.

Borradori. G. (2003) *Philosophy in a time of terror: Dialogues with Jurgen Habermas and Jacques Derrida*, Chicago, IL: University of Chicago Press.

Boswell, J. (1980) *Christianity, social tolerance and homosexuality*, Chicago, IL: University of Chicago Press.

Bourdieu, P. (2001) *Masculine domination*, Cambridge: Polity Press.

Boyarin, D. (1993) *Carnal Israel: Reading sex in Talmudic Judaism*, Berkeley, CA: University of California Press.

Boyarin, D. (1994) *A radical Jew: Paul and the politics of identity*, Berkeley, CA: University of California Press.

Brah, A. and Coombes, A. (eds) (2000) *Hybridity and its discontents: Politics, science, culture*, New York: Routledge.

Brah, A., Hickman, M. and Mac an Ghail, M. (1999) *Thinking identities: Ethnicities, racism and culture*, Basingstoke: Macmillan.

Braidotti, R. (1991) *Patterns of dissonance*, Cambridge: Polity Press.

Brake, M. (1987) *Comparative youth culture*, London: Routledge.

Brennan, T. (ed) (1989) *Between feminism and psychoanalysis*, London: Routledge.

Bright, M. (2000) 'A question of class', *The Observer*, 20 August, p 15.

Brittan, A. (1989) *Masculinity and power*, Oxford: Basil Blackwell.

Brockes, E. (2000) 'Boys in no-mans land', *The Guardian G2*, 18 August, p 4-5.

Brod, H. (ed) (1987) *The making of masculinities*, Boston, MA: Allen and Unwin.

Brod, H. and Kaufman, M. (eds) (1994) *Theorizing masculinities*, Thousand Oaks, CA: Sage.

Brophy, M. (2006) *Truth hurts: Report of the National Enquiry into self-harm among young people*, London: Mental Health Foundation.

Brown, P. (1990) *The body and society: Men, women and sexual renunciation in early Christianity*, London: Faber.

Brown, W. (1995) *States of injury: Power and freedom in late modernity*, Princeton, NJ: Princeton University Press.

Brown, W. (2006) *Regulating aversion: Tolerance in the age of identity and Empire*, Princeton, NJ: Princeton University Press.

Buck-Morss, S. (1978) *The origins of negative dialectics*, Brighton: Harvester.

Buck-Morss, S. (2000) *Dreamworld and catastrophe: The passing of mass utopia in East and West*, Cambridge, MA: MIT Press.

Buhle, M.J. (1998) *Feminism and its discontents*, Cambridge, MA: Harvard University Press.

Bull, M. (2003) *Sounds of the city*, Oxford: Berg.

Burgess, A. (1997) *Fatherhood reclaimed: The making of the modern father*, London: Vermillion.

Burke, J. (2006a) 'Third Reich epic starts bidding war', *The Observer*, 1 October, p 6.

Burke, J. (2006b) *On the road to Kandahar*, London: Allen Lane.

Burke, J. (2007) *Al-Qaeda: The true story of radical Islam*, London: I.B. Taurus.

Buruma, A. and Margalit, A. (2005) *Occidentalism*, London: Penguin

Butler, J. (1990) *Gender trouble: Feminism and the subversion of identity*, New York: Routledge.

Butler, J. (1993) *Bodies that matter: The discursive limits of 'sex'*, New York: Routledge.

Butler, J. (2004a) *Undoing gender*, New York: Routledge.

Butler, J. (2004b) *Precarious life*, London: Verso.

Butler, J. (2008) 'Sexual politics, torture and secular time', *British Journal of Sociology*, vol 59, issue 1, pp 1-23.

Butler, J. and Scott, J.W. (eds) (1992) *Feminists theorize the political*, New York: Routledge.

Campbell, K. (2004) *Jacques Lacan's feminist epistemology*, London: Routledge.

Canovan, M. (1996) *Nationhood and political theory*, Cheltenham: Edward Elgar.

Caplan, P. (ed) (1987) *The cultural construction of sexuality*, London: Tavistock.

Carby, H.V. (1987) *Reconstructing womanhood: The emergence of the Afro-American woman novelist*, New York: Oxford University Press.

Carby, H.V. (1998) *Race men*, Cambridge, MA: Harvard University Press.

Cavell, S. (1980) *The claim of reason: Wittgenstein, scepticism, morality and tragedy*, Oxford: Oxford University Press.

Caygill, H. (1998) *Walter Benjamin: The colour of experience*, London: Routledge.

Caygill, H. (2002) *Levinas and the political*, London: Routledge.

Chakrabarty, D. (2000) *Provincialising Europe: Postcolonial thought and historical difference*, Princeton, NJ: Princeton University Press.

Chapman, R. and Rutherford, J. (eds) (1987) *Male order: Unwrapping masculinity*, London: Lawrence and Wishart.

Chernin, K. (1983) *Womansize: Tyranny of slenderness*, London: The Women's Press.

Chodorow, N. (1978) *The reproduction of mothering: Psychoanalysis and the sociology of gender*, Berkeley, CA: University of California Press.

Chodorow, N. (1994) *Feminities, masculinities, sexualities: Freud and beyond*, London: Free Associations Books.

Clare, G. (2007) *Last waltz in Vienna*, London: Pan Books.

Clark, R.T. (1969) *Herder: His life and thought*, Berkeley, CA: University of California Press.

Clarke, S. (1982) *The nature of the beast*, Oxford: Oxford University Press.

Clatterbaugh, K. (1990) *Contemporary perspectives on masculinity: Men, women and politics in modern society*, Boulder, CO: Westview Press.

Cohen, J. (1982) *The friars and the Jews: The evolution of Medieval anti-Judaism*, Ithaca, NY: Cornell University Press.

Cohen, P. (1997) *Rethinking the youth question*, Basingstoke: Palgrave.

Cohen, P. and Bains, H. (eds) (1988) *Multi-racist Britain*, Basingstoke: Macmillan.

Collins, P.H. (1991) *Black feminist thought: Knowledge, consciousness and the politics of empowerment*, New York: Routledge.

Committee on Homosexual Offences and Prostitution (1957) *Report of the Committee on Homosexual Offences and Prostitution* (The Wolfenden Report), London: Her Majesty's Stationery Office.

Connell, R.W. (1987) *Gender and power: Society, the person and sexual politics*, Cambridge: Polity Press.

Connell, R.W. (1995) *Masculinities*, Cambridge: Polity Press.

Connell, R.W. (2000) *The men and the boys*, Cambridge: Polity Press.

Connolly, P. (1998) *Racism, gender identities and young people*, London: Routledge.

Connolly, W. (1991) *Identity/difference: Democratic negotiations of political paradox*, Ithaca, NY: Cornell University Press.

Cornwall, A. and Lindisfarne, N. (eds) (1994) *Dislocating masculinity: Comparative ethnographies*, London: Routledge.

Craib, I. (1989) *Psychoanalysis and social theory: The limits of sociology*, London: Harvester Wheatsheaf.

Craig, S. (1992) *Men, masculinity and the media*, Thousand Oaks, CA: Sage.

Crompton, L. (2003) *Homosexuality*, Cambridge, MA: Harvard University Press.

Croucher, S. (2004) *Globalisation and belonging: The politics of identity in a changing world*, Lanham, MD: Rowman and Littlefield.

Cruz-Malave, A. and Manalansan, M.F. (eds) (2002) *Queer globalisations: Citizenship and the afterlife of colonialism*, New York: New York University Press.

Dallmayr, F. (1998) *Alternative visions: Paths in the global village*, Lanham, MD: Rowman and Littlefield.

Daly, M. (1973) *Beyond God the Father: Toward a philosophy of women's liberation*, Boston, MA: Beacon Press.

Davidhoff, L. (1995) *Worlds between: Historical perspectives on gender and class*, Cambridge: Polity Press.

Davidhoff, L. and Hall, C. (1987) *Family fortunes: Women and men of the English middle class 1780-1850*, London: Routledge.

de Beauvoir, S. (1968) *The second sex*, London: Cape, republished by Penguin 1972.

de Vries, H. and Weber, S. (eds) (1997) *Violence, identity and self-determination*, Stanford, CA: Stanford University Press.

Deleuze, G. (1993) *Nietzsche and philosophy*, trans H. Tomlinson, Minneapolis, MN: University of Minnesota Press.

Deleuze, G. and Guattari, F. (1997) *Anti-Oedipus*, Minneapolis, MN: University of Minnesota Press.

Derrida, J. (1978) *Writing and difference*, Chicago, IL: University of Chicago Press.

Derrida, J. (2002) *Acts of religion*, New York: Routledge.

Dickens, P. (2004) *Society and nature*, Cambridge: Polity.

Dinnerstein, D. (1987) *The mermaid and the minotaur: The rocking of the cradle and the ruling of the world*, London: The Women's Press.

Disch, L.J. (1994) *Hannah Arendt and the limits of philosophy*, Ithaca, NY: Cornell University Press.

Dobash, R.E, Dobash, R.P., Cavanagh, K. and Lewis, R. (2000) *Changing violent men*, London: Sage.

Dobson, S. (2002) 'From silence to window view', *Street Signs: a CUCR Newsletter*, vol 1, issue 4, Spring, p 10.

Dollimore, J. (1998) *Death, desire and loss in Western culture*, London: Penguin.

Donald, J. and Rattansi, A. (eds) (1993) *'Race', culture and difference*, London: Sage.

Donzelot, J. (1979) *The policing of families*, London: Hutchinson.

Douglas, M. and Isherwood, B. (1979) *The world of goods*, New York: Basic Books.

Drescher, J. (2001) *Psychoanalytic therapy and the gay man*, London: The Analytic Press.

Dreyfus, H. and Rabinow, P. (1982) *Michel Foucault: Beyond structuralism and hermeneutics*, Brighton: Harvester Press.

Du Bois, W.E.B. (1903, 1989) *The souls of black folk*, London: Bantam Books.

du Gay, P. and Pryke, M. (eds) (2002) *Cultural economy: Cultural analysis and commercial life*, London: Sage.

Dunayer, J. (2004) *Speciesism*, Derwood, MD: Ryce Publishing.

Dunayevskaya, R. (1971) *Marxism and freedom*, London: Pluto Press.

Duncan, N. (ed) (1996) *Bodyspace: Destablising geographies of gender and sexuality*, London: Routledge.

Durkheim, E. (1893) *The division of labour in society*, trans W.D. Hall, published 1984, London: Macmillan.

Durkheim, E. (1925) *Moral education: A study in the theory and application of the sociology of education*, published 1973, London: Macmillan.

Easlea, B. (1981) *Science and sexual oppression: Patriarchy's confrontation with women and nature*, London: Weidenfeld and Nicholson.

Edwards, T. (1994) *Erotics and politics: Gay male sexuality, masculinity and feminism*, London: Routledge.

Eichenbaum, L. and Orbach, S. (1983) *Understanding women*, Harmondsworth: Penguin.

Eisenstein, H. (1985) *Contemporary feminist thought*, London: Unwin.

Elam, D. (1994) *Feminism and deconstruction*, London: Routledge

Elias, N. (1982) *The civilizing process: State formation and civilisation*, trans E. Jephcott, Oxford: Oxford University Press.

Elliot, A. (2008) *Subject to ourselves*, London: Paradigm.

Elliot, A. and Frosh, S. (eds) (1995) *Psychoanalysis in contexts: Paths between theory and modern culture*, London/New York: Routledge.

Elshtain, J.B. (1981) *Public man, private woman*, Princeton, NJ: Princeton University Press.

Epstein, D., Elwood, J., Hey V. and Maw, J. (eds) (1998) *Failing boys?: Issues in gender and achievement*, Buckingham: Open University Press.

Evans, S. (1980) *Personal politics: The roots of women's liberation in the civil rights movement and the new Left*, New York: Vintage Books.

Faludi, S. (2000) *Stiffed: The betrayal of modern man*, New York: Vintage.

Fanon, F. (1986) *Black skin, white mask*, London: Pluto Press.

Featherstone, M. (1991) *Consumer culture and postmodernism*, London: Sage.

Featherstone, M., Hepworth, M. and Turner, B.S. (eds) (1991) *The body: Social process and cultural theory*, London: Sage.

Flax, J. (1990) *Thinking fragments: Psychoanalysis, feminism and postmodern in the contemporary West*, Berkeley, CA: University of California Press.

Flax, J. (1993) *Disputed subjects: Essays on pscyhoanalysis, politics and philosophy*, New York, NY/London: Routledge.

Foucault, M. (1975) *Discipline and punish: The birth of the prison*, Harmondsworth: Penguin.

Foucault, M. (1976) *The history of sexuality, vol 1: The will to knowledge*, trans Robert Hurley, reprinted 1998, London: Penguin.

Foucault, M. (1978) *Language, counter-memory, practice: Selected essays and interviews*, edited by D.F. Bouchard, Oxford: Blackwells.

Foucault, M. (1980) *Power/knowledge: Selected interviews and other writings, 1972-1977*, New York: Pantheon.

Foucault, M. (1985) *The history of sexuality, vol 2: The uses of pleasure*, trans Robert Hurley, reprinted 1992, London: Penguin.

Foucault, M. (1986) *The history of sexuality, vol 3: Care of the self*, trans Robert Hurley, reissued 1990, London: Penguin.

Foucault, M. (1988) 'Technologies of the self', in L.H. Martin, H. Gutman and P.H. Hutton (eds) *Technologies of the self: A seminar with Michel Foucault*, New York: Tavistock.

Foucault, M. with Sennett, R. (1981) 'Sexuality and solitude', *London Review of Books*, 21 May.

Fox Kellner, E. (1992) *Secrets of life, secrets of death: Essays on language, gender and science*, New York: Routledge.

Frankenberg, R. (1993) *White women, race matters: The social construction of whiteness*, Minneapolis, MN: University of Minnesota Press.

Franklin, A. (2002) *Nature and social theory*, London: Sage.

Freud, S. (1930) *Civilisation and its discontents*, New York: W.W. Norton.

Freud, S. (1977) *On sexuality*, London: Penguin.

Friedman, J. and Lash, S. (1992) *Modernity and identity*, Oxford: Blackwells.

Fromm, E. (1991) *The fear of freedom*, London: Routledge.

Frosh, S. (1994) *Sexual difference: Masculinity and psychoanalysis*, London/ New York: Routledge.

Frosh, S., Phoenix, A. and Pattman, R. (2002) *Young masculinities*, Basingstoke: Palgrave.

Fullinwider R.K. (ed) (2008) *Public education in a multicultural society: Policy, theory, critique*, Cambridge: Cambridge University Press.

Fuss, D. (1995) *Identification papers*, New York: Routledge.

Fussell, S. (1992) *Muscle: The confessions of an unlikely bodybuilder*, New York: Harper.

Gallager, C. and Laqueur, T. (eds) (1987) *The making of the modern body: Sexuality and society in the nineteenth century*, Berkeley, CA: University of California Press.

Gallop, J. (1982) *Feminism and psychoanalysis: The daughter's seduction*, London: Macmillan.

Gallop, J. (1988) *Thinking through the body*, New York: Columbia University Press.

Game, A. and Pringle, R. (1984) *Gender at work*, London: Pluto Press.

Garcia-Canclini, N. (1995) *Hybrid cultures: Strategies for entering and leaving modernity*, Minneapolis, MN: University of Minnesota Press.

Gardner, L. (2000) 'Art and Soul', *Guardian Education*, 10 October, p 2.

Gates, H.L. Jr (ed) (1987) *'Race,' writing and difference*, Chicago, IL: University of Chicago Press.

Gay, P. (1988) *Freud: A life of our time*, London: Macmillan.

Geertz, C. (1973) *The interpretation of culture*, New York: Basic Books.

Giddens, A. (1971) *Capitalism and modern social theory*, Cambridge: Cambridge University Press.

Giddens, A. (1978) *Durkheim*, London: Fontana.

Giddens, A. (1990) *The consequences of modernity*, Cambridge: Polity Press.

Giddens, A. (1991) *Modernity and self-identity: Self and society in the late modern age*, Cambridge: Pluto Press.

Giddens, A. (1993) *The transformation of intimacy: Sexuality, love and eroticism in modern societies*, Cambridge: Polity Press.

Gilligan, C. (1982) *In a different voice: Psychological theory and women's development*, Cambridge, MA: Harvard University Press.

Gilligan, C. (ed) (1992) *Women, girls and psychotherapy: Reframing resistance*, Binghamton, NY: Harrington Park Press.

Gilligan, C., Lyons, N.P. and Hanmer, T.J. (1990) *Making connections: Relational worlds of adolescent girls at Emma Willard School*, Cambridge, MA: Harvard University Press.

Gilligan, C., Ward, J.V. and Taylor, J.M. (eds) (1988) *Mapping the moral domain: Contribution of women's thinking to psychological theory and education*, Cambridge, MA: Harvard University Press.

Gilligan, J. (2000) *Violence*, London: Jessica Kingsley.

Gillis, J. (1996) *A world of their own making: Myth, ritual and the quest for family values*, New York: Basic Books.

Gilmore, D.G. (1990) *Manhood in the making: Cultural concepts of masculinity*, New Haven, CT: Yale University Press.

Gilroy, P. (1987) *There ain't no black in the Union Jack*, London: Unwin Hyman.

Gilroy, P. (1993a) *The black Atlantic: Modernity and double consciousness*, Cambridge, MA: Harvard University Press.

Gilroy, P. (1993b) *Small acts: Thoughts on the politics of black culture*, London: Serpents Tail.

Gilroy, P. (2000) *Between camps: Nations, cultures and the allure of race*, London: Allen Lane.

Gilroy, P. (2005) *After empire: Multicultures or Postcolonial Melancholia*, London: Routledge.

Glazer, N. (1997) *We are all multiculturalists now*, Cambridge, MA: Harvard University Press.

Goldberg, D.T. (1993) *Racist culture: Philosophy and the politics of meaning*, Oxford: Basil Blackwell.

Goldstein, E.L. (2006) *The price of whiteness: Jews, race and American identity*, Princeton, NJ: Princeton University Press.

Gordon, C. (ed) (1980) *Power/knowledge: Selected interviews and other writings, 1972-1977*, Brighton: Harvester.

Gorz, A. (1985) *Paths to paradise*, London: Pluto.

Gramsci, A. (1971) *Selections from the prison notebooks*, London: Lawrence and Wishart.

Gray, G. (1988) *The warriors: Reflections on men in battle*, Lincoln, NE: University of Nebraska Press.

Gray, J. (1995) *Enlightenment's wake: Politics and culture at the close of the modern age*, London: Routledge.

Griffin, S. (1980) *Pornography and silence*, London: The Womens' Press.

Griffin, S. (1982) *Women and nature*, London: The Women's Press.

Grosz, E. (1994) *Volatile bodies: Towards a corporeal feminism*, Bloomington, IN: Indiana University Press.

Gutman, M.C. (1996) *The meaning of macho: Being a man in Mexico City*, Berkeley, CA: University of California Press.

Gutmann, A. (ed) (1994) *Multiculturalism*, Princeton, NJ: Princeton University Press.

Gutmann, A. and Thompson, D. (1997) *Democracy and disagreement*, London: The Belknap Press.

Habeck, M. (2005) *Knowing the enemy*, New Haven, CT: Yale University Press.

Hall, C. (2002) *Civilising subjects: Metropole and colony in the English imagination 1830-1867*, Cambridge: Polity Press.

Hall, L.A. (1991) *Hidden anxieties: Male sexuality 1900-1950*, Cambridge: Polity Press.

Hall, S. (1994) 'Cultural identity and diaspora', in P. Williams and L. Christman (eds) *Colonial discourse and post-colonial theory: A reader*, London: Harvester Wheatsheaf, pp 392–401.

Hall, S. (ed) (1997) *Representation: Cultural representation and signifying practices*, London: Sage.

Hall, S. and Jefferson, T. (eds) (1989) *Resistance through rituals: Youth subcultures in post-war Britain*, London: Hutchinson.

Haraway, D. (1991) 'A cyborg manifesto: science, technology, and socialist-feminism in the late twentieth century' in D. Haraway, *Simians, cyborgs and women: The reinvention of nature*, London: Free Association Books.

Hargreaves, A. (1995) *Immigration, race and ethnicity in contemporary France*, London: Routledge.

Hearn, J. (1987) *The gender of oppression: Men, masculinities and the critique of Marxism*, Brighton: Harvester.

Hearn, J. (1992) *Man in the public eye*, London: Routledge.

Hearn, J. (1998) *The violences of men*, London: Sage.

Hearn, J. and Morgan, D. (eds) (1990) *Men, masculinities and social theory*, London: Unwin Hyman.

Heckman, S.J. (1990) *Gender and knowledge: Elements of a postmodern feminism*, London: Routledge.

Hedges, C. (2003) *War is a force that gives us meaning*, New York: Anchor Books.

Heelas, P., Lash, S. and Morris, P. (1996) *Detraditionalization*, Oxford: Blackwell.

Hefner, R.W. (ed) (1993) *Conversion to Christianity: Historical and anthropological perspectives on a great transformation*, Berkeley, CA: University of California Press.

Hegel, G.W.F. (1807) *Phenomenology of mind*, 2004 edn edited by G.B. Bailey, Mineola, NY: Dover Publications.

Held, D. (1986) *Models of democracy*, Cambridge: Polity Press.

Held,V. (1993) *Feminist morality: Transforming culture, society and politics,* Chicago, IL: University of Chicago Press.

Hellinger, B. (1997) *Touching love,* ed by H. Beaumont, C. Beaumont and J.T. Herkel-Chaudhri, Heidelberg: Carl-Auer-Systeme Verlag.

Henry,W. (2006) *What the deejay said: A critique from the street!,* London: Nu-Beyond.

Herman, E. and McChesney, R. (1997) *The global media: Missionaries of corporate capitalism,* London: Cassell.

Hewitt, K. (1997) *Mutilating the body: Identity in blood and ink,* Bowling Green, OH: Bowling Green State University Press.

Hewitt, R. (1986) *White talk black talk: Inter-racial friendships and communication amongst adolescents,* Cambridge: Cambridge University Press.

Hirsch, M. and Fox Keller, E. (eds) (1990) *Conflicts in feminism,* New York: Routledge.

Hochschild,A.R. (1997) *The time bind,* New York: Metropolitan Books.

Hochschild, A.R. and Machung, A. (1989) *The second shift,* New York: Avon Books.

Hoffman, E. (1991) *Lost in translation: A life in a new language,* New York: Vintage.

Honig, B. (1993) *Political theory and the displacement of politics,* Ithaca, NY: Cornell University Press.

Hood, J. (ed) *Men, work and family,* Newbury Park, CA: Sage.

hooks, b. (1989) *Talking back: Thinking feminist, thinking black,* Boston, MA: South End Press.

hooks, b. (1990a) *Yearning: Race, gender and cultural politics,* Boston, MA: South End Press.

hooks, b. (1990b) *Sisters of the yam: Black women and self-recovery,* Boston, MA: South End Press.

hooks, b. (1992) *Black looks: Race and representation,* Boston, MA: South End Press.

hooks, b. (1995) 'Doing it for daddy', in M. Berger, B. Wallis and S. Watson (eds) *Constructing masculinity,* New York: Routledge, pp 98-106.

hooks, b. (2000) *All about love,* New York: Harper Collins.

hooks, b. (2001) *Salvation: Black people and love,* New York: Harper Collins.

Horton, J.O. and Horton, L.E. (2001) *The hard road to freedom: The story of African America,* New Brunswick, NJ: Rutgers University Press.

Howe, D. (2000) 'We are the future', *The Observer,* 10 September, p 29.

Hutton, W. (2000) 'Losing the ways of winning', *The Observer*, 20 August, p 29.

Ignatieff, M. (1998) *Isaiah Berlin: A life*, London: Chatto & Windus.

Ingram, G.B., Bouthillette, A.-M. and Retter, Y. (1997) *Queers in space: Communities, public spaces, sites of resistance*, San Francisco, CA: Bay Press.

Irigaray, L. (1985a) *The sex which is not one*, Ithaca, NY: Cornell University Press.

Irigaray. L. (1985b) *Speculum of the other woman*, Ithaca, NY: Cornell University Press.

Iwabuchi, K. (2002) *Recentering globalization: Popular culture and Japanese transnationalism*, Durham, NC: Duke University Press.

Jackson, S. (1999) *Heterosexuality in question*, London: Sage.

Jacobson, D. (1998) *Heshel's kingdom*, London: Hamish Hamilton.

Jacoby, R. (1975) *Social amnesia*, Boston, MA: Beacon Press.

Jaffrelot, C. (1996) *The Hindu Nationalist movement and Indian politics 1925 to 1990s*, London: Hurst.

Jagger, G. and Wright, C. (eds) (1999) *Changing family values*, London: Routledge.

Jameson, F. (1972) *The prison-house of language: A critical account of structuralism and Russian formalism*, Princeton, NJ: Princeton University Press.

Jimenez, L. (2002) '*Entendidos*: Young gay men and their friendships in Barcelona', PhD, Goldmiths, University of London.

Johnson, S. and Meinhof, U.H. (eds) (1996) *Language and masculinity*, Oxford: Blackwell.

Jordan, J. (1991) *Technical difficulties: African American notes on the State of the Union*, New York: Pantheon.

Kamen, H. (1985) *Inquisition and society in Spain in the 16th and 17th centuries*, Bloomington, IN: Indiana University Press.

Kaufman, M. (1987) *Beyond patriarchy*, Toronto: Oxford University Press.

Keat, R. and Abercrombie, N. (eds) (1991) *Enterprise culture*, London: Routledge.

Keith, M. (2006) *After cosmopolitanism*, London: Routledge.

Kelly, R.D.G. (2002) *Freedom dreams: The Black radical imagination*, Boston, MA: Beacon Press.

Kelly, R.D.G. and Lewis, E. (eds) (2000) *To make our world anew: A history of African Americans*, New York: Oxford University Press.

Kilby, J. (2001) 'Carved in skin: bearing witness to self-harm', in S. Ahmed and J. Stacey (eds) *Thinking through the skin*, London: Routledge.

Kimmel, M.S. (ed) (1987) *Changing men: New directions in research on men and masculinity*, Newbury Park, CA: Sage.

Kimmel, M.S. (ed) (1995) *The politics of manhood*, Philadelphia, PA: Temple University Press.

Kimmel, M.S. (1996) *Manhood in America: A cultural history*, New York: Free Press.

Kingston, M.H. (1976) *The woman warrior: Memoirs of a girlhood among ghosts*, New York: Random House.

Kingston, M.H. (1981) *China men*, London: Picador.

Kingston, M.H. (2003) *The fifth book of peace*, New York: Vintage.

Klein, M. (1950) *Contributions to psycho-analysis, 1921-1945*, London: Hogarth.

Klein, M. (1975) *Love, guilt and reparation, 1921-45*, New York: Free Press.

Knowles, C. (2004) *Race and social analysis*, London: Sage.

Kraidy, M. (2005) *Hybridity: Or the cultural logic of globalization*, Philadelphia, PA: Temple University Press.

Kruks, S. (2001) *Retrieving experience: Subjectivity and recognition in feminist politics*, Ithaca, NY/London: Cornell University Press.

Kymlicka, W. (1989) *Liberalism, community and culture*, Oxford: Clarendon Press.

Kymlicka, W. (1995) *Multicultural citizenship: A liberal theory of minority rights*, Oxford: Clarendon Press.

Laing, R.D. (1961a) *The divided self*, Harmondsworth: Penguin.

Laing, R.D. (1961b) *Self and others*, Harmondsworth: Penguin.

Laing, R.D. (1982) *The voice of experience: Experience, science and psychiatry*, Harmondsworth: Penguin.

Laqueur, T. (1990) *Making sex: Body and gender from the Greeks to Freud*, Cambridge, MA: Harvard University Press.

Lasch, C. (1977) *Haven in a heartless world: The family besieged*, New York: Basic Books.

Lasch, C. (1991) *The culture of narcissism: American life in an age of diminishing expectations*, New York: Norton.

Lash, S. and Urry, J. (1987) *The end of organised capitalism*, Cambridge: Polity Press.

Lash, S. and Urry, J. (1994) *Economies of signs and space*, London: Sage.

Lawson, M. (2000) 'So, where were you when Nasty Nick was kicked out of Big Brother?', *The Guardian 2*, 18 August, p 2.

Lea, H.C. (1906-07) *A history of the inquisition in Spain* (4 vols), London/New York: Macmillan.

Lennon, K. and Whitford, M. (eds) (1994) *Knowing the difference: Feminist perspectives on epistemology*, London: Routledge.

Levi, P. (1989) *The drowned and the saved*, New York: Vintage International.

Lewis, D.L. (2001) *W.E.B. Du Bois: The fight for equality and the American century, 1919-1963*, New York: Henry Holt.

Lloyd, G. (1984) *Man of reason: 'Male' and 'female' in Western philosophy*, London: Methuen.

Lloyd, T. (1990) *Work with boys*, Leicester: National Youth Bureau.

Lord, A. (1980) *Sister outsider: Essays and speeches*, Berkley, CA: Crossing Press.

Lovejoy, E.O. (1936) *The great chain of being*, New York: Harper and Row.

Lukes, S. (1983) *Emile Durkheim: His life and work*, London: Allen and Unwin.

Lukes, S. (2001) 'An unfashionable fox', in R. Dworkin, M. Lilla and R. Silvers (eds) *The legacy of Isaiah Berlin*, New York: New York Review of Books.

Lundqvist, S. (1997) *Exterminate all the brutes: One man's odyssey into the heart of darkness and the origins of European genocide*, trans J. Tate, New York: The New Press.

Lurie, S. (1997) *Unsettled subjects: Restoring feminist politics to poststructuralist critique*, Durham, NC: Duke University Press.

Lyotard, J.-F. (1979) *La condition postmoderne*, Paris: Les Editions de Minuit.

Lyotard, J.-F. (1994) *The postmodern condition: A report on knowledge*, Manchester: Manchester University Press.

McCarthy, M. (2008) 'Living in translation', MA dissertation, Sociology Department, Goldsmiths, University of London.

McLellan, D. (1980) *The thought of Karl Marx*, London: Macmillan.

McNay, L. (1992) *Foucault and feminism*, Cambridge: Polity Press.

McNay, L. (1994) *Gender and agency*, Cambridge: Polity Press.

McNulty, S. (2000) 'Equipping a people for the New Economy', *Financial Times*, 14 September, p 15.

McRobbie, A. (2007) 'Top girls?: young women and the post-feminist sexual contract', *Cultural Studies*, vol 21, nos 4-5, Jul/Sep, pp 718-37.

McRobbie, A. and Nava, M. (eds) (1984) *Gender and generation*, London: Palgrave.

Mac An Ghail, M. (1994) *The making of men: Masculinities, sexualities and schooling*, Buckingham: Open University Press.

MacInnes, J. (1998) *The end of masculinity*, Buckingham: Open University Press.

MacIntyre A. (1985) *After virtue: A study in moral theory*, London: Duckworth.

Macpherson, W. (1999) *The Stephen Lawrence Inquiry: Report of an inquiry by Sir William Macpherson of Cluny*, London: The Stationery Office.

Macey, D. (2001) *Frantz Fanon: A biography*, London: Vintage.

Macey, D. (1993) *The lives of Michel Foucault: A biography*, London: Vintage.

Maguire, M. (1995) *Men, women, passion and power*, London, Routledge.

Mahoney, P. (1985) *School for boys? Co-education reassessed*, London: Hutchinson.

Malcolm, N. (1986) *Ludwig Wittgenstein: Nothing is hidden*, Oxford: Basil Blackwell.

Manderson, L. and Jolly, M. (eds) (1997) *Sites of desire, economies of pleasure: Sexuality in Asia and the Pacific*, Chicago, IL: University of Chicago Press.

Mangan, J.A. and Walvin, J. (1987) *Manliness and morality: Middle class masculinity in Britain and America*, Manchester: Manchester University Press.

Marcuse, H. (1967) *Reason and revolution*, London: Routledge.

Marx, K. (1990) *Capital: A critique of political economy*, London: Penguin Books.

Mastnak, T. (2002) *Crusading peace: Christendom, the Muslim world and Western political order*, Berkeley, CA: University of California Press.

Mattar, P. (1998) *Islam in Britain, 1558-1685*, Cambridge: Cambridge University Press.

May, L. (1998) *Masculinity and morality*, New York: Cornell University Press.

Mayer, H. (1982) *Outsiders: A study in life and letters*, Cambridge, MA: MIT Press.

Mbembe, A. (2001) *On the postcolony*, Los Angeles, CA: University of California Press.

Meikle, J. (2000) 'BSE revelation confirms worst fears', *The Guardian*, 29 August, p 6.

Melucci, A. (1996a) *The playing self: Person and meaning in the planetary society*, Cambridge: Cambridge University Press.

Melucci, A. (1996b) *Challenging codes: Collective action in the information age*, Cambridge: Cambridge University Press.

Mendus, S. (1989) *Toleration and the limits of liberalism*, Basingstoke: Palgrave.

Mercer, K. (ed) (1994) *Welcome to the jungle: New positions in black cultural studies*, London: Routledge.

Merchant, C. (1982) *The death of nature: Women, ecology and the scientific revolution*, London: Wildwood House.

Messner, M.A. (1997) *Politics of masculinities: Men in movements*, Thousand Oaks, CA: Sage.

Middleton, P. (1992) *The inward gaze: Masculinity and subjectivity in modern culture*, London: Routledge.

Midgeley, M. (1979) *Beast and man*, Brighton: Harvester.

Midgeley, M. (1983) *Animals and why they matter*, Harmondsworth: Penguin.

Mies, M. and Shiva, V. (1993) *Ecofeminism*, London: Zed Books.

Miller, N. (1992) *Out in the world: Gay and lesbian life from Buenos Aires to Bangkok*, New York: Random House.

Miller, S. (1983) *Men and friendship*, London: Gateway Books.

Mills, K. and Grafton, A. (2003) *Conversion: Old worlds and new*, Rochester, NY: University of Rochester Press.

Minsky, R. (1998) *Psychoanalysis and culture: Contemporary states of mind*, Cambridge: Polity Press.

Mitchell, T. (ed) (2001) *Global noise*, Middleton, CT: Wesleyan University Press.

Mitscherlich, A. (1993) *Society without father: A contribution to social psychology*, New York: Harper Collins.

Modleski, T. (1991) *Feminism without women*, New York: Routledge.

Modood, T. (1992) *Not easy being British: Colour, culture, and citizenship*, Stoke-on-Trent: Trentham Books.

Modood, T. (ed) (1997) *Church, state and religious minorities*, London: Policy Studies Institute.

Modood, T. and Werbner, P. (eds) (1997) *The politics of multiculturalism in the new Europe: Racism, identity and community*, London: Zed Books.

Mohanty, C.T, Russo, A. and Torres, L. (eds) (1991) *Third world women and the politics of feminism*, Bloomington, IN: Indiana University Press.

Monk, R. (1990) *Ludwig Wittgenstein: The duty of genius*, London: Jonathan Cape.

Moore, M. (1996) *Downsize this! Random threats from an unarmed American*, New York: HarperPerennial.

Moore, M. (2002) *Stupid white men ...and other sorry excuses for the state of the nation!*, New York: Regan Books

Moore, R.I. (1987) *The formation of a persecuting society*, Oxford: Oxford University Press.

Morgan, D. (1992) *Discovering men: Sociology and masculinities*, London: Routledge.

Morgan, R. (ed) (1970) *Sisterhood is powerful: An anthology of writings from the women's liberation movement*, New York: Vintage Books.

Morrison, K.F. (1992) *Understanding conversion*, Charlottesville, VA: University of Virginia Press.

Morrison, T. (1970) *The bluest eye*, Austin, TX: Holt, Reinhart and Winstone.

Morrison, T. (1974) *Sula*, New York: Alfred Knopf.

Morrison, T. (1987) *Beloved*, New York: Alfred Knopf.

Morrison, T. (ed) (1992) *Race-ing justice, engendering power*, New York: Pantheon.

Morrison, T. (1993) *Playing in the dark: Whiteness in literary imagination*, London: Picador.

Mort, F. (1996) *Cultures of consumption: Masculinities and social space in late twentieth century Britain*, London: Routledge.

Mosse, G.L. (1996) *The image of man: The creation of modern masculinity*, New York: Oxford University Press.

Murdoch, I. (1970) *The sovereignty of good*, London: Routledge.

Naess, A. (1989) *Ecology, community and lifestyle: The outline of an ecosophy*, trans D. Rothenberg, Cambridge: Cambridge University Press.

Nancy, J.-L. (1993) *The experience of freedom*, Stanford, CA: Stanford University Press.

Narayan, U. (1997) *Dislocating cultures: Identities, traditions and third world feminism*, New York: Routledge.

Nardi, P.M. (ed) (1992) *Men's friendships*, Thousand Oaks, CA: Sage.

Nardi, P.M. (ed) (1999) *Gay men's friendship: Invincible communities*, Chicago, IL: University of Chicago Press.

Nardi, P.M. (ed) (2000) *Gay masculinities*, Thousand Oaks, CA: Sage.

Nash, K. (ed) (1999) *Readings in contemporary political sociology*, Oxford: Blackwell.

Nasr, S.H. (ed) (1991) *Islamic spirituality II; Manifestations*, New York: Crossroad Publishing.

National Foundation of Educational Research (2000) *Arts education in secondary schools: Effects and effectiveness*, Slough: NFER.

Nelson, C. and Grossberg, L. (eds) (1988) *Marxism and the interpretation of culture*, Urbana, IL: University of Illinois Press.

Nicholson, L.J. (ed) (1990) *Feminism/Postmodernism*, New York: Routledge.

Nicholson, L. and Seidman, S. (eds) (1996) *Social postmodernism: Beyond identity politics*, Cambridge: Cambridge University Press.

Nietzsche, F. (1887) *On the genealogy of morals: A polemic*, trans D. Smith, reissued 2008, Oxford: Oxford University Press.

Niezen, R. (2002) *A world beyond difference: Cultural identity in the age of globalisation*, Oxford: Blackwell.

Nixon, S. (1996) *Hard looks: Masculinities, spectatorship and contemporary consumption*, London: UCL Press.

O'Connor, N. and Ryan, J. (1993) *Wild desires and mistaken identities: Lesbianism and psychoanalysis*, London: Virago.

Olds, K. and Thrift, N. (2005) 'Cultures on the brink: reengineering the soul of capitalism on a global scale', in A. Ong and S.J. Collier (eds) *Global assemblages: Technology, politics and ethics as anthropological problems*, Oxford: Blackwell.

Oliver, K. (1997) *Family values: Subjects between nature and culture*, London: Routledge.

Ong, A. (1999) *Flexible citizenship: The cultural logics of transnationality*, Durham, NC: Duke University Press.

Ong, A. and Collier, S.J. (eds) *Global assemblages: Technology, politics and ethics as anthropological problems*, Oxford: Blackwell.

Orbach, S. (2009) *Bodies*, London: Profile Books.

Ordorika, T. (2003) 'Madness and heresy in the Spanish Inquisition', PhD thesis, London: Goldsmiths, University of London.

Pagels, E. (1982) *The Gnostic Gospels*, Harmondsworth: Penguin.

Painter, N.I. (2006) *Creating black Americans: African-American history and its meanings*, New York: Oxford University Press.

Parekh, B. (ed) (1990) *Law, blasphemy and the multi-faith society*, London: Commission for Racial Equality.

Parekh, B. (2000) *Rethinking multiculturalism: Cultural diversity and political theory*, Basingstoke: Palgrave.

Parkin, F. (1968) Middle class radicalism: The social bases of the British Campaign for Nuclear Disarmament, Manchester: Manchester University Press.

Pateman, C. (1988) *The sexual contract*, Stanford, CA: Stanford University Press.

Peters, E. (1980) *Heresy and authority in Medieval Europe*, Philadelphia: University of Pennsylvania Press.

Peters, E. (1989) *Inquisition*, Berkeley, CA: University of California Press.

Phillips, A. (1991) *Engendering democracy*, Philadephia, PA: University of Pennsylvania Press.

Phillips, A. (1993) *Democracy and difference*, Cambridge: Polity Press.

Phillips, A. (1995) *The politics of presence: Issues in democracy and group representation*, Oxford: Oxford University Press.

Phillips, T. (2000) 'The myth of gold chains and no brains', *The Observer*, 20 August, p 31.

Pieterse, J. and Parekh, B. (eds) (1995) *The decolonisation of imagination: Culture, knowledge and power*, London: Zed Books.

Plummer, K. (1995) *Telling sexual stories: Power, change and social worlds*, London: Routledge.

Plumwood, V. (1993) *Feminism and the mastery of nature*, London: Routledge.

Poster, M. (1998) *Critical theory of the family*, London: Pluto Press.

Probyn, E. (1990) *Sexing the self*, London: Routledge.

Proctor, R.N. (1988) *Racial hygiene: Medicine under the Nazis*, Cambridge, MA: Harvard University Press.

Putnam, R. (2000) *Bowling alone: The collapse and revival of American community*, New York: Simon & Schuster.

Puwar, N. (2004) *Space invaders: Race, gender and bodies out of place*, Oxford: Berg.

Rabinow, P. (ed) (1998) *Ethics: Subjectivity and truth. Essential works of Michel Foucault, 1954-1984*, trans. R.J. Hurley, New York: New Press.

Rajchman, J. (ed) (1995) *The identity in question*, London: Routledge.

Ramazanoglu, C. (1989) *Feminism and the contradictions of oppression*, London: Routledge.

Ramazanoglu, C. (ed) (1992) *Up against Foucault: Explorations of some tensions between Foucault and feminism*, London: Routledge.

Rawls, J. (1993) *Political liberalism*, New York: Columbia University Press.

Rée, J. (1974) *Descartes*, London: Allen Lane.

Rex, J. (1996) *Ethnic minorities in the modern nation state*, London: Macmillan.

Ricoeur, P. (1992) *Oneself as another*, Chicago, IL: Chicago University Press.

Rifkin, J. (1996) *The end of work: The decline of the global work force and the dawn of the post-market era*, New York: Putnam.

Rifkin, J. (2000) *The age of access*, London: Penguin Books.

Robinson, S. (2000) *Marked men: White masculinity in crisis*, New York: Columbia University Press.

Roof, J. and Wiegman, R. (eds) (1995) *Who can speak: Authority and critical identity*, Urbana, IL: University of Illinois Press.

Roper, L. (1994) *Oedipus and the devil: Witchcraft, sexuality and religion, 1500-1700*, London: Routledge.

Roper, M. and Tosh, J. (1991) *Manful assertions: Masculinities in Britain since 1800*, London: Routledge.

Rorty, R. (1989) *Contingency, irony and solidarity*, Cambridge: Cambridge University Press.

Rorty, R. (1991a) 'Feminism and pragmatism', *Michigan Quarterly Review*, vol 30, no 2, pp 231-58.

Rorty, R. (1991b) *Essays on Heidegger and others*, Cambridge: Cambridge University Press.

Rose, N. (1989) *Governing the soul: The shaping of the private self*, London: Routledge.

Rose, T. (1994) *Black noise: Rap music and black culture in contemporary America*, Hanover, NH: University Press of New England.

Rowbotham, S. (1972) *Woman's consciousness, man's world*, Harmondsworth: Penguin.

Rowbotham, S. (1973) *Hidden from history*, London: Pluto Press.

Rowbotham, S. (1983) *Dreams and dilemmas*, London: Virago.

Rubin, L. (1994) *Families on the faultline: America's working class speaks about the family, the economy, race and ethnicity*, New York: Harper Collins.

Ruddick, S. and Daniels, P (eds) (1977) *Working it out*, New York: Pantheon.

Rushkoff, D. (2000) 'Second sight', *The Guardian*, 28 September, pp 14-15.

Ruthven, M. (2002) *A fury for god*, London: Granta.

Ruthven, M. (2004) *Fundamentalisms*, Oxford: Oxford University Press.

Ryan, B. (1992) *Making capital from culture: The corporate form of capitalist cultural production*, New York: Walter de Gruyter.

Ryder, R. (2000) *Animal revolution: Changing attitudes towards speciesism*, Oxford: Berg.

Sacks, J. (1991) *The persistence of faith: Religion, morality and society in a secular age*, London: Weidenfeld and Nicholson.

Sacks, J. (2000) *The politics of hope*, 2nd edn, London: Vintage.

Sacks, J. (2002) *The dignity of difference: How to avoid the clash of civilisations*, London: Continuum.

Said, E. (1979) *Orientalism*, New York: Vintage.

Said, E. (1993) *Culture and imperialism*, London: Chatto and Windus.

Said, E. (2006) *Orientalism*, 2nd edn, London: Penguin Books.

Samuels, A. (1993) *The political psyche*, London: Routledge.

Sanchez-Eppler, K. (1993) *Touching liberty: Abolition, feminism and the politics of the body*, Berkeley, CA: University of California Press.

Sandel, M. (1982) *Liberalism and the limits of justice*, Cambridge: Cambridge University Press.

Satre, J.-P. (1948) *Anti-semite and jew*, trans G.J. Becker, Berlin: Schocken Books.

Sawhney, N. (1999) 'Beyond Skin', Zomba Music/Outcast Records, London.

Sawicki, J. (1991) *Disciplining Foucault: Feminism, power and the body*, New York: Routledge.

Schama, S. (2003) *A history of Britain: At the edge of the world*, London: BBC Books.

Schlapobersky, J. (2000) 'Obituary: Robin Skynner', *The Guardian*, 28 September.

Scholem, G. (1971) *The messianic idea in Judaism*, New York: Schocken Books.

Scholem, G. (1990) *Origins of Kabbalah*, Princeton, NJ: Princeton University Press.

Scott, S. and Morgan, D. (eds) (1993) *Body matters*, London: Falmer Press.

Seabrook, J. (1988) *The race for riches: The human cost of wealth*, Basingstoke: Marshall Pickering.

Searle, J.R. (1969) *Speech acts: An essay in the philosophy of language*, Cambridge: Cambridge University Press.

Sedgwick, E.K. (1990) *Epistemology of the closet*, Berkeley, CA: University of California Press.

Segal, L. (1990) *Slow motion: Changing masculinities, changing men*, London: Virago.

Seidler, V.J.J. (1986) *Kant, respect and injustice: The limits of liberal moral theory*, London: Routledge.

Seidler, V.J.J. (1989) *Rediscovering masculinity: Reason, language and sexuality*, London/New York: Routledge.

Seidler, V.J.J. (1991a) *The moral limits of modernity: Love, inequality and oppression*, Basingstoke: Macmillan.

Seidler, V.J.J. (1991b) *Recreating sexual politics: Men, feminism and politics*, London/New York: Routledge.

Seidler, V.J.J. (ed) (1991c) *The Achilles Heel reader: Men, sexual politics and socialism*, London: Routledge.

Seidler, V.J.J. (ed) (1992) *Men, sex and relationships: Writings from* Achilles Heel, London: Routledge.

Seidler, V.J. (1993) *Unreasonable men: Masculinity and social theory*, London: Routledge.

Seidler, V.J.J. (1994) *Recovering the self: Morality and social theory*, London/New York: Routledge.

Seidler, V.J.J. (2000) *Man enough: Embodying masculinities*, London: Sage.

Seidler, V.J.J. (2001) *Shadows of the Shoah: Jewish identity and belonging*, Oxford: Berg.

Seidler, V.J.J. (2005) *Transforming masculinities: Men, cultures, bodies, power, sex and love*, London/New York: Routledge.

Seidler, V.J.J. (2006) *Young men and masculinities: Global cultures and intimate lives*, London: Zed Press.

Seidler, V.J.J. (2007a) *Jewish philosophy and Western culture*, London: I.B. Taurus.

Seidler V.J.J. (2007b) *Urban fears and global terrors: Citizenship, multicultures and belongings after 7/7*, London: Routledge.

Seidman, S. (1996) *Contested knowledge: Social theory in the postmodern era*, Cambridge, MA: Blackwell.

Sennett, R. (1996) *Uses of disorder: Personal identity and city life*, London: Faber and Faber.

Sennett, R. (1998) *The corrosion of character: The personal consequences of work in the new capitalism*, New York: W.W. Norton.

Sennett, R. (2004) *Respect: The formation of character in an age of inequality*, London: Penguin Books.

Sennett, R. and Cobb, J. (1971) *The hidden injuries of class*, London: Knopf.

Sewell, T. (1996) *Black masculinities and schooling: How black boys survive modern schooling*, Stoke-on-Trent: Trentham Books.

Sharma, S. (2004) 'The sounds of alterity', in M. Bull and L. Back (eds) *The auditory reader*, Oxford: Berg.

Shilling, C. (1983) *The body and social theory*, London: Sage.

Silverman, K. (1992) *Male subjectivity at the margins*, New York: Routledge.

Skeggs, B. (1997) *Formation of class and gender: Becoming respectable*, London: Sage.

Skeggs, B. (2004) *Class, self, culture*, London: Routledge.

Skynner, R. (1976) *One flesh, separate persons: Principles of family and marital psychotherapy*, London: Constable.

Skynner, R. and Clease, J. (1983) *Families and how to survive them*, London: Methuen.

Slater, D. and Tonkiss, F. (2000) *Market society: Markets and modern social theory*, Cambridge: Polity Press.

Smart, C. (1992) *Regulating womanhood: Historical essays on marriage, motherhood and sexuality*, London: Routledge.

Smith, A. (1991) *National identity*, Harmondsworth: Penguin.

Smith, G., Cox, D. and Saradjian, J. (1999) *Women and self-harm: Understanding, coping, and healing from self-mutilation*, London: Routledge.

Spinner, J. (1994) *The boundaries of citizenship: Race, ethnicity and nationality in the liberal state*, Baltimore, NJ: John Hopkins University Press.

Spivak, G.C. (1990) *Postcolonial critic: Interviews, strategies, dialogue*, ed by S. Harasym, London: Routledge.

Spivak, G.C. (1999) *A critique of postcolonial reason: Towards a history of the vanishing present*, Cambridge, MA: Harvard University Press.

Squires, J. (1999) *Gender in political theory*, Cambridge: Polity Press.

Stacey, J. (1990) *Brave new families: Stories of domestic upheaval in late twentieth century America*, New York: Basic Books.

Stacey, J. (1996) *In the name of the family: Rethinking family values in the postmodern age*, Boston, MA: Beacon Press.

Stanley, L. and Wise, S. (1993) *Breaking out again: Feminist ontology and epistemology*, London: Routledge.

Staples, R. (1982) *Black masculinity: The black man's role in American society*, San Francisco, CA: Black Scholar Press.

Stecopoulos, H. and Uebel, M. (eds) *Race and the subject of masculinities*, Durham, NC: Duke University Press.

Steinberg, L., Epstein, D. and Johnson, R. (eds) (1997) *Border patrols: Policing the boundaries of heterosexuality*, London: Cassell.

Steiner, G. (1967) *Language and silence: Essays on language, literature and the inhuman*, London: Faber and Faber.

Steiner, G. (1975) *After Babel: Aspects of language and translation*, Oxford: Oxford University Press.

Stern, J. (2003) *Terror in the name of god: Why religious militants kill*, New York: Harper Collins.

Steyn, M. (2001) *"Whiteness just isn't what it used to be": White identities in a changing South Africa*, New York: State University of New York Press.

Sydie, R.A. (1987) *Natural woman, cultured men: A feminist perspective on sociological theory*, Milton Keynes: Open University Press.

Szasz, T. (1971) *The manufacture of madness*, London: Routledge & Kegan Paul.

Tamir, Y. (1993) *Liberal nationalism*, Princeton, NJ: Princeton University Press.

Tarr, C. (2005) *Reframing difference: Beur and banlieue filmmaking in France*, Manchester: Manchester University Press.

Taylor, C. (1979) *Hegel and modern society*, Cambridge: Cambridge University Press.

Taylor, C. (1989) *Sources of the self: The making of the modern identity*, Cambridge, MA: Harvard University Press.

Taylor, C. (2004) *Modern social imaginaries*, Durham, NC: Duke University Press.

Thorn, B. (1993) *Gender play: Girls and boys in school*, Buckingham: Open University Press.

Thrift, N. (2007) *Non-representational theory: Space, politics, affect*, London: Routledge.

Tiedemann, R. (2003) *Can one live after Auschwitz? A philosophical reader*, trans R. Livingstone, Stanford, CA: Stanford University Press.

Tomlinson, J. (1999) *Globalization and culture*, Chicago, IL: University of Chicago Press.

Trachtenberg, J. (1943) *The devil and the Jews: The Medieval conception of the Jew and its relation to modern anti-semitism*, Philadelphia: Jewish Publication Society.

Trimington, J.S. (1973) *The Sufi origins of Islam*, Oxford: Oxford University Press.

Turner, B. (1984) *The body and society: Explorations in social theory*, Oxford: Basil Blackwell.

Turner, B. (1992) *Regulating bodies: Essays in medical sociology*, London: Routledge.

Vanita, R. (ed) (2002) *Queering India: Same-sex love and eroticism in Indian culture and society*, New York: Routledge.

Varshney, A. (2001) *Ethnic conflict civil life: Hindus and Muslims in India*, New Haven, CT: Yale University Press.

Verushallami Zakhor, Y.H.Y. (1982) *Jewish history and Jewish memory*, Seattle, WA: University of Washington Press.

Walker, A. (1997) *Anything we love can be saved*, New York: Ballantine.

Wallace, M. (1979) *Black macho*, London: Calder.

Walter, N. (1999) *The new feminism*, London: Virago.

Walzer, M. (1983) *Spheres of justice: A defence of pluralism and equality*, New York: Basic Books.

Wandor, M. (1972) *The body politic*, London: Stage 1.

Ware, V. (1992) *Beyond the pale: White women, racism and history*, London: Verso.

Weber, M. (1930) *The Protestant ethic and the spirit of capitalism*, London: Allen and Unwin.

Weeks, J. (1977) *Coming out: Homosexual politics in Britain*, London: Quartet Books.

Weeks, J. (1985) *Sexuality and its discontents: Meanings, myths and modern sexualities*, London: Routledge.

Weeks, J. (1989) *Sex, politics and society*, Harlow: Longman.

Weeks, J. (1995) *Inventing moralities: Sexual Values in an age of uncertainty*, Cambridge: Polity Press.

Weeks, J. and Porter, K. (eds) (1998) *Between the acts: Lives of homosexual men 1885-1967*, London: Rivers Oram Press.

Weil, S. (1952) *Gravity and grace*, London: Routledge.

Weil, S. (1972) *The need for roots*, London: Routledge.

Weil, S. (2005) 'Human personality: between the personal and the impersonal', *Harvard Theological Review*, 1 April.

West, C. (1993) *Race matters*, Boston, MA: Beacon Press.

Whimster, S. (2006) *Max Weber: A Biography*, London: Routledge.

Wiegman, R. (1995) *American anatomies: Theorizing race and gender*, Durham, NC: Duke University Press.

Williams, B. (1978) *Descartes: The project of pure enquiry*, London: Penguin.

Williams, B. (1985) *Ethics and the limits of philosophy*, London: Fontana.

Williams, R. (1980) *Problems in materialism and culture*, London: Verso.

Willis, P. (1977) *Learning to labour*, Aldershot: Gower.

Willis, S. (1987) *Specifying: Black women writing the American experience*, Madison, WI: University of Wisconsin Press.

Wilson, A. (1978) *Finding a voice: Asian women in Britain*, London: Virago.

Winch, P. (1989) *A just balance: Reflections on the philosophy of Simone Weil*, Cambridge: Cambridge University Press.

Winnicott, D.W. (1974) *Playing and reality*, Harmondsworth: Penguin.

Wittgenstein, L. (1958a) *The blue and brown books: Preliminary studies for the 'Philosophical investigations'*, Oxford: Blackwell.

Wittgenstein, L. (1958b) *Philosophical investigations*, 2nd edn, Oxford: Blackwell.

Wittgenstein, L. (1980) *Culture and value*, Oxford, Blackwell.

Woodward, K. (ed) (1997) *Identity and difference*, London: Sage.

Wright, A. (2005) *Ripped and torn: Levi's Latin America and the blue jean dream*, London: Ebury.

Yegenoglu, M. (1998) *Colonial fantasies: Towards a feminist reading of Orientalism*, Cambridge: Cambridge University Press.

Young, I.M. (1990) *Justice and the politics of difference*, Princeton, NJ: Princeton University Press.

Young, I.M. (1990) *Throwing like a girl and other essays in feminist philosophy and social theory*, Bloomington, IN: Indiana University Press.

Young, R. (1990) *White mythologies: Writing history and the West*, London: Routledge.

Zangranado, R.L. (1980) *The NAACP crusade against lynching, 1909-1950*, Philadelphia, PA: Temple University Press.

Zizek, S. (1989) *The sublime object of ideology*, London: Verso.

Zizek, S. (2002) *Welcome to the desert of the real*, London: Verso.

Index